Issues in Music Teaching

Issues in Music Teaching is intended to stimulate critical reflection on a range of topics related to the teaching and learning of music. The chapters are written by experienced music educators representing a variety of perspectives in the field.

The issues addressed include:

- the historical and comparative context of music teaching
- the place of music in the curriculum
- the nature of music and music education
- ICT and music education
- music education and individual needs
- continuity and progression in music education

The book aims to prompt music teachers to be analytical and critical of theory and practice, and to help them to become autonomous professionals and curriculum developers in their own right.

Issues in Music Teaching will be of interest to student teachers, newly qualified teachers and music teachers engaged in professional development in both primary and secondary schools.

Chris Philpott is Principal Lecturer in Education at Canterbury Christ Church University College. **Charles Plummeridge** is Senior Lecturer in Education at the Institute of Education, University of London.

Issues in Subject Teaching series
Edited by Susan Capel, Jon Davison,
James Arthur and John Moss

Other titles in the series:

Issues in Music Teaching

Edited by Chris Philpott
and Charles Plummeridge

London and New York

First published 2001
by RoutledgeFalmer
11 New Fetter Lane, London EC4P 4EE

Simultaneously published in the USA and Canada
by Routledge
29 West 35th Street, New York, NY 10001

RoutledgeFalmer is an imprint of the Taylor & Francis Group

Selection and editorial matter © 2001 Chris Philpott and Charles
Plummeridge; © individual chapters, their contributors.

Typeset in Goudy by
Keystroke, Jacaranda Lodge, Wolverhampton
Printed and bound in Great Britain by
Biddles Ltd, Guildford and King's Lynn

British Library Cataloguing in Publication Data
A catalogue record for this book is available from the British Library

Library of Congress Cataloging in Publication Data
Issues in music teaching / edited by Chris Philpott and Charles Plummeridge.
  p. cm. — (Issues in subject teaching series)
  Includes bibliographical references.
  1. Music—Instruction and study. 2. School music—Instruction and study. 3. Teacher
effectiveness. I. Philpott, Chris, 1956– II. Plummeridge, Charles, 1939– III. Issues in
subject teaching.

MT1 .I84 2001
780'.71—dc21   00–066484

ISBN 0–415–23718–1 (hbk)
ISBN 0–415–23719–X (pbk)

Contents

Figures and tables

Figures

Tables

Contributors

Pauline Adams is a lecturer in music education at the Institute of Education, University of London. She is primarily responsible for co-ordinating the PGCE Secondary Music full-time and part-time courses, but is also responsible for the music education component of the Primary PGCE course. She also teaches on the MA Music Education course at Trinity College of Music and has wide experience of teaching music in primary and secondary schools. Her work has involved advising teachers in London and across Britain. She is a contributory author to books related to both secondary and primary education and is a member of the editorial boards of the *British Journal for Music Education* and *Music Education Research*.

Jonathan M. Barnes is a Senior Lecturer in Education at Canterbury Christ Church University College. He was a primary school headteacher for eight years, an Educational Officer for English Heritage and a District Council, a primary school class teacher for five years and a secondary school teacher for seven. He has also taught with his wife Cherry in Africa, Asia, in prisons and in Adult Studies. Throughout his career and in each context he has continued teaching music as a non-specialist enthusiast.

Tim Cain is Lecturer in Music Education at Kingston University. His publications include *Keynote: Music to GCSE* and *Fanfare* for KS2, both of which are published by Cambridge University Press. He has also taught children of all ages from 5–18 and for nine years was editor of the magazine *Music in the Curriculum*.

Gordon Cox is a subject leader of the PGCE (Secondary) Music and MA (Music Education) courses at the University of Reading. His research focuses upon the history of music education, and he is the author of A *History of Music Education in England 1872–1928* (1993). His recent work has encompassed studies of the BBC, *Music Education of the Under-Twelves Association*, the Schools Council, and the life histories of present-day secondary school music teachers and student teachers.

Lucy Green is Head of the Music and Drama Academic Group at the Institute of Education, University of London. Before working at the Institute she was a private piano teacher and then a secondary music teacher and Head of Department. She has written two books and a number of articles on music education and the sociology of music. She is the Co-ordinating Editor of the journal *Popular Music*, and an Editorial Board Member of *Music Education Research*.

Susan Hallam trained as a violinist at the Royal Academy of Music after which she spent ten years as a full-time professional musician. An interest in psychology led her to take a BA in Psychology externally with London University. This was followed by a career in teaching. Her PhD studies were completed at the Institute of Education, London University where she became a lecturer in 1991. In 1999 she was appointed as Professor in Education at Oxford Brookes University. She has published widely in areas as diverse as attendance at and exclusion from school, ability grouping, homework, and teaching and learning in secondary, further and higher education. Her work in music has two main strands: learning and performance in music and the effects of music on learning and behaviour.

Sarah Hennessy is a lecturer in music education at the University of Exeter. She teaches both specialist and generalist courses for undergraduate and postgraduate teacher training. She also works with higher degree and research students. Her research interests are focused on the professional development of teachers of music in primary schools, and children's musical creativity and its development. She is the author of *Music 7–11: Developing Primary Teaching Skills* (1994) and *Co-ordinating Music Across the Primary School* (1998). She is also editor of *Music Education Research* and director of the *International Conference for Research in Music Education*.

Richard Hodges studied at the Royal College of Music and developed his interest in ICT while undertaking postgraduate research at the University of London. He taught in schools and colleges in London before becoming Senior Lecturer in Music at Derbyshire College of Higher Education in 1988, assuming responsibility for developing the provision in music technology on initial and postgraduate teacher training courses. He has been Head of Music at the University of Derby since 1993, and is currently programme leader for the BA (Hons) Popular Music with Music Technology degree programme.

Robert Mawuena Kwami is a lecturer in music education at the Institute of Education, University of London. He is co-ordinator of music CPD/INSET courses and a PGCE Secondary Music tutor; he also teaches on the MA programme and supervises research students. His extensive teaching record includes higher education institutions in Ghana, Nigeria, England, Wales and Scotland where he was Deputy Director of Music at Northern College, Aberdeen. Robert Kwami has over fifty publications including books and academic articles. His research interests include educational management, inter-cultural aspects of music education and the use of technology in educational institutions.

Chris Philpott graduated as a music teacher in 1979. He then taught music and performing arts for sixteen years in secondary schools in Hertfordshire and Kent. He is currently a Principal Lecturer in Education at Canterbury Christ Church University College where his role includes PGCE tutor for secondary music and Director of the Key Stage 2/3 programme. He has written articles on school-based initial teacher education and is editor of *Learning to Teach Music in the Secondary School.*

Charles Plummeridge is a senior lecturer at the Institute of Education, University of London. His research interests includes the history of music education and the music curriculum; he has published widely in these fields. He is an organist, conductor and examiner and has lectured in Europe, South-East Asia and Southern Africa.

Gary Spruce was head of music at two Birmingham comprehensive schools from 1979 to 1995. He gained his first degree from London University and Masters degrees in music and in education from Birmingham University. He joined the Open University in January 1995 with responsibility for the PGCE music line. He has served on a QCA working group, auditing and evaluating published classroom music materials and is an examiner for A level and the international baccalaureate exam. In his spare time he is responsible for the music section at a Birmingham theatre where he has composed and directed music for a range of productions.

Philip Tate is an Assistant Professor of Music at the College of New Jersey, USA. He contributes to the undergraduate music teacher education programme and also directs the college orchestra. Before working in America he was Senior Lecturer in Music at St Martin's College, Lancaster. He is an experienced music educator, having previously taught school music at both primary and secondary levels. Philip Tate has also published materials for use in the music classroom. His recent research focuses on a comparison of school music between South-East England and New Jersey, USA.

John Witchell is County Adviser for Music in Hertfordshire. He leads the Hertfordshire Music Service, provides advisory support and inspection for schools and co-ordinates the work of arts advisers. In between teaching appointments in Northamptonshire and Hertfordshire he studied for an MA in music education at the Institute of Education. He is secretary of the Federation of Music Services and played a key role in the developing of the instrumental teaching curriculum document *A Common Approach.*

Vanessa Young is Senior Lecturer (Education) at Christ Church Canterbury University College. She has a number of roles across the Faculty including Coordinator of Primary Music within ITE courses and Deputy Director of the Key Stage 2/3 PGCE Programme. Drawing on her previous position in Kent LEA, she also co-ordinates Staff Development for the Faculty of Education. For many years she taught in primary schools in London and Kent.

Acknowledgements

We should like to thank Jill Dolphin and Denise Walker-Hutchinson of the Institute of Education, University of London, for their support in putting this volume together. Many thanks also to Gill Philpott for reading and commenting on drafts of chapters, and to the contributors for their energy and commitment to the project.

Chris Philpott
Charles Plummeridge

Introduction to the series

This book, *Issues in Music Teaching*, is one of a series of books entitled *Issues in Subject Teaching*. The series has been designed to engage with a wide range of issues related to subject teaching. The types of issues vary among the subjects, but may include, for example, issues that:

- impact on Initial Teacher Education in the subject
- are addressed in the classroom through the teaching of the subject
- are related to the content of the subject and its definition
- are related to subject pedagogy
- are connected with the relationship between the subject and broader educational aims and objectives in society, and the philosophy and sociology of education
- are related to the development of the subject and its future in the twenty-first century.

Each book consequently presents key debates that subject teachers will need to understand, reflect on and engage in as part of their professional development. Chapters have been designed to highlight major questions, and to consider the evidence from research and practice in order to find possible answers. Some subject books or chapters offer at least one solution or a view of the ways forward, whereas others provide alternative views and leave readers to identify their own solution or view of the ways forward. The editors expect readers of the series to want to pursue the issues raised, and so chapters include suggestions for further reading, and questions for further debate. The chapters and questions could be used as stimuli for debate in subject seminars or department meetings, or as topics for assignments or classroom research. The books are targeted at all those with a professional interest in the subject, and, in particular: student teachers learning to teach the subject in primary or secondary schools; newly qualified teachers; teachers with a subject co-ordination or leadership role, and those preparing for such responsibility; as well as mentors, tutors, trainers and advisers of the aforementioned groups.

Each book in the series has a cross-phase dimension. This is because the editors believe that it is important for teachers in the primary and secondary phases to look at subject teaching holistically, particularly in order to provide for continuity and progression, but also to increase their understanding of how children learn. The balance of chapters that have a cross-phase relevance, chapters that focus on issues that are of particular concern to primary teachers, and chapters that focus on issues which secondary teachers are more likely to need to address, varies according to the issues relevant to different subjects. However, no matter where the emphasis is, the authors have drawn out the relevance of their topic to the whole of each book's intended audience.

Because of the range of the series, both in terms of the issues covered and its cross-phase concern, each book is an edited collection. Editors have commissioned new writing from experts on particular issues who, collectively, will represent many different perspectives on subject teaching. Readers should not expect a book in this series to cover a full range of issues relevant to the subject, or to offer a completely unified view of subject teaching, or that every issue will be dealt with discretely, or that all aspects of an issue will be covered. Part of what each book in the series offers to readers is the opportunity to explore the interrelationships between positions in debates and, indeed, among the debates themselves, by identifying the overlapping concerns and competing arguments that are woven through the text.

The editors are aware that many initiatives in subject teaching currently originate from the centre, and that teachers have decreasing control of subject content, pedagogy and assessment strategies. The editors strongly believe that for teaching to remain properly a vocation and a profession, teachers must be invited to be part of a creative and critical dialogue about subject teaching, and should be encouraged to reflect, criticise, problem-solve and innovate. This series is intended to provide teachers with a stimulus for democratic involvement in the development of subject teaching.

Susan Capel, Jon Davison, James Arthur and John Moss
July 2000

Introduction

Chris Philpott and Charles Plummeridge

Everybody concerned with music in education will be aware of the considerable diversity of practice to be found in English and Welsh schools. Curriculum content and styles of teaching are obviously determined by many factors, but diversity is also indicative of the variety of beliefs, assumptions, values and ideals that inform practice. In spite of moves on the part of successive governments in recent years to establish a kind of educational orthodoxy, through centralised control, people continue to express a range of views and ideas on almost every aspect of education. There is a critical discourse that takes place in private and in public alongside the practical enterprise; as with all school subjects, the teaching and learning of music generate discussion and debate. Unfortunately, during initial and in-service education and training, the amount of time available for the critical examination of theoretical and practical issues is ever diminishing. Accordingly, many educators are of the opinion that such a state of affairs is stifling new thought and critical reflection; it is said that this can only be to the detriment of professional development. We hope that the chapters which follow will be of use to teachers in the process of becoming autonomous, reflective professionals and curriculum developers in their own right. Indeed, one of the purposes of this volume is to make a contribution to the music education debate by challenging some of the assumptions and principles that underpin national initiatives. However, we do not regard the book as being simply a critique of government policy and it is hoped that the content will be of interest and relevance, not only to teachers, but to all who are associated, both directly and indirectly, with the teaching of music in educational institutions.

The issues confronting music educators are frequently complex. This is clearly illustrated by the contributors to this collection, all of whom are experienced teachers and researchers and share a commitment to the growth and improvement of school music in its many forms. Some of the writers have concentrated on practical matters which are of daily concern to teachers in schools; others adopt a more theoretical approach. In each case the views expressed represent a personal perspective and at no stage has there been any attempt to adopt anything like a common 'philosophy'; in fact, this would have been entirely contrary to the general aim of the book which is primarily to highlight different positions and thereby stimulate discussion among members of the music education community.

In selecting topics we have attempted to identify and focus on some of the central issues of the day. Naturally, we are aware of certain omissions and recognise that others would perhaps have chosen to follow a different path.

The chapters that comprise Part I are devoted to an examination of the place of music in education and the nature of musical experience. Although music is one of the most ancient of curriculum subjects, its position in a system of general education has always been somewhat tenuous and surrounded by controversy. In his historical survey and analysis, Gordon Cox provides a fascinating account of changing attitudes over the past eighty years and demonstrates how educators have defended their theories and practices in the process of music becoming a recognised school subject. Charles Plummeridge also deals with justifications and considers the strengths and weaknesses of different arguments and their implications for practice. The chapters by Chris Philpott, Lucy Green and Susan Hallam represent philosophical, sociological and psychological viewpoints. In their different ways, studies rooted in these disciplines help to explain the significance of music as a fundamental mode of human experience. No longer regarded as a mere pastime or entertainment, music has come to be regarded as a language or way of knowing, and an understanding of its 'workings' is nowadays considered to be a necessary part of the educator's professional knowledge and expertise. Yet how musical competences are acquired and developed, and how meanings are determined by the social context in which music takes place, are rather more complicated matters than have sometimes been supposed. All these things are likely to have a bearing on the way that the subject is organised and taught in educational contexts.

The chapters in Part II are concerned with an examination of issues relating to the content, design, implementation and development of the music curriculum; they fall into three main groupings. In Chapters 6–9 the main area of inquiry is aspects of teaching and learning. Chris Philpott in Chapter 6 raises the question of how we can achieve musical literacy and develops a broad definition of what it is to be literate. Philpott's concern is essentially with musical cognition and he seeks to emphasise the dynamic relationship between body and musical consciousness as a basis for teaching and learning in school. Jonathan M. Barnes in Chapter 7 is committed to the preservation of creative teaching and the idea of creativity across the curriculum. He argues from a practical perspective and asserts that it is quite possible to interpret the National Curriculum in a way that will foster children's imaginative powers. The optimistic tone of this chapter will appeal to teachers who are looking for ways to sustain the ideals of an education that is more than just the 'delivery' of the official prescription. Continuity and progression are terms that feature constantly in contemporary educational language. Tim Cain in Chapter 8 identifies a number of problems associated with the notion of linear progression which, of course, permeates current curriculum thinking, at least as set out in official documents. He maintains that while this type of progression may have a place in some curriculum activities, it is certainly not applicable to all aspects of musical experience; far from it. Regrettably, in the present climate, continuity and progression have become generic terms and closely associated with the logical order of subject matter, and it is taken for granted that this order is the natural basis for the organisation of teaching and learning. Little thought seems to have been given to the extremely different subject matters that make up the curriculum. Another major issue that occupies the minds of teachers is assessment. Gary Spruce in Chapter 9 takes a refreshingly new look at some long-held assumptions and practices and argues that much assessment in music education is dominated by a mainstream, but limited, Western model of achievement. This, he suggests, is far from appropriate in a curriculum that is supposed to be multi-stylistic and providing an education in and for a pluralist society. Spruce sees a need for alternative models that will complement existing assessment techniques.

In Chapters 10–13 the writers explore changes in the content and organisation of the music curriculum over the past twenty years or so. Less than a decade ago there was much enthusiasm for combined arts programmes, but this practice no longer fits comfortably with the present tendency towards the compartmentalisation of knowledge. Charles Plummeridge in Chapter 10 suggests that there are, of course, arguments for and against combined arts programmes but there is much to be said in favour of children being involved in different types of arts projects; sufficient evidence exists to indicate that such projects are likely to motivate many of those students who do not respond positively to studies in the separate disciplines. Robert Kwami's writings on introducing music from non-Western cultures and his practical work in this area will be known to many readers. Here, in Chapter 11, he argues in favour of divergent approaches to the development of curricula which incorporate a variety of musical traditions. This is not always an easy task. Teachers are required to extend their subject knowledge and exercise sensitivity in order to avoid the misrepresentation of different genres.

In Chapter 12, Chris Philpott takes a critical look at the role of instrumental provision in schools and points to the rather strange anomaly whereby, in music, it is often the most able and socially advantaged children who are likely to receive and benefit from extra tuition. In other subject areas it is usually the 'less able' who are thought of as being in need of additional help and support. He suggests that prevailing views of musical achievement, together with lack of access to instrumental tuition for many students, all too frequently lead to a situation which actually militates against the cherished ideal of music as a subject for the majority.

The most remarkable and dramatic change to have occurred over the past twenty years must surely be the growth of information and communications technology. For music teachers and their students, the new technology provides for previously unimagined possibilities, and in Chapter 13 Richard Hodges reviews some of the ways in which hardware and software are being used in primary and secondary schools. These developments are very exciting, but Hodges warns against the dangers of music teaching being dictated by technology and the ready availability of electronic equipment. Undoubtedly, technology offers many new opportunities for all children, but the message is that it must not be allowed to replace genuine musical experience.

One of the most notable developments in recent years has been the increase in contacts between schools and professional musicians. Indeed, many orchestras, opera companies and other professional groups have established educational policies and set up their own education departments. Pauline Adams outlines and discusses some of these initiatives in Chapter 14 and shows how they can add an important new dimension to children's musical encounters.

John Witchell in Chapter 15 discusses one of the most difficult practical realities in class music teaching, namely, the construction and implementation of programmes which meet the needs of individuals. He considers the complex issue of differentiation with reference to the design and implementation of curricula for children with different abilities and backgrounds. Drawing on his wide experience as a practitioner he offers thoughtful advice and suggestions which will be welcomed by all teachers of music.

The main themes of Part III are teacher education and research. Vanessa Young in Chapter 16 raises some searching questions about teacher education and training at both initial and in-service levels. The situation in the primary sector is particularly disturbing since interest in music is increasingly overshadowed by the emphasis on the core subjects. Young maintains that many teachers often do not have sufficient training in the skills and techniques required for the successful operation of class music programmes. At one time a teacher might have attended in-service music courses as part of his or her personal development plan; with so much attention now being given to mathematics, language and science there is little time for the arts subjects. Although there is a statutory curriculum for music, its implementation is becoming increasingly problematic.

The fear is constantly expressed that in the present educational climate teachers are losing their professional autonomy and are regarded solely as technical operatives who are expected to deliver a curriculum designed by those in positions of power. Certainly, the professional model of curriculum development and the notion of teachers as researchers, in the Stenhousian sense, are no longer uppermost in people's minds. Yet there is a growing interest in research in music education and over the past twenty years we have witnessed the employment of a greater number of methodologies in the field.

Philip Tate considers comparative studies in Chapter 17. He reminds us that music educators have always been interested in systems other than their own. In the eighteenth century the renowned Dr Burney travelled extensively in Europe, as did John Hullah and John Spencer Curwen a hundred years later. These educators sought to gather ideas that could be introduced in England, a procedure which has come to be known as 'cultural borrowing'. However, as Tate so rightly points out, it would be most unwise to put too much faith in such a practice. He goes on to consider the possible dangers and pitfalls and proposes an alternative methodology. This includes both macro and micro studies that together can unravel some of the intricacies of music education and offer insights which can be of use to the discerning practitioner.

Sarah Hennessy also focuses on research as a way of bringing about developments in teaching and learning in Chapter 18. Many people will agree with her observation that there are important areas of music education about which we know very little. They will also support her claim that there is a need for independent research particularly at a time when widely publicised inspection findings often go unchallenged. However, it is necessary for researchers to present their findings in a language that is meaningful to the professional community. To what extent this is happening at present is, of course, rather questionable.

Throughout the book there is much reference to the National Curriculum and official policies. This is hardly surprising since over the past ten years all teachers have had to respond to a plethora of government directives. Centralisation and bureaucratisation have not only resulted in increased workloads but also major changes in the nature of professional dialogue. Nevertheless, there are many issues that are likely to resonate with teachers working in other educational systems. Indeed, at international gatherings it soon becomes apparent that music educators the world over share many common aspirations and face similar problems. Therefore, although the discussions are closely related to the English and Welsh scene, it is hoped that the treatment of issues will also be of interest to colleagues in other countries.

Part I

The nature of music and music education

1 Teaching music in schools
Some historical reflections

Gordon Cox

On 24 April 1998 *The Times Educational Supplement* carried the headline 'Primary music in decline'. A 'horrifying' survey had uncovered that one in five primary schools in England and Wales were cutting down on music, and some were dropping the subject altogether. There was no doubt about the culprit: it was the government's insistence that schools concentrate on the teaching of numeracy and literacy. *The Times Educational Supplement* (*TES*) mounted a campaign to save music in schools entitled Music for the Millennium.

This crisis prompted me to chart historically the continuities and discontinuities in the teaching of music in schools in order to understand more clearly the shifting alliances and struggles which have characterised the process of music 'becoming a subject' (see Goodson, 1994). In order to place my thinking within a wider context I found Kliebard's (1995) categorisation of the four major influences on the American curriculum helpful: first, the humanists, who were the keepers of the tradition, tied to the finest elements of the Western canon, and committed to the traditional skills associated with it; second, social efficiency educators who looked upon the curriculum as directly functional to the adult life-roles of future citizens, they applied the standardised techniques of industry to the business of schooling; third, the developmentalists, who were committed to a curriculum in harmony with children's real interests; fourth, the social meliorists who maintained that schools and the curriculum should act as major forces for social change and justice. I shall refer to these curriculum traditions in my conclusion.

Through reading the *TES* columns relating to Music for the Millennium, I identified three main questions that I wanted to pursue historically with the intention of discerning some underlying patterns: how have the aims and justifications for the teaching of music changed and developed? What have been the principal innovations in the music curriculum over the years? What do we know about music teachers and the teaching of music in classrooms in relation to these aims and innovations? Change and continuity have been examined by comparing press coverage of music education at 25-year intervals over a span of seventy-five years, commencing in 1923–24, through until 1998–99. The journals selected for consultation I have taken to be representative of music teachers' reading during these years, and include: *The Times Educational Supplement*

(1998–99), *Music Teacher* (1923–24, 1948–49, 1973–74, 1998–99), *Music in Education* (1948–49, 1973–74), *School Music Review* (1923–24).

I shall discuss the three main questions through snapshots taken at these four 25-year intervals. In comparing the accounts no doubt at times my chosen themes will elide, at other times they will collide. Each particular year will necessarily contain different emphases. Finally, I shall present a conclusion which will point to some of the main currents and conflicts I have identified.

1923–24

The justifications for the teaching of music in the early 1920s ranged from the idealist to the pragmatic. We read of a high-minded view in a critique (*School Music Review*, July 1923) of a book by Ernest Hunt entitled *Spirit and Music* (1922). Hunt believed that music should be valued as a subject, not merely as a part of life, a means of earning a living or of relaxation, but also more importantly as 'a manifestation of the divine spirit' (ibid.: 51). Music in schools, particularly folk tunes and dances, could provide an outlet for the emotions, and stimulate imaginative play. Consequently, it might be socially regenerative:

> the prosaic life and surroundings of the slum child are sufficiently deadening and the new mental picture this gives are in the nature of windows opening on new vistas of life. They suggest views that could come to the child's mind in no other ways.
>
> (ibid.: 97)

This rhetoric contrasts with the more down-to-earth advice given to music teachers as regards classroom principles by Walter Carroll, the music adviser of Manchester (*School Music Review*, February 1924). He outlined eight aims for elementary schoolchildren up to the age of 14. These included the cultivation of a love of music for its own sake; good breathing habits; a sweet voice with forward tone and no breaks or registers; a sensitive ear for pitch and rhythm; a facility in reading simple tunes from staff notation; a large number of good songs; an appreciation of music through rhythm, melody and harmony; and knowledge of music literature through hearing standard works performed well. The relation between such statements of rhetoric and practice did become closer in some of the curriculum innovations of these years, particularly in tune building, musical appreciation, and concerts for children.

Walford Davies was convinced that the majority of children could be tune-builders (*Music Teacher*, January 1923). However, he observed that remarkably few children in schools were taught the simple rules of the game of melody, although he emphasised that like any game it was not enough to be merely taught in books and classrooms. While one-third of a music course might be found in instruction books, the most exciting two-thirds should be spent in the activity of making music. Davies believed in the simple truth that 'melody is our real mother-tongue' (ibid.: 194), and consequently the tune building of the pupils may enable them to inhabit 'the little creative heaven of sound' (ibid.). Davies was to preach this gospel not only through the gramophone, but increasingly through the wireless: in 1924 he presented the first schools broadcast on the BBC.

Perhaps the most significant innovation, however, was music appreciation. It was Carroll's opinion (*School Music Review*, February 1924) that school music needed both action (music by doing) and contemplation (listening), but in his opinion the latter received much less attention than the former. Appreciation certainly raised the profile of listening. However, the apostle of the new movement, Stewart MacPherson, in an article entitled 'The Position of the Appreciation Movement' gave a warning: there was a danger that the aesthetic element in general education could be too loose and debased (*Music Teacher*, January 1923). He welcomed the fact that musical appreciation had caught on, but like all new movements it also suffered from 'the zeal, untempered by discretion, of not a few of its supporters' (ibid.: 203). Appreciation should certainly not be the province of every teacher, its purpose was not to amuse or provide anecdotes. Much of the teaching associated with it was, in MacPherson's opinion, profoundly bad. The teacher needed enthusiasm – 'it is impossible to kindle a fire from an icicle' (ibid.) – but, above all, a deep appreciation and grasp of the art of music itself. Whilst the primary school teacher might deal with the rudimentary stages of class singing and ear training well, appreciation work needed specialised teachers.

The third development during these years was related to musical appreciation, and provided an expansion of opportunities for children to hear music outside the school. On 29 March 1924, the inaugural concert for children promoted by Robert Mayer was presented at Westminster Central Hall (*School Music Review*, May 1924):

> In spite of strike difficulties some 1500 children were present . . . Mr Mayer had in mind the children's concerts conducted by Mr Walter Damrosch in the United States and desires to arrange a series along similar lines in London.
> (ibid.: 333)

This movement gained momentum fast. Manchester City Council approved a series of municipal orchestral concerts with 500 seats reserved for elementary and secondary school pupils, while official recognition had been given to children's concerts by the Board of Education, with the proviso that local education authorities (LEAs) had to provide the money.

These innovations helped to develop creative music making, and to reinforce the effectiveness of musical appreciation by affording masses of children the opportunity to listen to music played by professionals on the gramophone and wireless, and in real life.

But the conditions for implementing such innovations in schools were not ideal. In an article entitled 'Appreciation in an Elementary School', E.R. Lewis (*Music Teacher*, August 1924) informs us that of the three classes in his school, two numbered 65 pupils each, while the third had 40 pupils. Each group was assigned two half-hour periods weekly for music. Much of the time was taken up with vocal training in tonic sol-fa and staff notations. This work was regarded as difficult by both teachers and pupils. Appreciation was therefore a welcome innovation, but it had to be approached circumspectly. At first it comprised one in six lessons, and later was extended to include a short piece of pianoforte music played three days a week to the whole school assembly, while on a fourth morning a gramophone record was played.

There were, however, more highly favoured schools which blazed the trail of musical excellence. One of the key centres for developing the music curriculum in secondary schools was the Mary Datchelor School in Camberwell, London, the subject of one of the Board of Education's pamphlets (*School Music Review*, July 1923). A special grant had been awarded to the school from 1919. It provided for a two-year course of further study for those girls who, having reached the standard for the General School Certificate Examination, demonstrated that they possessed special musical ability. These pupils spent between twenty and thirty periods per week in music. Eventually most of them took up music professionally, and some entered teaching. But the school laid the foundation of this advanced course early on in the curriculum. In a demonstration of the musical work of the school to the Music Teachers Association (*Music Teacher*, January 1923), it is evident that improvisation and composition played a key role. This was a scheme which provided hope for the future, and enhanced the status of the subject.

Questions of status and professionalism and training were in the forefront of music teachers' concerns at this time. Proper training was one of the keys to enhanced professionalism. There was a need for a new diploma (*School Music Review*, June 1923) which would ensure that teachers, who otherwise had had little musical experience apart from that gained in training college, could both improve and update themselves in order to cope successfully with the host of new developments in the teaching of music which were on the horizon. The School Music Teachers Certificate was reckoned to be too narrow, too tied to a textbook. Perhaps LEAs could increase the musical scope of qualifications: why not an LCC (London County Council) Diploma of Music? The dilemma was that the LRAM was too difficult. A relevant diploma needed to cover ear training, sight singing, rhythmic movement, musical appreciation, history, musical form and harmony. The *School Music Review* reported the following month that the Tonic Sol-fa College had set up a special committee 'instituting a new diploma for school teachers whose needs will be specially remembered in the light of modern developments in school methods' (*School Music Review*, July 1923: 29–30).

1948–49

A thoughtful reassessment of music teaching in the post-war years was provided by A.H. Radcliffe in an article entitled significantly 'Education through Music' (*Music in Education*, January–February 1948). He expressed concern about the institutionalisation of music: 'while school education is handled as a thing apart, as it all too often is, while it is undertaken in a social vacuum, it can strike children only as unreal and completely non-vital' (ibid.: 165). If education was a process, rather than merely having content, it followed that a music teacher's concepts of education were at least as important as his or her musical capacities. The problem with music was that its objectives in schools were ill-defined and ill-considered: we had lost sight of education in our concentration on pure technique.

In some ways this theme was developed by one of the pioneers of the Percussion Band movement, Louie de Rusette. She believed in the importance of the present moment. The child should be encouraged to express himself or herself through rhythm, melody and harmony (*Music in Education*, May–June 1948). Mere imitation killed initiative, forestalled nature and dwarfed the personality. She asked, why should music be different from art in schools? Children were encouraged to paint and draw according to their present powers of observation and experience. Too often in school music, children were penalised because they were not felt ready to produce accurate sounds. On the contrary, de Rusette declared: 'We shall not become a musical nation until music is treated as a creative art in the Primary school' (ibid.: 62).

If such views were growing, they were still not generally representative of the majority. More characteristic was Reginald Hunt's (*Music Teacher*, June 1948) listing of the four essential aims of school music teaching: to ensure musical literacy; to afford practical experience of music and music making; to promote a knowledge of and liking for the best music; ultimately to bring about a cultivated and urbane outlook on life, as a result of musical training.

Instrumental teaching was clearly in the ascendant. Area and youth orchestras began to represent unrivalled opportunities for children to take part in music. The National Youth Orchestra made its first appearance in 1948 (*Music Teacher*, June 1948), while at a more local level Elizabeth Lumb wrote about her secondary modern school brass band in Bradford, which within four years had gained fourth place in the appropriate section of the National Championships (*Music Teacher*, September 1949).

Classroom instruments too were gaining in importance and popularity. While sight reading still played an essential role in the scheme of things, it was not necessarily taught through the voice. Snell (*Music Teacher*, March 1948) maintained it could be taught more effectively using the whole range of instrumental resources available to a teacher: percussion bands, string classes, the recorder, bamboo pipes. '

The link between orchestras and 'musical appreciation' had been considerably strengthened in 1946, the year in which the Crown Film Unit produced a film called *Instruments of the Orchestra*, specifically for use in the classroom (*Music in Education*, March–April 1947). Composed by Benjamin Britten, it was directed by Muir Mathieson. Mathieson was enthusiastic about the potential of film for delivering an effective music education. He extended his love of film, to the context of cinemas, where he was conducting a series of children's morning symphony concerts in Middlesex. In his opinion, the cinema could assist the cause of music education, and he desired the fullest possible use 'of this vast potential source of education and instruction' (*Music in Education*, May–June 1948: 40).

A penetrating insight into teaching during these years was provided by Gordon Reynolds in an article entitled 'The Secondary School Music Master'

(*Music Teacher*, October 1948). Reynolds had intended to be a church organist, but as a result of his work in the Forces found himself organising choral groups and music clubs. Consequently, he took a school music diploma, and became the sole music master in a school. Every class, he tells us, was allocated 40 minutes per week, and the teaching extended from tonic sol-fa, to the School Certificate, the Higher School Certificate, and Scholarship work. Because of an overcrowded timetable, everything else, including choirs and orchestras took place after school. His working day extended therefore until 5.30 p.m. and longer on a Friday. He bemoaned having to teach the ABC stage, pupils had little experience in primary school. But for Reynolds the greatest joy was the choral work: 'don't expect to grow rich or fat, but you would be dull indeed if you were not at least occasionally spiritually warmed by your endeavours' (ibid.: 380).

During these years the training of music teachers was a preoccupation reflected in the columns of *Music in Education*. A portrait of the Southern Music Training Centre in Ewell (*Music in Education*, November–December 1948) provides us with evidence of the variety of training procedures. The range of courses included a three-year programme for young people leaving school who wished to train immediately as music specialist teachers, a supplementary course for ordinary or emergency trained teachers wishing to specialise in music teaching, and a one-year course for trained musicians wanting to teach in schools and qualify for Burnham rates of pay. In addition to the full-time courses of training colleges, there was a plethora of vacation courses. As an example, we might take the school music training course held at Stockwell Training College for the Music Teachers Association (*Music in Education*, May–June 1948: 37–8). The lecturers and their subjects provide a list of current concerns and significant music educators: Watkins Shaw, 'A Practical Music Syllabus for the Junior School'; Frederick Green, 'Voice, Ear and Eye Training'; Doris Gould, 'Percussion Bands'; Dorothy Smith, 'Music in the Infant School'; Edgar Hunt, 'The Recorder'; Leslie Russell, 'The London Plan on School Music'.

1973–74

The 1970s witnessed the ascendancy of creative music making. It was fast becoming the new orthodoxy. Creativity became a focus for re-defining the aims of music in the curriculum. Propelled by the publication of *Sound and Silence* (Paynter and Aston, 1970), the columns of the periodicals were peppered with references to it and the Schools Council project, 'Music in the Secondary School Curriculum' directed by John Paynter at the University of York. In *Music Teacher* (May 1974) we find an advertisement for a course at York, 'New Music in Action', designed for teachers of music, dance and drama. The course contributors read like a roll-call of the movement: Harrison Birtwistle, Wilfrid Mellers, John Paynter, Bernard Rands, George Self and Trevor Wishart.

A keyword in the 1970s is 'aesthetic', although we noted its use by MacPherson in 1924. It was connected in a series of four articles in *Music Teacher* (March–June 1974) by Keith Swanwick, with the feeling of crisis that was afflicting secondary music teachers, caused by the barrage of criticism in the wake of the publication by the Schools Council in 1968 of *Enquiry One* (1968) in which music, in the opinion of young school leavers, was the most boring and useless subject on the school curriculum.

Swanwick's four articles were entitled 'Class Music in the Secondary School – A Perspective', and in the first of these he attempted to clarify the nature of musical activity, by identifying its three vital processes (*Music Teacher*, March 1974). First, the sounds we use in music are selected from an enormous range of possibilities; second, we have to engage in the process of relating sounds together; finally, and most crucial of all, is the intention that there shall be music. Essential to this intention was an aesthetic response: the ability to perceive and feel something which becomes self-enriching, a response to something on its own terms. Although music may be a part of cultural heritage, and is a skill-learning activity, nevertheless its central core is the aesthetic experience: 'music without aesthetic qualities is like a fire without heat' (ibid.: 13).

It would be misleading, however, to characterise the 1970s as single-minded as far as aims and purposes were concerned. George Odam in 'Music in the Secondary School' (*Music Teacher*, January–February 1974) felt that agonising choices lay ahead as far as music education was concerned. He believed strongly that pupils should be taught to read music, and there were some hopeful signs on the horizon, notably the advent of classroom orchestras which could do much to teach basic music literacy. In this connection, William Salaman developed a systematic approach to the classroom orchestra in a series which was featured in *Music Teacher* in 1974.

But what was going on in schools? On the one hand, there was a feeling of exhilaration in developing the innovatory ideas stemming from the Schools Council secondary music project, but, on the other hand, there was a mood of desperation. Like Odam, Swanwick (*Music Teacher*, April 1974) identified the present moment as being a crisis. Now was the time to act decisively: either stop music as a class activity, or develop a sense of purpose about it. He outlined some problematic scenarios of music teaching which encapsulated the experience of fairly common practice in classrooms during this time. First, was an attempt to engage children in 'experimental' music:

> after an hour the children are still listlessly exploring, bored to tears by an activity that has neither skill achievement nor aesthetic content . . . The teacher does not know the transformation spell of selection, relation and intention, and so is not able to change the drab Cinderella of sound materials into a beautiful Princess, a musical experience.
>
> (*Music Teacher*, March 1974: 13)

Next was the 'Novelty' structure:

> when-in-doubt-change-the-activity . . . so activities are launched on waves of enthusiasm and as they degenerate other verses are sent off down the

slipway . . . I have seen more classes driven to distraction by monotonous strings of novelties without any feeling of achievement or musical purpose than by whole periods spent on a single activity.

(*Music Teacher*, May 1974: 20)

And finally an approach which was 'pupil-generated': 'where we assume that classes can be split into groups and sent off into various rooms and corners to make their own music . . . without first establishing a starting-point' (ibid.).

As a consequence of reading Swanwick's articles a music teacher wrote a letter to the editor of *Music Teacher* (August 1974) confessing that she felt angry and ashamed. It nicely encapsulates the frenetic pace of the period, and much of the underlying frustration of music teachers:

I have allowed my judgement to be clouded by an over-riding desire to stimulate interest . . . I am a slave to the Top Twenty – every Sunday. During my lessons, the tape recorder lies visible on my desk – blatant bribery, a fifteen minute reward after one hour of flogging one dead horse after another. I weep to see a trunk-load of broken instruments, quite beyond repair . . . I twang on a wretched guitar, and seethe when a very expensive copy of modern folk song is stolen. I never liked them – but still – why worry? . . . 'Improvisation and composition' – this produces a hollow laugh. I have found all Hell let loose when fifth year boys (ROSLA's first products) found a way into the Music Room and blew and banged everything available . . . 'Listening skills' – who listens? . . . there is an all-pervading restlessness; desks and chairs are constantly on the move as ungainly bodies shift uneasily. As teachers we are reduced almost entirely to dependence on personality values. Combine a forceful personality, a strong physique, boundless nervous energy, unlimited time and ingenuity, and one has a chance of survival – with some success . . . The fact remains, that this teacher at least, is a weak echo of what she might be, both in enthusiasm and consequently in achievement.

(ibid.: 17)

1998–99

In spite of the perceived threat to music in schools in the 1990s, the *TES* ('Opinion', 22 May 1998) reported that David Blunkett, the Secretary of State for Education and Employment had a considerable personal commitment to music. It had played an important part in his own life and he wanted young people to have access to its enormous benefits: 'Learning an instrument, singing, or simply enjoying the music of others, can help develop an awareness of the spiritual dimension of life' (ibid.: 13). What generally characterised the search for a convincing justification for music during this time was an exploration of the transfer of learning. In the first issue of the *TES* campaign to save music in schools, Anthony Everitt wrote an extended article entitled 'Cerebral Software' ('Opinion', 24 April 1998) in which he drew upon recent research which explored the fundamentals of music. What distinguished music from the other arts was that it was more than art: 'It reaches beyond aesthetics into ethics and the nature of intelligence' (ibid.: 15). Everitt tells us there is nothing new in this: Plato had elaborated on the profound impact music exerted upon our individual personalities. But what was new, according to Everitt, was that scientific research demonstrated that music played a key role in the functioning of the brain. Behavioural psychologists had shown how music could aid the learning process. Consequently, Everitt concluded that giving more time to the 3 R's was counter-productive if it led to fewer music classes. In other words, music is fundamental to human experience:

> Underneath the elaborations of civilised life and the birth of reason, lies music – the primary language. It is only as we grow up that it dwindles into an art. We forget at our peril its original, underpinning function as cerebral software.
>
> (ibid.)

A critical view of this notion of transferability was raised in a letter from Richard Staines which accused Everitt of simplistic assumptions and errors. Everitt's approval of some Swiss research into the benefits of extended music teaching was challenged, because in fact the supposed benefits were of an affective nature rather than in effects which were tangible, measurable and scholastic (*TES*, 15 May 1998). This particular debate continues.

The two most apparent curriculum innovations chronicled in the 1990s in *Music Teacher* have been music technology and popular music. Adrian York in his article 'Be Brave about the New Sound World' (*Music Teacher*, February 1999) encouraged music teachers to put in the time and effort needed to embrace technology. After all, many children have access to electronic keyboards or PCs with relatively sophisticated sequencing, sampling and editing software. The technophobia felt by many music educators may be unsurprising but it has to be addressed for three reasons: undoubted demand from pupils; to break the out-moded chain of music education; to accept the primacy of popular musical culture, itself permeated by technology, in the twentieth century.

The increasing importance of popular musical culture and its implications for music teaching were explored by Norton York (*Music Teacher*, April 1999). He pointed to the measure of respectability pop music had achieved with New Labour clearly understanding its economic importance. Music educators, according to York, should feel confident with the progress they had made, particularly in opening up the music room and curriculum to pop, particularly through the GCSE. What was required, however, was a debate about teacher training, and how it might adapt to the musical aesthetic of pop music, as well as to its technology. We note a direct parallel here with the concerns of teachers of music in the 1920s who wanted to update their skills in order to cope with a rapidly changing educational environment.

However, *Music Teacher* also witnessed a good deal of support for traditional music teaching. In particular, Andrew Peggie, a respected music educator, wrote an impassioned letter (*Music Teacher*, January 1999) protesting about the obsession of the Music National Curriculum with an inclusive, maximum breadth approach, which resulted in virtually no progression and even less context. He suggested three strategies: (a) to ensure all pupils develop a confident vocal identity through speech, singing and movement; (b) to ensure pupils experience a wide range of music through listening, implying that curriculum music reverts to music appreciation; and (c) to ensure pupils achieve Grade 5 level fluency in reading notation by the end of Key Stage 3.

As part of its Music for the Millennium campaign the *TES* focused on schools which provided exemplars of good practice, frequently drawing on those identified as outstanding by OFSTED Inspectors. These examples illustrate a more positive view of the inclusiveness fostered by the National Curriculum than Peggie's more negative stance. For example, Kates Hill School in Dudley had a music programme that influenced other crucial areas of the curriculum. Its head believed that there were other ways of delivering the literacy hour than a wholesale concentration on literacy type work. Music, for example, could play a key role (*TES*, 1 May 1998). The variety and scope of music provision at the school were impressive: Year 6 pupils were encouraged to write compositions from scratch, using percussion, electronic keyboards, ethnic instruments and music software; multi-cultural approaches were fostered through the Asian Dance Group, and the school steel band. It was reckoned that participation in the steel band had helped save some pupils from exclusion.

A secondary school that was singled out was the Duchess's County High School in Alnwick, Northumberland (*TES*, 22 May 1999). Its choir of ninety pupils which included forty boys, demonstrated an evident sense of commitment, and its repertoire was refreshingly eclectic, ranging from Zulu songs to Andrew Lloyd-Webber, Tammy Wynette to Vivaldi. There was notable success in curriculum terms too: GCSE numbers had increased from twenty to seventy in three years.

But as far as the plight of music teachers was concerned, there was the serious worry that too few music graduates were becoming classroom music teachers. Tony Knight of the Qualifications and Curriculum Authority (QCA) (*Music Teacher*, April 1999) outlined five factors that might dissuade a youngster from entering the music teaching profession: the hugely exhausting balance of curricular and extra-curricular work; the isolation of frequently being a one-person department; the low status of the subject in schools; ineffective timetabling for the subject; poor resources and accommodation. His conclusion was that the nature of the job and attitudes towards it needed to change, before more young people were attracted to it.

Conclusion

What conclusions can we draw from these historical snapshots? We recognise aspects of Kliebard's humanist curriculum tradition in the constant concern about the teaching of basic musical skills associated with the Western canon, particularly musical notation. But there were shifts within this position. In the 1920s the teaching of sight reading through vocal work was the prevailing orthodoxy, while in the 1940s there was a move towards an instrumental approach. The development of new perspectives in the 1970s were perceived as a threat to such traditional concerns, yet for Odam and Salaman, the teaching of music literacy was still central. More recently in the 1990s the letters to the *TES* have re-emphasised concerns about the necessity of teaching musical literacy.

There are certain ideas that permeate the justifications and aims of music education. The belief in music as a 'spiritual' or 'divine' force was being expressed at the start and end of our chronological survey and in many ways is connected with the humanist tradition centred on a belief in the transcendence of music. But there is also a link to the social meliorist position: music has the power to regenerate society. After all, if music is so elemental and fundamental there is no limit to its power. A conviction that melody is 'our mother-tongue' (1923), that music is 'our primary language' (1998) reinforces the belief that it has the power to effect a cultivated outlook on life (1948), and to play a key role in a pupil's performance in other subjects (1998).

The notion shared by MacPherson (1923) and Swanwick (1974) of music as 'aesthetic' education essentially moved away from extrinsic outcomes to an emphasis on encountering music on its own terms. It becomes self-enriching through the ability to perceive and feel. In turn this connected with de Rusette's conviction (1948) in the importance of children expressing themselves through music according to their own powers of observation and experience. This meant that children could form their own 'little creative heaven of sound' (Davies in 1923). Such thinking dominated music education in the 1970s, and established itself as the new orthodoxy. There was a direct connection in all this with Kliebard's developmentalist tradition.

There has been no shortage of curriculum innovations during these years. The development of different technologies has frequently propelled these, ranging from the wireless, gramophone, film, to 'classroom instruments' and ICT. But again we note continuities between the percussion bands of the 1940s and the classroom orchestras of the 1970s, between MacPherson's pioneering work on appreciation in the 1920s, and Peggie's plea for a return to such work in the 1990s.

Finally, what of teachers and classrooms? There has been a tendency for curriculum historians not to look behind the schoolhouse door (Goodson, 1994). But running through the accounts in this chapter are stories of hard-pressed teachers who nevertheless gain satisfaction from their work against often overwhelming odds. The lack of status and recognition afforded school music teachers is a constant theme, still being expressed in the 1990s, together with the needs for relevant training. And yet what is achieved is sometimes outstanding, and reports from the Mary Datchelor School in the 1920s, to the Kates Hill School and the Duchess's County High School in the 1990s give us reason to hope.

To conclude, Goodson (1994) compares the making of curriculum to the process of inventing tradition. But it is not a once-and-for-all given, it has to be defended and reconstructed both in terms of prescription and practice. Music educators in the UK in 1998 were given a jolt when their subject had to fight for its life in a battle with the social efficiency tendencies of a government determined to prioritise 'the basics'. Fortunately by the end of 1999 the *TES* (26 November 1999) was welcoming music's return to the primary National Curriculum. But we would do well to develop a historical perspective towards music in education, as it provides pause for thought and a space for scepticism about the taken for granted and seemingly inevitable nature of the curriculum.

Questions for discussion

1   What in your opinion are some of the problematic scenarios of classroom music that may be observed frequently today? How do they relate to examples of 'experimental', 'novelty' and 'pupil-generated' lessons (see pp. 15–16 in this chapter)?
2   What historical continuities and discontinuities can you discover contained within the present Music National Curriculum document, particularly with reference to aims and methods?
3   In what ways has the job of the music teacher changed for better or worse since the 1920s?

References

Goodson, I.F. (1994) *Studying Curriculum*, Buckingham: Open University Press.
Hunt, E.B. (1922) *Spirit and Music*, London: Kegan Paul, Trench, Trubner and Co; J. Curwen and Sons.
Kliebard, H.M. (1995) *The Struggle for the American Curriculum 1893–1958*, 2nd edn, London: Routledge.
Music in Education (1948–49, 1973–74).
Music Teacher (1923–24, 1948–49, 1973–74, 1998–99).
Paynter, J. and Aston, P. (1970) *Sound and Silence: Classroom Projects in Creative Music*, Cambridge: Cambridge University Press.
School Music Review (1923–24).
Schools Council (1968) *Enquiry One: Young School Leavers*, London: HMSO.
The Times Educational Supplement (1998–99).

Further reading

Cox, G. (1993) *A History of Music Education in England 1872–1928*, Aldershot: Scolar Press.
Pitts, S. (2000) *A Century of Change in Music Education: Historical Perspectives on Contemporary Practice in British Secondary School Music*, Aldershot: Ashgate.
Rainbow, B. (1989) *Music in Educational Thought and Practice: A Survey from 800 BC*, Aberystwyth: Boethius Press.

2 The justification for music education

Charles Plummeridge

Introduction

Music education is an enterprise that takes many forms and is provided for in a wide variety of settings; discussions relating to its justification focus almost exclusively on the issue of music as a school curriculum subject. In view of the existence of the National Curriculum it might reasonably be concluded that the topic is not especially relevant at the present time. After all, music is a foundation subject and the arguments for its inclusion in the curriculum must surely have been won; it is no longer what the Assistant Masters and Mistresses Association (1984) once described as an 'endangered subject'. But is this really the case? Individuals and professional bodies regularly issue earnest statements about the educational significance and value of music studies and express concerns over limited staffing and resources. While there appears to be a steady supply of secondary specialists, the Music Education Council (MEC) (2000) is understandably disappointed by the scant attention now being given to music in the education and training of primary school teachers. It may seem to some observers as if musicians and music educationists constantly need to protect their subject against the philistine attitudes of people who still regard the arts as little more than dispensable extras or mere entertainments. Whether or not there are any educational policy-makers who would subscribe to such an extreme view is questionable, but music educationists often appear to be on the defensive. And in an age of transparency and accountability many teachers report that they are often required to explain, to different audiences, why music is of value within the context of a general education.

A survey of the literature reveals that current justifications fall roughly into two categories. First, there are those which are rooted in ideas about the transfer of learning. For example, it is often asserted that engagement in music promotes the growth of intellectual capacities and worthy dispositions: accordingly, this is taken to be an indisputable reason for its inclusion in curriculum programmes. Such views are attractive and have received considerable media coverage in the past few years. Second, there are justifications which arise from, or are part of, a certain conception of education; these are likely to receive less publicity but will obviously be of interest to professional educationists. There is frequently a tendency on the part of those who advocate a justification of the first type to assume that it is, *de facto*, of the second type; when this is the case, genuine discussion of educational issues can all too easily be replaced by rhetoric and propaganda.

It may be that educators do need to highlight the importance of music within the curriculum for all sorts of professional and pedagogical reasons. The purpose of this chapter, however, is not to outline some new argument as a basis for an ultimate or foolproof justification since such an undertaking would be impossible. The content of the curriculum can be viewed in different ways and is therefore always problematic; there is nothing that is fixed and immutable. The intention here is to examine critically a number of past and present ideas about the position of music in the curriculum and discuss some of their strengths, limitations and likely practical implications.

Extrinsic justifications

There exists a very long-held belief in the 'power' of music to improve the human condition. It is a belief that has appeared in numerous guises, and while receiving widespread acceptance has just as often been scorned and rejected. Nevertheless, it has been influential in educational circles since earliest times. The ancient Egyptians, who established the first formal systems of schooling, initially regarded musical activity, as an educational pursuit, with some suspicion. Certainly, music and the arts featured strongly in society and were much enjoyed and supported by the aristocracy, but it was often thought that too much direct exposure to the performing arts might weaken the character of those destined to become the future rulers. However, over time, the singing of carefully chosen songs gained approval as a means of fostering sound moral attitudes and good behaviour. It is well known that the Greeks also associated the arts with moral development. Plato is customarily thought of as the great champion of arts education because of the views expressed in *The Republic*: through musical experience the young would acquire a sense of grace and an appreciation of beauty. Many of the Greek philosophers (although certainly not all) regarded instruction in literature and the fine arts (*mousike*) as a necessary part of a liberal education and a means of preserving the culture, but there was almost always a link between music and a concern for moral rectitude. Furthermore, the ability to appreciate beauty in the arts was, for Plato, a preparation for the eventual recognition of the beauty of reason, the highest form of cognitive functioning. Music as a component of a liberal education for philosopher kings, the men of gold, thus remained related to some extrinsic end.

A number of the nineteenth-century social reformers in Britain were inspired by Greek ideals and the notion of making people 'better' through the study of music pervades the Victorian writings on education. William Hickson's famous assertion that music has a tendency to wean the mind from vicious and sensual indulgences is a typical example of nineteenth-century thought. At the same time, other reasons emerged for including music in the curriculum. Several leading figures in the English Church, perturbed by the dismal singing at Sunday services, advocated the teaching of music as a way of raising standards of worship. In some European states emphasis was placed on the performance in schools of those songs which would promote a sense of national pride and identity, and hopefully a more harmonious society. How far these various social, political and religious aims were ever realised is unclear. Even so, it is not difficult to identify vestiges of some nineteenth-century views, and also ancient precepts, in present-day curriculum rationales.

The idea of music being educationally valuable because of its spin-off effects has gained increasing appeal in recent years. Much publicity is given to what is declared to be a direct connection between engagement in musical activity and academic achievement. It has often been accepted, almost without question, that the accomplishments of cathedral choristers provide the exemplar of the link between musical and scholastic performance. These children's overall attainments serve to demonstrate, so it is said, that concentrated studies in music actually nurture general cognitive capacities and abilities. One of the most frequently cited examples of the effects of learning in music on the growth of intellectual skills is the information provided by Hungarian music educators, and first publicised in a celebrated book by Frigyes Sandor (1965). It is claimed that there is substantial evidence to show that the overall academic achievements of children attending the special music primary schools are superior to those of their contemporaries in the regular primary schools. This Hungarian research features prominently in a most optimistic and enthusiastic booklet entitled *The Fourth 'R'* published by the organisation known as the Campaign for Music in the Curriculum (1998). The purpose of the document is to draw attention to the 'empirical evidence' and 'proof' of the academic and social benefits of musical studies. It is argued that the government's mission to raise standards (which the Campaign fully supports) would be further strengthened if greater emphasis were placed on the values of teaching music in schools.

The most immediate and obvious reaction to these sorts of empirical claims about the educative power of music is to wonder to what extent they can be verified. What is the quality of the research methodology in the various studies and therefore the status of the findings? It is striking that nowhere in the Hungarian research is there any mention of those established psychological theories of transfer that have been formulated as a result of continuous research over the past eighty years. The findings, as reported by Sandor, could, in fact, all be explained in the light of some very well-known and recognised theories: identical elements, generalisation, learning to learn (see Klausmeier, 1985). These theories would actually lend some support to the general proposition. The trouble with the Hungarian research, which is completely overlooked in *The Fourth 'R'*, is a reliance on formal discipline theory and faculty psychology. In spite of the fact that this theory was shown to be seriously flawed over eighty years ago it still has a popular appeal: studying certain subjects helps to train and develop the 'faculties'. There are even traces of the theory in the latest version of the National Curriculum (DfEE, 1999); the study of music is said to promote thinking skills, self-discipline and creativity across the curriculum. At first sight this may seem convincing but there is no evidence to show that creative behaviour developed in music makes children more creative in mathematics, home economics or history.

Many of the benefits associated with studies in music can be accounted for in terms of learning to learn: good study skills and habits acquired in music transfer to other activities. But such skills could just as likely transfer from studies in any other discipline. It is one thing to say that the study of music has transfer effects but quite another to claim that this makes music unique which in turn provides its justification as a curriculum subject. The point is that transfer of skills, attitudes, techniques and knowledge from one discipline to another occurs all the time in everyday life and is, of course, a vital part of the educational process. For Bruner (1966) transfer was central to a theory of instruction.

There continues to be a good deal of psychological and neurophysiological research into the effects of music on brain functions and cognitive operations (see, for example, Overy, 1998; Rauscher, 1998). While there is undoubtedly some evidence to suggest that musical studies can result in extra-musical benefits, it soon becomes obvious that there are limitations, and even dangers, in using such evidence for the purpose of justifying the inclusion of music in the curriculum. The main problem is that if musical activities are to be part of children's general education because they improve intellectual performance and promote social skills, then any evaluation of music education in an institution would have to be undertaken with this in mind. Music programmes would only be considered to be successful if it could be shown that they had in some ways contributed to enhanced intellectual skills in subjects other than music. Equally, poor performance in, say, mathematics might be attributed to inadequate music teaching. But how would it be possible, in a school context, to show any such connection? Attempting to judge music education in terms of students' achievement in other areas of the curriculum would obviously be quite ludicrous, but this would be the logical outcome arising from a justification which relies on transfer theory.

It is certainly the case that many teachers will be able to give examples of how individual students appear to have gained much from taking part in musical activities. Nobody with experience of teaching in school would want to deny that music can be 'good' for children in any number of ways and that participation in music pursuits can contribute to their personal and social education. But it does not follow that this constitutes a sufficient reason for supporting its inclusion in the curriculum. Any proper justification for music, or anything else, has to be with reference to broader educational principles

Justifications, theories and practices

The well-known diversity of practice in the English system is partly due to the multitude of ideas about the nature and purpose of musical studies in a general education that have emerged over the past hundred years. Widely publicised arguments about the structure and content of the National Curriculum, following the publication of the Interim Report (DES, 1991) reflected alternative and often conflicting views of music education. And it would be most unwise to assume that there was now a consensus position and all differences had been laid aside.

In reality, classroom practices have usually developed in a fairly pragmatic fashion and not as part of a clearly formulated overall scheme; teachers employ material and techniques that 'work'. Nevertheless, it is apparent that individual teachers have particular ideas about aims, content and methods and several writers have identified alternative conceptions, or theories, of class music teaching. Keith Swanwick (1988) talks about three theories based respectively on traditional values, a focus on children and a respect for alternative traditions. Graham Vulliamy (1977) critically reviews what he calls the traditional and avant-garde paradigms of music teaching, and Marion Metcalf (1987) distinguishes between the 'trads' and the 'rads'. Teachers are often understandably sceptical about these sorts of typologies for the reason already stated: practice tends to be a mixture of styles and traditions. However, through an examination of the music education literature, research findings and published classroom materials, it is possible to identify distinct theories of music education. For the purpose of analysis and discussion these may be described as the *traditional*, the *progressive* and the *eclectic*. Each is characterised by an underlying view regarding the justification of music in the curriculum which in turn leads to specific aims, the realisation of which is dependent on certain types of content and teaching styles. Furthermore, these three 'ideal' types (which, of course, do not exist in a pure form) can be linked to more general theories of education or educational ideologies from which, in a sense, they arise. It might be argued that since there is now a National Curriculum, there is now only one view of music education, namely that which is stated in the Order. However, one only has to visit a few classrooms to appreciate that there are still marked differences of opinion regarding the ideas that inform the practice of music teaching. This is something that seems not to be fully understood by the present policy-makers. Central control and official views, as stated in documents, do not necessarily bring about changes in people's thinking and value positions. Professional educationists have minds of their own; they are not merely operatives who deliver the product.

The major feature of the traditional approach to music education is that it is underpinned by a particular, and some would say limited, view of music itself. This leads to a form of practice that emphasises the development in students of an operational competence that is in keeping with the conventions of the post-Renaissance classical tradition. Students are expected to acquire aural, manipulative and literacy skills that will enable them to participate with growing assurance in activities such as class singing, class orchestra and music listening or appreciation. Repertoire for these activities is likely to include classical songs, folk songs, hymns and works of the 'great' European composers. In this scheme of things the teacher is *the* authority whose aim is to introduce children to the recognised 'rules' and procedures that constitute the discipline of music. This is a form of music education that is associated with accepted practices in the 1950s and 1960s and is exemplified in the many excellent published classroom materials of the period (e.g. Smith and Renouf, 1968). The wider principles of education which relate to this style of music teaching are those which Martin Skilbeck (1976) defines as classical humanism. Education is concerned with the

development of intellectual skills, the preservation of the best of the cultural heritage, and the preparation of students who, as responsible citizens, can contribute to society according to their abilities and interests. For the classical humanist, knowledge is hierarchically structured and the arts hold only a lowly place in a system that is dominated by subjects such as mathematics, science and languages. On this view, music for the vast majority will be a small part of their general education; it will have a place in the curriculum but not a particularly important one. Inherent in classical humanism is an academic elitism that supports and maintains the status quo; ability is distributed across the population. Such a view leads to the idea that 'real' success in music can only be achieved by the talented few. In those schools where this ideology is predominant there is likely to be an inclination towards high-level extra-curricular activities rather than music as a class subject.

Whereas the traditional music educator emphasises the importance of students acquiring recognised skills, techniques and knowledge, the progressivist is more concerned with the development of certain qualities of mind such as sensitivity, imaginativeness, creativeness and a sense of the aesthetic. One of the ways of realising these aims is through the exploration and discovery not just of existing forms but of the basic materials of music. Children are encouraged to be composers rather in the way that Herbert Read (1943) maintained that students could and should be regarded as visual artists. The teacher is no longer *the* authority who dispenses conventional wisdom but essentially a guide whose task it is to set up an appropriate learning environment that will facilitate students' creative self-expression. This does not mean that the teacher no longer has an instructional function, although opponents of progressivism are inclined to make this sort of unwarranted claim: children are allowed to do as they like. The progressive movement in music education is sometimes regarded as having grown out of the ideas of Carl Orff, but the seeds were sown much earlier. In modern times, progressivism is particularly associated with innovations of the 1970s and early 1980s in which the emphasis was on children as 'creators' rather than 'performers'. One of the best examples of this type of thinking was the Schools Council Project, *Arts and the Adolescent* (Ross, 1975). The progressive ideology in education has a long history but it is the Plowden Report (Central Advisory Council, 1967) that is often cited as its most influential manifestation in modern times. Above all, progressivism represents an optimistic view of human nature and children's abilities, and a belief in the value of allowing children to 'grow' into fulfilled individuals. Education is a process that enables children to adapt both cognitively and affectively to their environment. The arts have an important function in this process since they are seen as being directly related to the life of feeling; for this reason early progressive thinkers such as Rousseau, Pestalozzi and Froebel all attached an importance to musical activity in their educational theories. In a significant sense, progressive education questions and challenges the established order and consequently has often been subject to attack and even abuse. Music educators such as Murray Schafer (1965) and John Paynter (1970) who espouse progressive principles have not only developed a range of innovative strategies but also done much to demonstrate and publicise the significance of the arts in a system of general education. They have extended ideas about what counts as music in an educational context and constantly argued that musical education should be available for all children. Progressivism represents an egalitarian ideal.

At first sight it may well seem that the eclectic theory of music education is simply a fusion of traditional and progressive approaches since it is based on the principle of children exploring a wide range of music (or musics) through the modes of performing, composing and listening. This conception of music education has been supported by many educationists; it has become something of an orthodoxy and an almost unquestioned starting point for curriculum planners. Indeed, the various versions of the National Curriculum conform to the general principle. The idea of the three experiential modes as a foundation for music programmes is by no means new, but the distinctive feature of recent formulations of the eclectic theory (see, for example, Swanwick, 1999) is that music is regarded as a way of knowing or a realm of meaning with a cognitive content that is equal to that of mathematics and the sciences. Furthermore, the discipline of music is taken to be more than the 'classical' tradition; education in music will involve engaging students in a range of styles and genres. This particular conception of music and music education has been influenced by developments in theory of knowledge, the sociology of music, ethnomusicology and cognitive psychology, as well as ideas about education in and for a pluralist society. It fits well into a *reconstructionist* ideology. Education is conceived of as a process that aims to develop children's individual capacities through the provision of broad experiences; a wider educational aim is the improvement of society as a whole through the promotion of democratic principles. The reconstructionist ideology has its roots in the philosophy of John Dewey for whom the arts were the highest form of human expression and communication.

One of the best known exponents of a reconstructionist approach to education in Britain is Denis Lawton (1989) who portrays the school curriculum as a 'selection from the culture'. Using the device of cultural analysis, Lawton identifies a number of experiential systems as a framework for curriculum design and planning. He maintains that all societies have some kind of aesthetic (artistic) system; accordingly, the arts have a secure position in a broad common curriculum, the purpose of which is to introduce all students to the range of customs, experiences and meanings that constitute the culture. On this view of education, failure to provide for experiences in the arts would be to deny children access to a significant aspect of the culture and therefore contrary to the principles of equality of opportunity and social justice that are embodied in reconstructionism.

Current government thinking and policy on education appear to be a curious mixture of reconstructionist and traditional ideals. On the one hand, there is much reference to education as a force which can transform individuals and society, while on the other there is an almost obsessional emphasis on the raising of standards in the core curriculum subjects. Indeed, education seems sometimes to be equated with 'standards'. The consequence is that although education in music and the arts is recognised as being of value, the position of these subjects in the curriculum remains fairly peripheral; they are certainly not priorities. And this is likely to remain so all the while schools are under pressure to see that they retain a good profile in terms of test and examination results especially in the core subjects. Arts activities can, of course, make a very useful contribution to a school's public image, and this has always been recognised to some extent and especially where the traditional ideology has been dominant. Following a survey of music in forty primary schools, Lawson *et al.* (1994) suggest that there is some evidence to support the view that concerts, plays, productions and other presentations are being increasingly valued in these terms. It would clearly be most undesirable if this became the main reason for including music in schools; attempts to use the arts for solely extrinsic purposes have often led to the most disastrous outcomes.

Justifications in practice

In the days before the National Curriculum, the position of music in the curriculum depended very much on the traditions of the individual and the attitudes of its decision-makers; usually, decisions rested with the headteacher. There were some teachers, often working in a relatively unsympathetic environment, who believed that if they could develop a strong and convincing rationale for music, then their headteacher, and senior colleagues, would undergo a conversion and give the subject much more attention and support. This type of outlook was common among those following higher degree courses who sometimes saw the writing of a dissertation as a way of changing the views of people who controlled the curriculum. Whether or not this course of action was ever successful is unknown but it would seem unlikely. Even with the National Curriculum in place, the support for music still varies from school to school. Differences in attitudes and policies are due to the fact that ideological and cultural traditions, referred to earlier and which are much more powerful than is often appreciated, continue to influence the organisation and management of curricula in individual institutions. If it is necessary to bolster the position of music in a particular school, it may well be that this will be achieved through practice rather than some sort of elegant theoretical exposition.

   Professor Louis Arnaud Reid (1980), one of the most imaginative and respected of educational philosophers and with a particular interest in the arts, has made the point that it is only really possible to understand the value of the arts from within. The implication arising from Reid's position is that if one is trying to justify music to a group of sceptics, the best way of doing this would be to engage them in a musical activity. This might seem to be a slightly romantic and even fanciful point of view and removed from the tough realities of educational practice. But anyone who engages in artistic pursuits will acknowledge that, in a very real sense, what Reid said was true. In those schools where music is being taught effectively, questions of justification seldom seem to arise. To see children taking part in activities and working with a sense of commitment, purpose and delight is to recognise that they are participating in something worthwhile and of intrinsic value. *The practice is the justification.*

Over the past fifty years there have been numerous individuals and professional groups who have contributed to the expansion and development of class teaching and thereby the enhancement of the quality of students' musical experiences. Practical innovation (rather than theoretical argument) has been a major factor in the improved status of music as a curriculum subject and its eventual inclusion in the National Curriculum. But having achieved the status of a foundation subject obviously does not guarantee that it will be well taught. As always, the effectiveness of music within the curriculum depends on the skills of the practitioner. One of the limitations of the National Curriculum is that it is basically a planning model. Furthermore, and to use Stenhousian language, the specification is seen as 'correct' and to be 'delivered', rather than a framework that is to be 'tested' in practice. To what extent the current view of theory and practice might actually inhibit innovative teaching remains the subject of debate. The developments in music teaching which have led to the increased status of the subject occurred at a time when teachers were not obliged to work within the apparent constraints of a statutory curriculum. They were free to experiment and explore new ideas and practical activities, take risks and even make mistakes. The fact that music is a component of the National Curriculum is obviously welcomed by those who believe in the importance of musical studies as an integral part of a liberal education. But the existence of an 'official' conception of music education which must be the basis of *all* curricula in *all* schools may in the end be detrimental to the future of music as a curriculum subject. Of course, to arrive at such a conclusion is likely to be interpreted as a kind of heresy, and people who dare to criticise current policy are usually condemned as trouble-makers living in the past. They will be reminded of HMI's findings as reported to the 1999 conference of the National Association of Music Educators (NAME, 1999); since 1995 there has been a marked improvement in the standard of class music teaching. Who would want to deny that this is good news? However, one cannot help but wonder if the innovations of the 1960s and 1970s, which did so much to establish a place for music in the curriculum, would have been possible in a more tightly controlled and bureaucratic system.

Conclusion

Music is one of the oldest of curriculum subjects but there has always been divided opinion over its educational value. Now that there is so much concern for mathematics, science and language studies, it is understandable that many people express the fear that those arts subjects which do not have an instrumental value will be marginalised or even omitted from the curriculum altogether. Consequently, music educationists seek to highlight the significance of their subject and often emphasise its possible extrinsic outcomes. However, in so doing there is always the danger of making claims that will not stand close scrutiny. Furthermore, justifications based on dubious arguments may well prove self-defeating.

It is, of course, necessary to have a strong rationale for music in the curriculum since this provides the basis for practice. Any consideration of justifications inevitably leads to discussion of wider issues and no doubt, there will be practitioners who feel that 'theorising' about music education is something of an academic luxury which in the end has little bearing on practice. There is much to be said for this point of view, hence the argument that one of the best forms of justification is through good practice. What actually constitutes good practice will inevitably be determined by views regarding aims, content and teaching methods, factors that are directly linked to justifications. And since there are different sorts of justifications for music there will never be complete agreement on how it should be taught within the context of a general education. But this is something that people have been arguing about for well over two thousand years.

Questions for discussion

1   What are the *educational* reasons for including music in the school curriculum?
2   To what extent can different conceptions of music education be reconciled in theory and practice?
3   How far is the National Curriculum in Music a suitable basis for *all* classes in *all* schools?

References

Assistant Masters and Mistresses Association (AMMA) (1984) *Music: An Endangered Subject?* London: AMMA.

Bruner, J. (1966) *The Process of Education*, New York: Vintage Books.

Campaign for Music in the Curriculum (1998) *The Fourth 'R'*, London: Campaign for Music in the Curriculum.

Central Advisory Council for England (1967) *Children and their Primary Schools*, London: HMSO.

Department for Education and Employment (DfEE) (1999) *Music: The National Curriculum for England*, London: DfEE and QCA.

Department of Education and Science (DES) (1991) *National Curriculum Music Working Group Interim Report*, London: DES.

Klausmeier, H.J. (1985) *Educational Psychology*, 5th edition. New York: Harper and Row.

Lawson, D., Plummeridge, C. and Swanwick, K. (1994) 'Music and the National Curriculum in primary schools', *British Journal of Music Education* 11, 3–14.

Lawton, D. (1989) *Education, Culture and the National Curriculum*, London: Hodder and Stoughton.

Metcalf, M. (1987) 'Towards the condition of music', in P. Abbs (ed.) *Living Powers: The Arts in Education*, London: Falmer Press.

Music Education Council (MEC) (2000) *Newsletter*, February.

National Association of Music Educators (NAME) (1999) *Conference Report '99*, NAME Magazine. Issue No. 3.

Overy, K. (1998) 'Discussion note: can music really "improve" the mind?' *Psychology of Music*, 26, 1, 97–9.

Paynter, J. (1970) *Sound and Silence*, Cambridge: Cambridge University Press.

Rauscher, F. (1998) 'Response to Katie Overy's paper'. *Psychology of Music*, 26, 2, 197–9.

Read, H. (1943) *Education Through Art*, London: Faber and Faber.

Reid, L.A. (1980) 'The intrinsic value of the arts in the education of children'. *National Society for Arts Education* III, 2, 11–14.

Ross, M. (1975) *Arts and the Adolescent*, London: Evans.

Sandor, F. (1965) *Musical Education in Hungary*, London: Boosey and Hawkes.

Schafer, R. Murray (1965) *The Composer in the Classroom*, Ontario: Canada BMI.

Skilbeck, M. (1976) 'Curriculum design and development. Units 3–4' in *Culture, Ideology and Knowledge*, Open University Course E203. Milton Keynes: Open University Press.

Smith, E. and Renouf, D. (1968) *Approach to Music: A Course for Secondary Schools*, London: Oxford University Press.

Swanwick, K. (1988) *Music, Mind and Education*, London: Routledge.

Swanwick, K. (1999) *Teaching Music Musically*, London: Routledge.

Vulliamy, G. (1977) 'Music as a case study in the "new sociology of education"', in J. Shepherd, P. Virden, T. Wishart and G. Vulliamy, *Whose Music?: A Sociology of Musical Languages*, London: Latimer.

Further reading

Campaign for Music in the Curriculum (1998) *The Fourth 'R'*, London: Campaign for Music in the Curriculum.

Overy, K. (1998) 'Discussion note: can music really "improve" the mind?' *Psychology of Music*, 26, 1, 97–9.

Swanwick, K. (1999) *Teaching Music Musically*, London: Routledge.

3   Is music a language?

Chris Philpott

Introduction

This chapter assumes that a 'language' is a symbolic medium through which knowledge is held, understood and articulated. The arts have a problematical relationship with language and knowledge which apparently rests on their non-discursive nature. Thus the arts are not regarded as languages at all, except in a very special sense, and therefore cannot be regarded as 'ways of knowing'. Past attempts at making a case for music as a language (and thereby comparing it with spoken and written language) have failed because it has been assumed that there needs to exist a foundational link between word/sounds (signifier) and the object of meaning (signified). This 'logical' view of language has also been a cosy partner for a 'scientific', mind-independent vision of knowledge. The consequence for music and the arts has been an epistemological barrier to them being regarded as forms of knowledge. If music (and the other arts) cannot show that meanings are somehow 'objective' and testable against logic or observation, they cannot be taken seriously as media in which knowledge can be held and expressed. In any case, it is argued, the arts are part of the subjective realm which is an essential counter-balance to the objectivity of the sciences. In a culture, society and education system which promotes and trusts 'objectivity' above 'subjectivity', music is seen at best as being equal (but different), and at worst a less valid form of knowledge than the sciences. However, a careful analysis of the assumptions upon which the music–language comparison has been made, calls into question the 'logical' view as an adequate account of knowledge, meaning and understanding. Recent work in semiotics and literary theory can help to reformulate what constitutes a language. For example, some semioticians suggest that the relationship between signifier and signified is an ever shifting, unstable horizon and consequently any signifier is open to many interpretations of its meaningful significance. Such research into alternative visions of language might provide a more fruitful account of human knowledge, where many more symbolic modes are regarded as epistemologically sound, and also an interesting basis for the music–language comparison.

This chapter will explore the ways in which music has been written about as a 'language'. It will also examine different ways in which language can be viewed and the significance of this analysis for music. Finally, some implications for music education will be discussed.

Music is a language

The comparison between music and spoken/written language has always been a fruitful area for philosophical speculation. Sloboda (1985), has suggested that there are many similarities between music and language:

- both are particular to humans;
- both contain the potential for infinite combinations of possibilities;
- both can be learned by listening to models;
- both use vocal and auditory sound processes as their natural medium;
- both involve the use of notational systems;
- both require necessary skills to be received and absorbed before they can be used;
- both share some universality of form across cultures;
- both can be examined in terms of phonetic, syntactic and semantic structure;
- both contain an underlying structure over which various transformations can take place (there is a parallel here between the work of the linguist Chomsky and the musicologist Schenker).

While Sloboda feels unable to move beyond these points, authors such as Cooke (1959) have attempted to propose music as a 'language' of the emotions with its own 'vocabulary'. Composers, Cooke argues, can communicate, through a musical vocabulary, the emotions they feel themselves and there is no problem in understanding the composer once we understand the 'vocabulary', i.e. the language of the music. The 'expressionist' view of art has also been taken up by writers such as Collingwood (1938) and Tolstoy (1930). This approach to music as a language of the emotions assumes that: 'Beethoven's Ninth Symphony as performed is an externalisation of Beethoven's intuition; in appreciating it I come to grasp again the intuition that Beethoven grasped, I reproduce his expression in myself' (Sheppard, 1987: 25, summarising Collingwood). Tolstoy argues that an object is a work of art if (a) it causes the audience to experience feeling; (b) it is intended to do so by the author; and (c) the maker has himself lived the feelings aroused.

This approach is analogous to the view of language in which there is a causal link between signifier and signified. In the case of music, most eloquently articulated by Cooke, the use of particular musical ideas has the power to evoke and make us feel particular emotions. In this analysis music can operate like the 'logical' view of language for there is a direct conduit between musical sounds and specific meanings. Cooke bases his work on the nuances of major and minor as the elements of a vocabulary which 'refers', after Freud, to shades of pleasure and pain. However, despite the attractiveness and tidiness of such a position for education, not least because there is a 'correct' meaning to a piece of music and a 'vocabulary' to be learned, there have been some devastating criticisms.

Music is not a language

Criticisms of these positions have been well trodden (see Langer, 1942; Swanwick, 1979; Sheppard, 1987). In particular Cooke's brave attempt at a musical vocabulary has been questioned, for example:

- Why can we find contrary examples, e.g. when major feels sad?
- Has the theory any validity outside the 'western' classical frame?
- Is it really possible for a composer to 'download' feelings to us via a piece of music, given the amount of time it might take to write one composition?
- Why should music be exclusively bound up with emotion? What of other types of meanings, e.g. cognitive, social, cultural, ideological?

It is because of the difficulty of developing a sustainable musical vocabulary that both Sloboda (1985) and Bernstein (1976) worry that the analogy falls down at the semantic level. Bernstein, in a famous set of lectures, tried to analyse the relationship of music to language in terms of *phonetics* (the sounds), *syntax* (how these sounds are combined and put together) and *semantics* (the meaning of the sounds once this has happened). He felt that at the phonetic and syntactic level there is a great deal of cross-cultural acceptance of what counts as music, and at the semantic level he found the transformations which make *different meanings to different cultures*, as with spoken language. However, Bernstein and others have found many more detailed problems here, and these are summarised below:

1   There are no stable denotations between individual signifiers (sound) and a signified (object of significance). It is difficult to see how music could have specific referents; 'things' that it was pointing to, e.g. 'this door' or 'this feeling' or 'this colour'. In short, there are no dictionary definitions of musical meaning.

2   Music is not translatable. For example, how can Mozart be translated into Aboriginal music with the new audience understanding the precise meanings intended by him?

3   Our spoken or written language can be used to express and analyse truth claims: to reject, revise or accept them. However, there is no sense in which music can be negated, i.e. a musical assertion that proved somehow to be 'wrong'.

4   Dewey (1934) used the language analogy when talking of the arts as modes through which human meanings could be shared, exchanged and communicated in a unique way. However, the sciences (he argues) 'state' meanings while the arts uniquely 'express' them. He suggests that we imagine flags on a ship as signals and flags on a ship as decoration – here is the difference between denotative language and art!

5   Susanne Langer (1942) argues that through *discursive symbols* we can be analytical, precise and give reference, i.e. the languages of rational inquiry. The *non-discursive symbols* of music and the arts are non-referential in this sense. The arts, according to Abbs (1989), are sensuous and perceptual rather

than conceptual, and music is one of the disciplines in which our sensory and perceptual experience is elaborated and given patterned import. This import is, however, embedded in the symbols themselves and cannot be usefully separated from them.

6   Finally, Bernstein (1976) points to the double life of language at the semantic level, which can be both metaphorical and denotative. Music, he argues, has no equivalent of the sentence in written language. A prose sentence may or may not be a work of art, for language leads a double life of communication and the aesthetic, while art can only exist in the aesthetic realm. Words can make a metaphorical leap making them art, whereas music can only operate on a level of meaning which is metaphorical. Music can express but not assert meanings.

While the expressionists find it difficult to sustain a vocabulary for music, there is something about their work which resonates with us. After all, music must *mean* something or why else would we listen to it? In order to resolve this apparent contradiction (precise meaning or no precise meaning), various writers have proposed that music can be viewed as a 'type' of language, not fully analogous to spoken language.

Music as a type of language

The antithesis to the 'expressionist' argument of Cooke is that of the 'absolutist' Hanslick (1854), who believed that music had no semantic content; it does not refer to anything other than itself. The referential dimension to music is in fact music, i.e. how the sound changes in strength, motion, ratio and intensity. The meaning of music lies in the contemplation and appreciation of the relationships between the sounds as they pass us by. Referents, feelings and emotions may accompany the experience but they are *not* the meaning of the experience itself! In this analysis, language expresses something else, while music expresses itself.

A resolution of these two positions is found in 'Absolute Expressionism', most coherently argued in the work of Susanne Langer. Music cannot refer to specific emotions or ideas but it does present human feelings in symbolic form; it is a metaphor for human feeling and experience and *not* this feeling or *that* emotion. Music and human feeling share similar shapes and structures and this is why music is significant to us. Langer (1942: 204–45) characterises music in the following ways:

- It shows a composer's 'knowledge of feeling'.
- It 'logically resemble[s] certain dynamic patterns of human experience'.
- It 'reflect[s] only the morphology of feeling'.
- It is an 'unconsummated symbol'.
- '[A]rticulation is its life, but not assertion; expressiveness, not expression.'
- It can be known but not named.

• Music has significant form in relation to the world of feelings; the meaning is implicit but not conventionally fixed.

Langer's argument is for music as a 'type' of language in which we recognise a congruence between life (feeling) and music. The essence of each is movement: both physical and in terms of consciousness, taking place in time and space. Thus, feeling has form, e.g. growth and decay, birth and death, ebb and flow, intensity and resolution, excitement and calm, struggle and fulfilment, and music is a tonal version of this felt life. In a poignant metaphor Langer asserts that the 'rhythms of life are the prototypes of musical structure'.

Leonard Meyer (1956) has also written from the absolute expressionist position. He has built a theory of musical meaning out of a psychology of the emotions called 'inhibition of tendency'. The theory holds that emotion is felt in life, to a greater or lesser degree, when deviations to our expectations occur. In music of a certain style we might expect certain things to happen. When contrasting material occurs and norms are deviated from, we experience this as a tendency inhibited or emotion. Some deviations will be minor while others will be dramatic and, as Langer suggests will reflect the ebb and flow of our existence.

The work of the absolute expressionists has been used to underpin the work of many eminent music educators (Swanwick, 1979; Reimer, 1989) and is one of the most powerful arguments for music (and other arts) as a type of language; different from, but just as significant as discursive 'logical' models of language and knowledge. Indeed, this work has raised the epistemological status of the arts as sensuous non-discursive ways of knowing. However, it has also been accused of being over-concerned with subjectivity and feeling (Best, 1992) and of being unconcerned about the role of cognition. The philosophy also assumes certain aspects of musical meaning are cross-cultural, and like that of Cooke does not fully embrace social and ideological dimensions.

However, much sociological and anthropological writing also models music as a 'type' of language. Music, it is argued, has the power to encode aspects of the society or culture from which it originates and can only really be understood by the culture which produces it (see Shepherd, 1977). For example, tonality, with its emphasis on a dominant central key, can be likened to the strict power relations of the society from which it originates, and is not shared by all cultures (see Small, 1977).

Finally, there is the vision of music as a type of language enshrined within the National Curriculum for Music (1999), a vision which is common to many popular approaches to music education. The various working parties have chosen to interpret music as a 'type' of language through the 'elements' and the musical concepts which make them up. This approach is at the same time controversial (is musical understanding really conceptual?) and useful (in terms of notating curriculum content). The ephemeral and elusive 'language' of music is pinned down, if not to the satisfaction of all (see Swanwick, 1988). While some argue that music is reduced here to a series of isolated conceptual 'facts', there are many precedents for music being described in this way. Many planned music programmes in the past have regarded music as a 'type' of language articulated via the elements and the musical concepts contained within them, e.g. The Manhattanville Music Curriculum Program (1970). The National Curriculum regards the elements as underpinning universal musical processes which are cross-cultural. This conceptual (technical) view of music as a 'type' of language can be contrasted with the more intuitive vision of Langer.

The wide and variable literature on music as a type of language is testament to a desire to give music epistemological status, and yet it is clear that music is inadequate when compared to our written and spoken language *as* a language. However, the paradigm through which language is defined has meant that this is as far as the analysis can go. At best we have emerged with music as a 'type' of language, i.e. music is not a real language and as such will always be epistemologically inferior to spoken/written words and the 'hard' subjects of the school curriculum.

If the comparison is to be revisited, then a new analysis is needed. Perhaps there is scope for a more fruitful resurrection of the music–language comparison following Wittgenstein's rather enigmatic assertion that 'Understanding a sentence is much more akin to understanding a theme in music than one may think' (1953: 143). This prompts us to view the original problem in a new and different way. For example, what if the original comparison was based on false assumptions about the nature of the language itself? What if the original assumptions about the nature of spoken and written language were wrong? What if there is no one-to-one correspondence of signifier to signified in language? What if language has no 'pure' communicative, denotative function at all? What if language is always metaphorical? What if some of our assumptions about the nature of meaning in music are applied to language itself? Such an analysis might provide a more optimistic basis for comparison. If we can modify the central assumptions of a 'logical' view of language, then perhaps the comparison can rise from its philosophical death bed!

Revisiting the comparison

More recent aspects of literary theory provide a more encouraging basis for a comparison of music and language. Goodman (1976; Goodman and Elgin, 1988) offers a clue to the possibility of such a comparison in his work on a theory of symbols. He suggests that there are two fundamental misconceptions about understanding symbols of any type. First, that understanding a symbol is an 'all or nothing affair' and, second, that a symbol must have one single and correct interpretation. Goodman argues that these misconceptions constitute a false analysis of the way in which symbols, language and knowledge work.

We have seen that notions of language based on these misconceptions have been important in the epistemological hierarchies which have dominated modernity. The arts have often been questioned as forms of knowledge due to their inability to live up to measures of truth in discursive language, i.e. what is said or written has a logical and verifiable meaning. Thus, if the arts are not real languages, then their truth claims are problematic. However, more recent work in semiology has questioned the view of language upon which this proposition is based (see Derrida, 1978). The assumptions of some 'postmodern' philosophers of language are that 'texts, like language, are marked by instability and indeterminacy of meaning' and 'that interpretation is a free-ranging activity more akin to game playing than analysis' (Sim, 1992: 425). While these assertions are contentious, research into alternative accounts of language might provide a more fruitful account of human knowledge, where many more symbolic modes are regarded as epistemologically sound.

Early work on semiotics was carried out by Saussure (1916) in a famous treatise on linguistics. He postulated the concept of *signifier* (the word or sound) and the *signified* (object of signification) and together these form what he calls the *sign* (see Figure 3.1). The relationship of signifier to signified is arbitrary in as much as any word or sound could apply to a *dog*. However, while the relationship between signifier and signified might change, at any one time they are conceived of as the same thing. As we have seen, the stable relationship of signifier to signified has been difficult to sustain when applied to music, and it is difficult to see how this early approach to semiotics could provide a parallel between spoken/written language and music.

Figure 3.1 Stable semiotics

Hodge and Kress (1988) have highlighted the inadequacy of the 'old school' of semiotics and argue that Saussure ignored many important aspects of meaning because he felt them to be impossible objects for systematic study. Saussure's 'scientific' vision of linguistics thus disposed of the need to study the processes of culture, society, ideology, history and other semiotic systems in addition to verbal language. The Saussurean epistemology assumes both stability and a direct causal relationship between signifier and signified.

Barthes (1957) has used this type of analysis to maintain that there is a semiotic structure in all types of networks of signification from a glass of red wine to wrestling! However, he shows that while on one level the 'sign' has a role of denotation, there is a second level in which every denotation can be seen as connotation for something else. Denotations are vehicles for connotation! Barthes calls these connotations 'myths'. Myth, he maintains 'is a type of speech . . . is a system of communication that is a message . . . [and that] . . . the universe is infinitely fertile in suggestion . . . everything can be a myth provided it is conveyed by a discourse' (1957: 117).

Hodge and Kress draw on the work of C.S. Peirce to make a similar point and argue that 'Interpretants (*myths*) are further ideas linked to a sign . . . The process of generation of interpretants is seemingly limitless, an infinite semiosis, rather like the process of free association' (1988: 20). Peirce sees the making of meaning as intrinsically a dynamic and interpretative process. However, he insists that 'interpretation' is not merely a free for all and is controlled by material reality and by cultural 'habits'. However, the argument that language functions through a dynamic, interpretative relationship between sign and signifier/signified, opens up interesting possibilities for a comparison between music and language (see Figure 3.2).

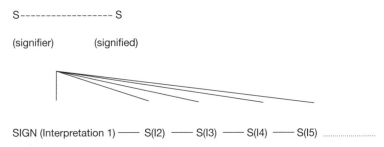

Figure 3.2 Dynamic, interpretative semiotics

In relation to music, Nattiez (1987) has adapted the work of Peirce on the semiotics of language. Indeed, his notion of musical meaning is grounded in the 'infinite and dynamic interpretant' of Peirce. He argues that the sign (interpretation) sparks off many other signs (interpretations) and each interpretation adds to a web of musical meaning. However, these interpretations are not utterly random, as we have seen, but neither are they fixed on a precise sound–meaning basis. The web is part of a complex interpretative process and philosophers of musical meaning have known this for a long time. The additional idea is that language also operates in this way!

By way of summary Sim (1992) speculates that:

- Language is ultimately never purely denotational; it never refers directly to something without there being a complex web of meaning surrounding it, pointing to other meanings.
- Language is not a simple matter of one word to one meaning (against which music falls down) but again a matter of complex webs of meaning depending upon context and interpretation.
- Texts, language and words are marked by instability and indeterminacy of meaning.
- Given such indeterminacy and instability, no one can lay any special claim to authority with regard to interpretation.
- Interpretation is a free-ranging activity more akin to game playing than analysis of the 'truth'.

Meaning is no longer stable and 'easy', but a difficult and interpretative (hermeneutical) process, which takes account of the interaction between the text (words) and the predispositions (cultural context) of writer (speaker) and reader. Meaning is never one-dimensional and words are constantly pointing to something beyond themselves and the simple objects of meaning become caught in a web of understanding.

This appears to be a more hopeful basis for comparison of language and music. However, we need to speculate how the webs of meaning are constructed and sustained in language (and in music) through the dynamic, playful processes of *différance*, the hermeneutics of understanding and metaphor. These are, it must be stressed, speculative ideas in need of significant research if they are to make sense in a coherent theory of musical language and meaning.

Three themes from new approaches to language applied music

Différance *in language and music*

Différance is a difficult and slippery concept borrowed from Derrida (1978) which nonetheless seems a promising point of contact for language and music, especially in relation to its potential for explaining the dynamic process of making meaning. Sarup explains *différance* in the following terms:

> Derrida has developed a concept which he calls 'différance' and which refers to 'to differ' – to be unlike or dissimilar in nature, quality or form – and 'to defer' – to delay, to postpone (the French verb *différer* has both these meanings) . . . Language is thus the play of differences.
>
> (Sarup, 1988: 48)

And Derrida himself explains that 'each element is . . . related to something other than itself but retains the mark of a past element and already lets itself be hollowed out by the mark of its relation to a future element' (1996: 450). It is important to draw from this difficult concept some implications for the dynamic processes behind the making of meaning in music. First, the meaning of music is constructed through the relationships between the parts. A musical tone only has meaning in relation to that which has gone before and that which comes after. It is important to note here the role of 'play' for Derrida in the construction of meaning; the parts 'play' with each other in time and make meaning through their relationships and their differences. Green seems to be making a similar point when she suggests that at any one point in a piece of music 'the present can point to the past, and thence to itself, just as it can the future' (1988: 24).

Second, when applied to music, *différance* suggests that the meanings in a piece of music are endlessly deferred, i.e. we never arrive at a final definitive and authoritative meaning. The complex web of interpretation is constantly shifting, changing, moving as past and present interact with each other and the listener (reader). Understanding is a playful and dynamic process of interpretation.

Hermeneutics

The themes of dynamic and interpretative construction of meaning can also be found in the work of Gadamer (1975) whose treatise on hermeneutics argues that understanding is always an interpretative act. Furthermore, he maintains the primacy of 'play' in interpretation. Not only is there 'play' within the work itself (as described by Derrida), but this is inextricably linked with the 'play' between the audience and the work. Bernstein (1983) describes the nature of 'play' as the basis of interpretation:

> [T]here is a to-and-fro movement, a type of participation characteristic of our involvement with a work of art . . . A work of art is not thought of as a self-contained object that stands over against a spectator . . . There is a dynamic interpretation or transaction between a work of art and the spectator who 'shares' in it.
>
> (1983: 122–3)

Meaning is not only dynamic in the act of interpretation, it is also dynamic over historical time:

> It is thus of the very nature of dramatic or musical works that their performance at different times and on different occasions is, and must be, different . . . The viewer of today not only sees in a different way, but he also sees different things.
>
> (Gadamer, 1975: 130)

Each piece of music (work of art) comes with an 'attitude' and along with our own values and beliefs (which Gadamer calls prejudices) is engaged in a playful dialogue in order to construct meaning. When we engage with a situation (work of art) we understand it in the light of values and beliefs derived from a tradition which historically locates both us and the 'object' of our attention. Meaning is not an objective quality but is a historically located consciousness; not an objective property or subjectivity but a play between a work of art and the interpreter. For Gadamer, there are no general or extrinsic standards of truth about meaning, for different vantage points provide different viewpoints; there is no such thing as an independent 'natural attitude'. While Gadamer maintains that there is no sovereign rationality which transcends any situation, he does assert the sovereignty of interpretation itself. Gadamer developed the concept of 'fusion of horizons' to describe this moment of playful interpretation. These themes of dynamism and 'play' in making meaning are also important features of metaphor, which relates to the final and most important point of contact between new definitions of language and music.

Metaphor and music

Metaphor and denotation have often been regarded as different functions of language and there is a sense in which the art – science, truth – myth has been founded upon this assumption. However, alternative approaches to language suggest that the relationship between signifier and signified is always metaphorical. This revelation is less of a problem for music than language which seems to lose its literal dimension through this analysis. Sarup argues that:

> Language works by means of transference from one kind of reality to another and is thus essentially metaphorical . . . Metaphors evoke relationships and the meaning of relationships is very much the task of the hearer or reader . . . meaning shifts around, and metaphor is the name of the process by which it does so.
>
> (1988: 52)

Thus, there is a sense in which metaphor is the defining feature of languages of all types, i.e. we are seeing one thing in terms of another. The moment we use language(s) to understand our world, we see it through the symbols we use and not as some raw unmediated presence. Cognition thus has a metaphorical dimension; seeing one thing in terms of another.

Here again, we find dynamic themes, i.e. metaphor involves a cognitive shift and there is 'play' in the construction of meaning when seeing one thing in terms of another. In this definition, cognition relies on metaphorical processes and metaphor is dynamic; it 'moves' us to understand. There is a play in the construction of meaning when seeing one thing in terms of another; this is how we construct meaning. Metaphor is literally moving.

There is nothing new in seeing music as essentially metaphorical. Indeed, Langer's work suggests that music is a metaphor for our felt world. Scruton also asserts that 'our experience of music involves an elaborate system of metaphors – metaphors of space, movement, and animation' (1997: 80). Swanwick extends Langer's ideas when he argues that:

> in musical engagement the metaphorical process functions on three cumulative levels. These are: when we hear 'tones' as though they were 'tunes', sound as expressive shapes; when we hear these expressive shapes assume new relationships as if they had a 'life of their own'; when these new forms appear to fuse with our previous experience, when, to use a phrase of Susanne Langer's, music 'informs the life of feeling'.
>
> (1999: 13)

It is metaphor that gives a meaningful life to *différance*; metaphor gives meaning to our dynamic interpretations of music as we recognise the 'play' of meaning as a dynamic shift to something new.

What, then, are the implications for music education of music as a language? As a language which seems to use the very same processes for the construction of meaning as our spoken and written language?

Some implications for music education

There are some important implications for music education both at the philosophical level and at the level of pedagogy if we accept the arguments made above. On the philosophical level we might conclude that:

1 The act of understanding a piece of music is remarkably similar to the understanding of any text; understanding requires a *cognitive* act of interpretation, of engagement with the dynamic process of meaning construction.
2 Music is not simply a 'language of the emotions' but a language for human cognition; a way of knowing, thinking and feeling, and as such has epistemological parity with other 'disciplines'.
3 If music is a language, then it is a mode of discourse and 'a medium in which ideas about ourselves and others are articulated in sonorous shapes' (Swanwick, 1999: 2).

These points contribute to the justification of music in the curriculum both in terms of its uniqueness as a discipline and what it shares with other symbolic modes. Furthermore, if we accept Reimer's (1989) maxim that the nature of music should be reflected in the nature of music education then at the pedagogical level the implications seem to be that:

- Music lessons should primarily involve pupils in the construction of meaning both during the formative process of learning and when engaging with the discipline of music.
- Music as language necessarily involves music lessons to be conducted as a 'conversation' (about music and with music).
- There is a clear sequence of learning from using the language to notating it in written form.
- What counts as being musically literate is complex in the context of different cultural models, i.e. reading and writing may not always constitute 'being literate'; there are many different types of musical 'literacies'.
- Pupils come to school having developed their musical language as part of their 'culture'.
- In the light of this, what counts as the 'basics' of musical learning are problematic in the school music curriculum.
- Musical achievement constitutes having a 'voice' in musical discourse and needs to be open to all pupils.
- Approaches to the assessment of musical achievement should be consistent with the notion of music as a language and form of discourse, e.g. the formative processes of the 'conversation'.
- Given the dynamic, 'playful', moving processes of meaning making in language and musical language, we must recognise the importance of our bodily, kinaesthetic sense in the development of cognition (which Jacques-Dalcroze seemed to know instinctively).

If we follow the argument and treat music as discourse, Ross offers a vision of how this might appear in the classroom:

> Learning music is acquiring musical speech. Having musical speech means being able to have musical ideas, and being able to give voice to them . . . If musicking is speech, then it follows that musical learning will be speaking. Of course, in learning to speak we learn to listen too, and there are times when our speech impulse is completely satisfied in attending to the conversation of other performers. But no language user is prepared to be seen and not heard for long. So it is with kids and music, and so it should be.
>
> (1995: 194, 197)

Learning musical language, as with language learning itself, takes place largely outside the classroom. We learn through our natural engagement with the 'culture', our parents, our peers and our teachers. A problem for music education in the past has often been a dissonance between our learning of the language outside the classroom and our learning inside (see Ross, 1995 and Schools Council, 1968). This dissonance has often caused alienation from a school music seen as out of kilter with the more 'natural' learning experience outside of school. For the music curriculum to be both successful and useful to the majority of pupils in school, it could do worse than accept the implications of music as language, and the need for a genuine musical 'conversation' and discourse in class between pupils, teachers and the culture.

Conclusion

It is clear that a theory of language based upon interpretations, webs of meaning and metaphor is altogether more amenable to the resurrection of a music–language comparison than the 'logical' version. Furthermore, this comparison can shed some light on the nature of musical discourse and the implications for the actions of teachers and pupils in the classroom. However, it would be premature to suggest complete rehabilitation! It is still difficult (and not necessarily desirable) to pin down a precisely analogous relationship between music and language, yet if we revise commonly held beliefs about language, then the debate can at least re-open, and might shed more light on the nature of human discourse. Such a debate might also embrace the possibility of music as a paradigm and exemplification of all human knowledge, meaning and understanding.

Questions for discussion

1   What are the implications for learning in the classroom if we consider music to be a language?
2   Which of the theories of music as a language do you find most attractive or convincing in relation to your own practice?

3 How can music teachers reconcile a pupil's learning of musical language outside the classroom with their learning in it?
4 Many postmodern theories of language imply that truths in all forms of human discourse are essentially relative. Do you think that this strengthens or weakens the case for music in the school curriculum?

References

Abbs, P. (ed.) (1989) *The Symbolic Order*, London: Falmer.

Barthes, R. ([1957], 1973) *Mythologies*, London: Paladin.

Bernstein, L. (1976) *The Unanswered Question*, Cambridge, MA: Harvard University Press.

Bernstein, R. (1983) *Beyond Objectivism and Relativism*, Philadelphia: University of Philadelphia Press.

Best, D. (1992) *The Rationality of Feeling*, London: Falmer.

Collingwood. R.G. (1938) *The Principles of Art*, Oxford: Oxford University Press.

Cooke, D. (1959) *The Language of Music*, Oxford: Oxford University Press.

Department for Education and Employment/Qualifications and Curriculum Authority (1999) *The National Curriculum for England: Music*, London: DfEE/QCA.

Derrida, J. (1978) *Writing and Difference*, London: Routledge and Kegan Paul.

Derrida, J. (1996) 'Différance', in R. Kearney and M. Rainwater (eds) *The Continental Philosophy Reader*, London: Routledge.

Dewey, J. ([1934] 1958) *Art as Experience*, New York: Capricorn Books.

Gadamer, H.G. (1975) *Truth and Method*, New York: Seabury Press.

Goodman, N. (1976) *Languages of Art*, Indianapolis: Hacket.

Goodman, N. and Elgin, C.Z. (1988) *Reconceptions in Philosophy*, London: Routledge.

Green, L. (1988) *Music on Deaf Ears: Musical Meaning, Ideology and Education*, Manchester: Manchester University Press.

Hanslick, E. (1854) *The Beautiful in Music*, trans. 1957, New York: Liberal Arts Press.

Hodge, H. and Kress, G. (1988) *Social Semiotics*, Cambridge: Polity Press.

Langer, S. (1942) *Philosophy in a New Key*, Cambridge, MA: Harvard University Press.

Manhattanville Music Curriculum Program (1970) Bardonia, New York: Media Materials Inc.

Meyer, L.B. (1956) *Emotion and Meaning in Music*, Chicago: University of Chicago Press.

Nattiez, J.-J. (1987) *Music and Discourse: Towards a Semiology of Music*, Princeton, NJ: Princeton University Press.

Reimer, B. (1989) *A Philosophy of Music Education*, Englewood Cliffs, NJ: Prentice-Hall.

Ross, M. (1995) 'What's wrong with school music?', *British Journal of Music Education*, 12, 3: 185–201.

Sarup, M. (1988) *An Introductory Guide to Post-Structuralism and Postmodernism*, London: Harvester Weatsheaf.

Saussure, F. de (1916) *A Course in General Linguistics*, trans. R. Harris, London: Duckworth.

Schools Council (1968) *Enquiry One: The Young School Leavers*, London: HMSO.

Scruton, R. (1997) *The Aesthetics of Music*, Oxford: Oxford University Press.

Shepherd, J. (ed.) (1977) *Whose Music? A Sociology of Musical Languages*, London: Latimer, reprinted by New Brunswick (1980).

Sheppard, A. (1987) *Aesthetics: An Introduction to the Philosophy of Art*, Oxford: Oxford University Press.

Sim, S. (1992) 'Structuralism and post-structuralism', in O. Hanfling, *Philosophical Aesthetics: An Introduction*, Oxford: Blackwell/Open University.

Sloboda, J.A. (1985) *The Musical Mind: The Cognitive Psychology of Music*, Oxford: Oxford University Press.

Small, C. (1977) *Music – Society – Education*, London: John Calder.

Swanwick, K. (1979) *A Basis for Music Education*, Windsor: NFER Nelson.

Swanwick, K. (1988) *Music, Mind and Education*, London: Routledge.

Swanwick, K. (1999) *Teaching Music Musically*, London: Routledge.

Tolstoy, L. (1930) *What is Art?*, Oxford: Oxford University Press.

Wittgenstein, L. (1953) *Philosophical Investigations*, Oxford: Blackwell.

Further reading

Bernstein, L. (1976) *The Unanswered Question*, Cambridge, MA: Harvard University Press.

Cooke, D. (1959) *The Language of Music*, Oxford: Oxford University Press.

Hodge, H. and Kress, G. (1988) *Social Semiotics*, Cambridge: Polity Press.

Nattiez, J.-J. (1987) *Music and Discourse: Towards a Semiology of Music*, Princeton, NJ: Princeton University Press.

4 Music in society and education

Lucy Green

Forty or so years ago, the music curriculum in Britain was built largely on musical appreciation and class singing, involving a mixture of mainly post-seventeenth-century Western classical music and settings of folk songs collected by early twentieth-century composers. Despite the existence of Orff instruments, in most schools instrumental tuition took place outside the classroom during extra-curricular time. Although some pupils studied rudiments, harmony and counterpoint, virtually no-one studied composition until they were in Higher Education. By contrast, as we enter the new millennium, teachers have become quite accustomed to incorporating all sorts of musical activities into the classroom, involving everyone in not only singing, but playing an array of instruments, composing and improvising as well as listening to a huge variety of musical styles including popular, folk and classical music from all over the world.

Such rapid and radical changes in the music classroom go hand in hand with music's roles in the wider society; and these roles are themselves bound up with much broader social developments concerning, for example, demography, technology, globalisation, gender, social class and race relations. The increased flow of peoples across national borders has brought a number of differing musical styles and cultures into close proximity. Ever more efficient, effective and cheap equipment for sound-recording and reproduction, along with the expansion of the music industry, have made a huge variety of global musical styles available, at the flick of a switch, to large numbers of listeners from almost any walk of life. Electronic musical instruments and computers have profoundly affected the ways in which music is performed, composed and stored. The relationships of people from differing social groups to music have changed: women are less restricted in their musical roles than they once were; certain styles of music, such as folk and classical, are no longer exclusively associated with certain social classes; and particular musics no longer 'belong' solely to particular ethnic groups.

In the first part of this chapter I will examine some concepts which can help to increase our understanding of the connections between music and wider social factors such as some of the examples mentioned above. The discussion will concentrate on various ways in which different social groups can be understood to relate to music. Then, in the second part, I will illustrate how the relationships of different social groups to music impinge upon the music classroom. Finally, I will suggest that an understanding of such factors can be helpful in the development of teachers' sensitivity to our own and our pupils' musical abilities, values and needs.

Music in society

Social groups

Some of the most familiar and well-researched social groups are those of social class, ethnicity, race, gender, age, religion, nationality, the family and sub-culture. We can understand society as being made up of different groups such as these, but at the same time, social groups are bound to overlap each other. It is helpful to distinguish three different ways in which this overlap occurs.

One way concerns the identification of groups. I will take as examples the two groups of ethnicity and social class. An ethnic group can be identified by a combination of the cultural practices, educational backgrounds, language, religion, race, nationality, geographical location, and related issues concerning the people in the group. A social class can be identified also by the cultural practices and educational backgrounds, as well as the economic status of its members, or the kind of jobs they have. Thus cultural practices and education play a part in the identification of both these groups: or in other words, similar characteristics may at times be relevant in identifying different social groups. Second, overlap also occurs in terms of how groups fit in with each other. Using the same two examples, some ethnic groups might be found mainly within one social class – such as gypsies in certain European countries; while other ethnic groups might be spread across several different classes – such as Welsh-speaking people living in the United Kingdom.

A third way in which social groups overlap is through the individuals who are their members. It makes no sense to conceive of social groups as being contrasted to, or juxtaposed with, individuals. Each person is always simultaneously a member of several different social groups, some of which may correspond with each other, some of which may conflict, and some of which may change. For example, a person may move from one social class to another over the course of time, or may live in a working-class family situation while holding a middle-class job; a person may have mixed ethnicity, but may identify more with one ethnic group than another; a person may even undergo a sex-change operation. Nonetheless, in all these examples it would be impossible for the person to altogether avoid being in some relation to the social groups of class, ethnicity and gender. Even a person who is explicitly committed to a position of extreme individualism has acquired his or her individualist perspective through social interaction, enculturation and membership of a variety of social groups. When considering social groups, it is necessary to look at how individuals negotiate their positions within groups, and how they are actively involved in constructing and defining the groups they are in.

Social groups relating to music

How do social groups relate to music? A summary response to this question might be, that to varying degrees, people in different social groups are often found to engage in different musical practices, and to attach different meanings and values to different kinds of music. Three simple examples would be: the majority of listeners to BBC Radio 3 (the well-established, mainly classical music station) are white, middle class and over the age of 35; most rap artists (not all) are black and male; most famous classical composers are white and male. But even in these brief examples, I have referred to four social groups (race, social class, age and gender), three musical practices (listening, performing and composing), and two kinds of music (classical music and hip-hop). Implicit in the examples are also further issues concerning the meanings and values placed upon the music, the manner in which the groups form around the music, and the ways in which individuals within the groups see themselves in relation to the music. Because of all this complexity and diversity, it is helpful to break down the question of how social groups relate to music, into areas. Here, I will consider the question in terms of four areas: musical practices, musical meaning, music itself, and individuals' musical identity.

Musical practices

We can conceive of musical practices in three broad ways. One concerns the *production* of music, and involves considering *who* produces *what* music and *how* they go about it. Social groups such as those already mentioned can be looked at in these terms: different social classes, ethnic groups, gender or age groups and other similar groups, are characteristically involved in producing different types of music in different ways, depending on the historical era, geographical location and other contexts. At the same time, musical production throws up new, specifically musical groups, not identified in general sociological terms: these include groups of performers, composers, recording engineers, students, as well as sub-groups within each of these such as trumpeters, singers, professors of composition, freelance song-writers, and so on. For the sake of clarity, from here I will refer to non-musical social groups such as ethnicity or gender, as large-scale social groups, and to groups of musical producers as more specific, smaller-scale musical groups.

A second area of musical practice involves *distribution*: how music is passed from the producer to the consumer. Different distribution mechanisms are, for example, sound-recordings, live concerts, TV and radio, busking on the streets, religious ceremonies, or teaching. Different large-scale social groups may be involved in different modes of distribution, and again, as with musical production, the modes of distribution themselves imply more specific, smaller-scale groups of people putting them into action, such as people working in the recording industry, music administrators, teachers, and so on.

A third area of musical practice concerns *reception*, or in other words, how people use music. They might listen to CDs in their homes, listen to the radio at work, go to concerts or dance to music. Again, different large-scale social groups tend to take part in different reception practices, and different reception practices throw up smaller groups specifically related to music: Radio 1 listeners, opera-goers, ballroom dancers or clubbers are examples.

Musical meaning

In the philosophy of music, questions are raised about what music means or how it takes on its meaning. But when considering the relationships of social groups to music, we would be more interested in asking how different social groups *construct* musical meanings, what those meanings are, how groups come to agree upon them, and how they come to contest them, both within and between groups. To some extent, musical meanings are articulated by lyrics or libretti, but word-setting can on no account be said to be necessary for musical meanings to arise. Meanings also derive from the social groups, musical practices, and other factors with which music is conventionally associated. Some music takes on meanings by virtue of its repeated use within certain contexts: the National Anthem is associated with the Queen; a theme from Tchaikovsky's *Nutcracker Suite*, because of its use in an advertisement over several years ('Everyone's a fruit and nut-case') makes many people think of Cadbury's chocolate. But music also takes on vaguer, more contestable meanings arising from its social contexts. Some such meanings will be generally understood, others will be more personal and individual. For example, on hearing the opening of a heavy metal number, the majority of people in this country could, if they were asked, make a fairly accurate guess as to the likely clothes and hair-styles of the band-members, their gender, or the probable ethnicity and age of their fans. At the same time, opinion is likely to be divided as to whether the music is good, bad, indifferent, immoral, ethical, aggressive or sensitive. Whatever each individual's position is on such factors, they are a part of the meanings which the music transmits to that person, and they will affect the uses to which that person puts the music.

Music itself

As already observed, different social groups to varying extents engage in different musical practices involving different kinds of music. It is important to take note of the characteristics of the music itself, otherwise we could end up leaving out of consideration the very object which is so central to our concerns. A friend of mine who is a music sociologist was amused when she consulted some market research on musical taste. Under the category 'dance music' the statistics showed that this was the favourite music of people over the age of 55, and of people under the age of 25. What the statistics did not say, was that the nature of what is called 'dance music', and the musical practices and meanings associated with it, are so different for each of these age groups, as to be virtually unrelated to each other. The statistical information on its own, without reference to the nature of the music involved, would represent only a partial, and possibly misleading picture.

Most importantly, music itself is not merely a symptom of our musical practices and meanings, but it acts back on us, through its capacity to *afford* certain beliefs, values, feelings or behaviour. For example, if a primary-school teacher asks children to dance to some fast, loud music with an explicit beat and a prominent drum-kit, the children will jump around vigorously; if they are asked to dance to soft, slow string music, they will glide about gracefully. The music itself affords these responses. By the same token, certain types of music have formal, textural or other such characteristics, which render the music more or less suitable for certain uses or meanings.

Individuals' musical identity

Finally, for many people, music helps in defining their identity as an individual within a group or groups. Individual members of peer groups and sub-cultural groups, for example, use music as one way in which to affirm their identity within the group. This, in turn, aids group cohesiveness. Once again, the music itself is not arbitrarily chosen, but it carries appropriate meanings by dint of convention, it affords certain responses and behaviour, and it is suitable to different degrees, for certain uses and meanings.

Music in education

If we look at music in schools, we can discern a number of patterns related to some of the issues discussed above. In brief, children from different large-scale social groups tend, by varying degrees, to be involved in different musical practices, to attach different meanings to music, to prefer different kinds of music, and to relate differently to music as individuals within their groups. These differences occur not only in their lives outside the school, but also in their engagement with music in school. Teachers are of course themselves members of diverse social and musical groups, and they also relate to music as individual members of larger groups. I will now provide some illustrations of how such factors can impinge upon the content and effects of music education. The illustrations will focus on just three social groups – class, gender and ethnicity.

Social class

I have already indicated that a class division exists in relation to musical style: although people from all social classes, especially nowadays, are quite likely to enjoy popular music (think of the late Princess Diana, for example), it is mainly upper- and middle-class people who listen to classical music. During the 1970s and 1980s, research in the sociology of music education (Vulliamy, 1977a, 1997b; Green, 1988) suggested that even though schools were beginning to incorporate a variety of musical styles into the curriculum, the majority of teachers, curriculum planners and examination boards nonetheless presented classical music as the most important and legitimate musical style. In 1982 I conducted a questionnaire in sixty-one schools which included, among other things, asking teachers whether they taught classical music and popular music, and to give reasons for their answers. As examples of the prime place of classical music in education at that time, here are some responses to the question 'Do you teach classical music?':

> Yes. It is part of our heritage. It contains valuable musical elements. It is essential for public examinations.

> Yes. The heritage should be presented before young pupils since the opportunity would not otherwise exist. Seeds sown now may well bear fruit in later years.

> Yes. It offers the widest field of musical discovery – affords the greatest satisfaction to sing, play and listen to. Any musician worth his/her salt *must* pass on the source of his/her *lifetime* enjoyment in the hope that others will derive the same pleasure from it.

> Of course! The reasons should be obvious: basic grounding; techniques; standard background to any other musical developments.

> Yes in so far as 'classical' = expressive, and in so far as it is an art form, and is the style of music that a) requires the greatest concentration and b) requires the greatest explanation and c) requires the greatest sensitivity.

Only three out of the sixty-one randomly selected teachers said they did not teach classical music, two without giving a reason, and the other one on the grounds that the ethnicity and the low intelligence of her pupils made it unsuitable.

Regarding popular music, teachers often used it at the end of the lesson as a 'treat', to entertain children, or to pacify 'low ability' pupils, rather than studying it seriously. Overall, their attitudes towards it contrasted starkly with those towards classical music. To illustrate this, here are some further examples of answers to the same question ('Do you teach classical music?'):

> Yes. Since children have very little knowledge of any music apart from disco/pop etc. and therefore teaching classical music broadens their musical knowledge.

> Yes. I introduce children to classical music. Pop music they listen to anyway, there seems little point in teaching it therefore.

> Yes. Children have 'pop' thrust upon them everyday and therefore we try to broaden their musical appreciation.

> Yes. . . . My 'boss' talks about 'the adolescent deviation around the arts'.

Yes. I think it important that children should hear music other than the pop diet that they have fed off since they were infants.

And in response to 'Do you teach popular music?':

No. The pupils seem sufficiently saturated in this cultural area to warrant its exclusion from the curriculum.

No. Most teenagers surround themselves with pop music 24 hours a day. Music lessons give the opportunity to show other music exists.

In order to succeed at music in school – in terms of gaining praise, being given the opportunity to have extra-curricular instrumental lessons, passing exams, and so on – it was normally necessary for pupils to accept the superiority of classical music. Not only that, but pupils who opted for music at 14+, normally required instrumental tuition, and although this was available free of charge to some extent, for a large number of children it was arranged on a private, fee-paying basis. Research suggests that one of the most significant factors in the development of young classical musicians is support and encouragement from their parents (Sloboda and Howe, 1991). Some children came from families who did not have much interest in classical music and these children lacked such support. Furthermore, many children who did not have access to free instrumental tuition, could not afford private lessons. Therefore, while music education was in theory offered to all children equally, in practice, children from some particularly interested, committed or better-off social classes were more likely to benefit from and succeed at music in school, to the detriment of children from other social classes.

As mentioned at the beginning of this chapter, music-making opportunities in schools have increased massively for all pupils since the research described above was carried out, and one particularly significant factor in the context of the present discussion is the introduction of a greater variety of music, including 'world music', into the curriculum, along with a more serious and inclusive approach towards all kinds of music. However, very little research has been conducted since the 1980s to ascertain whether these curriculum changes have affected patterns of social class interest or success in music education.

Gender

Recent research has enquired into the musical practices, meanings, the kinds of music and the musical identities associated with boys and girls in schools (see *British Journal of Education*, 1993; Green, 1997; O'Neill, 1996, 1997). In 1992 I conducted a questionnaire involving music teachers in seventy-eight English secondary schools, who gave their views about boys' and girls' musical practices, abilities and inclinations, and I interviewed sixty-nine pupils aged 11–16, in small, single-sex friendship groups in two mixed inner-London comprehensives. Clear patterns emerged, both in the perceptions of teachers, and in the practices and attitudes of girls and boys.

Singing is one curriculum area towards which secondary boys are notoriously disinclined, and this was verified by both the survey and the interviews. Of the seventy-eight teachers, sixty-five said that girls were better at singing than boys, thirteen said they were equal, and no-one said boys were better. Further, the teachers overwhelmingly characterised girls as willing vocalists who enjoy singing lessons and who volunteer in large numbers for extra-curricular choral and other group singing activities, sometimes to the total exclusion of boys. The pupils agreed: a large number of girls expressed a readiness to sing, and many said that singing was seen as a girls' activity, or in the words of one 11 year old, 'singing is girls' jobs'.

Teachers also said that far more girls than boys play orchestral instruments, mainly the flute and violin, and the piano, all of which were associated largely with classical music. One teacher mentioned that out of fifty flautists in her school, not one was a boy! Again, the pupils' responses were entirely commensurate with those of the teachers. For example, boys said things such as, 'Most girls like to play the violin and the cello', and 'they don't branch out much from classical music', whereas girls said things like:

> Boys don't like music lessons.
> LG: Why do you think that is?
> Well, basically, in the music lessons all we do is listen to classical music . . . and that sort of thing.
> It might make a difference if the music [the teachers] played was more for our age group.
> Yes, so the kind of things they played were sort of electric guitar and that sort of thing.
> Like not orchestras and that sort of thing. . . .

In general, girls actively avoid performance on highly technological or electric instruments, especially those associated with popular music, most notably, drums and electric guitars. But boys are responding very differently to the contemporary treatment of popular music in schools. Boys in every 11–14 age group to whom I spoke, without exception, chorused that either they already play the drums, or that they would like to play the drums. Many complained that they were not given the chance.

> I like playing the drums but it's just that we never get a chance to express ourselves. It's just xylophones, xylophones. We would like to play drums, we would like to play guitar, we would like to play lots of things.

This interest in drumming was associated with a desire to be involved in other popular musical instruments and in sound-reproduction technology.

Whereas girls' music was understood as 'slow', popular music in which boys expressed interest, was characterised as 'fast' or 'having a beat'. A group of boys were saying that 'most girls play classical instruments':

> There are two girls in our class who play the cello, I think it is.
> LG: Why do you think that is?
> 'Cos they like slower music.

Not only were girls represented as preferring 'slow', 'classical' music, but teachers also characterised them as wanting to use music in order to express their feelings, and as having an interest in the sensitive, delicate side of music. Boys, on the other hand, were not only seen to prefer 'fast' 'pop' music, but to decry music lessons mainly for fear of appearing 'cissy' or 'unmacho' (both these words were used by several teachers). Girls were seen to be lacking in confidence, but to be co-operative, hard-working and conformist; whereas boys were thought to be generally over-confident, extrovert, unco-operative, and to place more importance on what their peers thought of them than on what their teachers told them to do.

The most striking thing about teachers' responses was that, despite this characterisation of boys as uninterested, unco-operative and negative towards music lessons, they regarded boys as excelling at composition. Contrastingly, they saw girls as dull and lacking in creative spark. Here, for example, are some comments by teachers:

> On the whole, boys produce more imaginative work than girls.

> Boys are not so afraid to be inventive, and experiment. Girls tend to stick to set forms.

> Girls tend to be more traditional and conservative in their compositions.

> Girls seem to have to work harder and don't have as much natural ability.

> Boys seem to have a greater creative spark than girls . . . The girls seem often to be devoid of ideas, and have a problem developing musical ideas.

When talking about composition to GCSE pupils, I found that although they did not use the same terms as teachers – 'conformity' or 'creativity', for example – they once again nonetheless adopted these same characteristics in different ways. They also adopted attitudes mentioned by teachers above, such as girls expressing a lack of confidence, an interest in feelings, and doing what the teacher tells them, or boys appearing confident, unco-operative and more interested in peer-group norms than in lessons.

Some of the girls expressed a strong dislike and a debilitating lack of confidence in composition. Others viewed their compositional work with pleasure and pride. But in both cases they confirmed the teachers' descriptions. For example:

Well, I like composition when it's doing what you feel and everything, but I don't so much like the theory because you've got to learn it . . .

When I like a piece [of mine] it's more, like I get this feeling, I know it's really silly but I get this feeling I think, you know, 'Ah, self-satisfaction', and I sort of like have this big glow on my face.

Some of them characterised themselves as 'incompetent' or 'confused'. All of them indicated a reliance on the teacher, and several said they had 'done their best'. Even those who liked composition were prone to denigrate at least some of their own work or their own feelings about it in numerous asides when they described their work as 'silly', 'boring', 'horrible' and 'terrible'.

Boys displayed a completely different attitude to composition. All but one of them were positive, confident and carefree, whether or not they saw themselves as 'good' composers. They demonstrated not merely a confidence in their ability and a lack of reliance on the teacher, but a rejection of the teacher's advice and values; they presented themselves as less hard-working, yet more 'clued up' about what they needed and what they were aiming for. Rather than having 'done their best', they all indicated that they 'could have done better'. None of them mentioned his feelings.

Both teachers and pupils displayed sets of assumptions concerning the musical practices, instruments, values, and the kinds of music associated with boys and girls respectively. These assumptions cannot be dismissed as mere prejudices, for they are based on reasonable evidence from everyday life in the school. But one of the complexities of the situation arises from a tendency for *beliefs*, about others and about ourselves, to act as labels and self-fulfilling prophecies (see Green, 1997, for further discussion of this). Even though many teachers today are aware of gender patterns in music, the power of musical gender relations retains a very strong pull not only inside but outside the school. Teachers' good intentions and interventionary practices cannot be expected to alter the situation radically, but by encouraging boys to join the choir, or making efforts to recognise and reward girls who do show imagination in their compositions, teachers can go some of the way towards breaking down the implicit divisions which are currently preventing both girls and boys from engaging in and excelling at certain musical practices.

Ethnicity

The following example is taken from research for an MA dissertation in which Andrew Alden (1998) interviewed children in a mixed-race, inner-city London primary school where about 70 per cent of the pupils spoke English as a second language. He was familiar with the school and had been a teacher there previously. The school had a written anti-racist policy and a multicultural curriculum, in which Alden observed lessons and curriculum materials involving music from around the world, including the rehearsal of a Hindi song for assembly on the very morning of the events related below.

During a whole-class, mixed-ethnicity session, he asked pupils about their musical tastes and the kinds of music they listened to at home. The picture that emerged was of a listenership that was almost entirely committed to charts music such as *Top of the Pops* or BBC Radio 1. But when he interviewed Asian children in small, single-ethnicity groups, Alden was presented with a very different picture. He states: 'although they were familiar with "pop" music and sometimes listened to *Top of the Pops*, they were all very clear that Hindi film music was the substance of their experience at home and they stated that this was their preferred music' (ibid.: 84). They also told him they listened mainly to local radio stations broadcasting Hindi popular music.

Alden then conducted another whole-group session in which pupils worked together to devise a curriculum and resources that they would like to have for music in their school. At the end of the session their suggestions included only mainstream charts music, instruments associated with such music, and some of the classroom percussion instruments with which they were already familiar. During discussion afterwards, the Asian pupils in the group were silent.

> I pointed out that pupils in the school listened to a much wider range of music than those which had been suggested and asked if this range should be included. Even with such a clear lead, there was no voice strong enough to say 'Yes'.
>
> (ibid.: 88)

Later on, he asked the Asian pupils separately why they had not spoken up, and they attributed the reason explicitly to negative peer pressure (ibid.: 85).

A great deal has recently been made of music's ability to cross national borders, and to communicate to all people regardless of the language they speak, their cultural practices or beliefs. The multicultural music curriculum has grown up partly in response to the demographic changes that have brought different ethnic and national groups into close contact, as well as the developments in the music industry that have brought us 'world music', as referred to in the introduction of this chapter. One claim which is often made is that studying world music can inculcate tolerance and respect for 'other' cultures in pupils, and many teachers will verify the beneficial effects of a global musical perspective. But very little research has so far been conducted to ascertain how successful the multicultural music curriculum is being in furthering inter-ethnic tolerance and understanding.

There are also issues of a different nature confronting the relationship between ethnicity and the music curriculum. At the moment it is an entitlement of the National Curriculum that all children should compose, perform, appraise and listen to music, individually and in groups. But this ruling has not taken account of the fact that in a small number of families from certain ethnic and/or religious backgrounds, such musical engagement is problematic. For example, some Muslim families disapprove of girls and boys making music together, or even making music at all. Very little research has yet been undertaken as to the overall social significance of this situation, although it can quite clearly put some teachers and some pupils in awkward situations.

Some implications for teachers

The diversity of the contemporary music curriculum is both an effect of, and a response to, wider social patterns and changes in musical engagement in the world outside the school, such as have been discussed in this chapter. For example, the curriculum has responded to an opening-up of social class relations in music-listening habits, by including not only classical music but also popular music. Some teachers are demonstrating increased awareness of gender relations by ensuring that music composed by women is introduced, that boys are encouraged to join the choir, or girls to play the drums. Most schools are meeting demographic changes by including not only Western music but also music from other parts of the world. In such ways, teachers can appeal to and aid pupils from a larger variety of social groups than used to be the case. It is not possible, in a chapter of this length, to go into details about classroom strategies that might ameliorate some of the problem-areas discussed. I am sure readers will already have thought of various possibilities, and a consultation of some of the books in the reference list will yield other ideas. Here, I can only emphasise that, although teaching strategies which aim to combat prejudices and inequalities are of course of enormous potential value, perhaps over and above explicit practical strategies, teachers need to be continuously sensitive and responsive to the social groups and the personal musical meanings, values and identities of their pupils. Such awareness is necessary if the fullest potential of a broad curriculum is to be realised in practice and possible dangers avoided.

Whether you play music, sing, listen, compose, study or teach it, music can be taken on and worn rather like a piece of clothing, to indicate something about your class, ethnicity, gender, your sexuality, age, religion, sub-culture, political values, and so on. It can be worn by pupils as a public expression within the school, which may reveal or may indeed conceal part of the pupils' private identity; or alternatively musical 'clothing' may be worn only in the privacy of the home or other situations beyond the school. Particularly in the case of children and adolescents who are searching for identity as new adults in a changing society, music offers a powerful cultural symbol which aids in their adoption and presentation of a 'self'.

Coming to an increased understanding of the social processes involved in music can help to reveal some reasons why pupils from different groups engage in certain musical practices, why they avoid others, and how they respond to music in the classroom. It can help us to appreciate that pupils' responses and attitudes towards music are not just to do with innate musical ability, but also derive from the listening habits, the values and the cultural norms of the large-scale social groups to which they belong, their public and private identities and desires. In this way, we are less likely to label students 'unmusical', without first considering the deep influence of social factors on the surface appearance of their musicality. Such awareness can also contribute to increasing our own understanding of ourselves as musicians and teachers within the complex web of musical practices, meanings, styles and identities with which we all negotiate.

Acknowledgements

I would like to thank Andrew Alden for permitting me to refer to his dissertation, Sarah Thornton for the anecdote about statistics on dance music, and Charlie Ford for reading and commenting on a draft of this chapter.

Questions for discussion

1 To what extent should the music taught and studied in classrooms reflect the musical experiences and tastes associated with the social groups to which the pupils belong?
2 How might teacher awareness and sensitivity concerning the social contexts of music affect our approaches in the classroom?
3 Is it possible that teachers' estimations of pupils' musical ability might be negatively influenced by the teachers' own lack of familiarity with pupils' musical culture?
4 What are the resource implications of considering music's social contexts and social meanings?

References

Alden, A. (1998) 'What does it all mean? The National Curriculum for Music in a multi-cultural society', unpublished MA dissertation, London University Institute of Education.

British Journal of Music Education (1993) 10, 2 (Special issue on music and gender).

Green, L. (1988) *Music on Deaf Ears: Musical Meaning, Ideology and Education*, Manchester and New York: Manchester University Press.

Green, L. (1997) *Music, Gender, Education*, Cambridge and New York: Cambridge University Press.

O'Neill, S. (1996) 'Boys' and girls' preference for musical instruments: a function of gender?', *Psychology of Music* 24, 171–83.

O'Neill, S. (1997) 'Gender and music', in D. Hargreaves and A. North (eds) *The Social Psychology of Music*, Oxford, New York and Tokyo: Oxford University Press.

Sloboda, J.A. and Howe, M.J.A. (1991) 'Biographical precursors of musical excellence: an interview study', *Psychology of Music* 19, 3–21.

Vulliamy, G. (1977a) 'Music and the mass culture debate', in J. Shepherd, P. Virden, T. Wishart and G. Vulliamy, *Whose Music?: A Sociology of Musical Language*, London: Latimer New Dimensions.

Vulliamy, G. (1977b) 'Music as a case study in the "new sociology of education"', in J. Shepherd, P. Virden, T. Wishart and G. Vulliamy, *Whose Music?: A Sociology of Musical Language*, London: Latimer New Dimensions.

Further reading

Green, L. (1997) *Music, Gender, Education*, Cambridge and New York: Cambridge University Press.

Martin, P. (1995) *Sounds and Society*, Manchester and New York: Manchester Univesity Press.

Scott, D.B. (ed.) (2000) *Music, Culture and Society: A Reader*, Oxford: Oxford University Press.

5 Learning in music

Complexity and diversity

Susan Hallam

What is there to learn in music?

Man created music. The means of making it were readily available – the voice, materials for making instruments – but it was human ingenuity that generated ways of making different sounds and organising and combining them into coherent, meaningful wholes. While we do not know at what exact point in our history this process began, there is evidence of the use of instruments as far back as 3000 BC. Pictures in bas-relief at Susa, the capital of Sumeria, dating from 2600 BC show musicians at the temple gate playing flute, oboe, horn and bow-string instruments. Evidence of use of these relatively advanced instruments suggests a lengthy period of previous development. Music has been an important part of human existence for a very long time. Why? This question has provoked considerable intellectual debate. On the face of it, music serves no obvious purpose which is perhaps why its place in the compulsory school curriculum is constantly questioned. Although evolutionary theory is now delving into cultural issues, to date, no clear evolutionary or survival purpose has been identified. Nevertheless, it must satisfy some very important human needs. If it doesn't, why are there so many radio stations devoted to playing music 24 hours a day? Why is there such a huge market for recorded music? So, what might these human needs be? For the individual, music can be an outlet for emotional expression, can influence moods and arousal levels and be therapeutic. It can entertain and inspire. For those who become actively involved in its performance, publicly or privately, it can provide intellectual stimulation, the challenge of mastery, and emotional fulfilment. Within society, it provides a means of communicating which goes beyond words and provides us with shared, unspoken understandings. It enables particular groups to reinforce their identity whether they be football supporters, members of political parties or members of particular ethnic or cultural groups. No major state occasion is without music. Finally, it provides opportunities for numerous shared social activities, formal and informal. Looked at in this way, a society without music is unthinkable.

The many functions that music serves in society reflect, to some extent, the complexities of what is to be learned. But the most important lesson may be that music has a crucial role to play in human existence and has a very powerful impact on our emotions in ways we may not consciously be aware of. Music can be experienced in many different ways. What might be perceived as a single activity, listening, may involve a range of different processes. Listening can be undertaken holistically with the individual deriving pleasure from the emotion engendered. It may be used to change or indulge a mood or make a boring task more palatable. Listening can be undertaken at an intellectual level, identifying structure, harmony, timbre, dynamic. Alternatively, a critical stance to the actual performance or work may be adopted. Composing and arranging can be approached intellectually, as problem solving or intuitively. Improvising draws on creativity and automated, over-learned skills utilised within a specific, immediate time frame. Performing presents intellectual, technical, musical, communication, and expressive challenges, usually with the added complexity of working with others. Music offers other opportunities for learning through analysis, the study of musical history, instrument making, acoustics, the physics of sound, the effects of music, its role in relation to the other arts, technology, dance, and so on. The list is seemingly endless.

There is also a growing body of evidence that being actively involved in making music may be beneficial to the development of non-musical skills. Early research in the USA made claims that listening to or actively making music had a direct and positive effect on spatial reasoning, one aspect of the measurement of IQ (Rauscher *et al.*, 1997). While this has not been successfully replicated, other evidence from Europe has indicated that an increase in class music lessons can have positive effects on social relationships in school (Spychiger *et al.*, 1995). Research in the UK has shown that concentration in primary school children and those with emotional and behavioural difficulties can be improved when 'calming' music is played in the background (Hallam and Price, 1998). Ongoing research is investigating to what extent playing an instrument encourages the development of transferable skills.

Music also offers many employment opportunities. The music industry is one of the major generators of income in the UK and having a high level of musical expertise is currently perceived as important in preparing individuals not only to work as music specialists but in related careers, e.g. in TV and radio, in the record business, advertising. This brief résumé has outlined the extent to which music offers a wide variety of opportunities for learning which are diverse in nature and require the utilisation of a very wide range of skills. In short, music has something to offer everyone.

How do we learn in music?

Learning appears to be a natural process for human beings. We learn constantly in a wide range of circumstances often in spite of all kinds of obstacles. In educational institutions the problem is not that pupils do not learn, it is that they do not learn what teachers want them to learn. Most learning requires time and engagement, but some learning occurs in a relatively automatic way. This is particularly true of emotional responses which can be conditioned through the association of two events in time. This can be maladaptive in relation to academic learning. Many pupils are prevented from learning because of their emotional responses and attempts to cope with them. If they are made to look foolish, feel inadequate or the learning situation creates anxiety, they may either become de-motivated or develop a 'block' to learning in that domain.

Humans are also naturally generative (Newell, 1990). As a species we continually create, recreate and develop new ideas and materials, new recipes, new games, new dances, new music. Given the natural human propensity to learn and create, the question that educators need to consider is why, in our institutions of learning, the process is often far from optimal and in some cases goes drastically and irretrievably wrong.

Towards a model of learning in music

The factors which influence learning and development are many and complex. At one time, it was believed that an individual's learning capabilities depended on their ability. The outcome of learning could be predicted from what the learner brought with them to the learning situation. This relationship is illustrated in Figure 5.1. The ability of the learner led directly to the learning outcome.

Figure 5.1 A model of learning

We now know that this is not the case. Learners bring to the learning situation a complex set of prior learning experiences and the support available to them in their family environment. Once in the learning situation, their learning will be further influenced by the teaching environment, what they are expected to learn, how it is to be assessed, and their teacher and his or her methods. Learning outcomes are also determined by the nature of the learning task to be undertaken and the processes which are adopted to achieve the desired end. Figure 5.2 outlines a model which provides a framework for considering the factors which influence learning in music and the interactions between them. The model is dynamic and change in one element affects the others. The next sections consider each

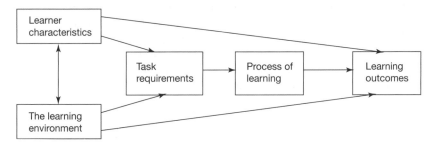

Figure 5.2 Towards a model of learning in music

group of elements: learner characteristics; the learning environment; learning requirements; the process of learning; and learning outcomes, in more detail.

Learner characteristics

Level of expertise and prior knowledge

The individual brings to each new learning situation a range of previous musical experiences. These begin in the womb (Lecanuet, 1996). From infancy, the developing child embarks on the process of musical enculturation in the home. In some homes there may be little or no music. Others may provide a very rich musical environment. During this period the young child will begin to develop aural templates of the way that music sounds – the language of music – from absorbing the music occurring in the environment. This learning takes place automatically without conscious awareness in much the same way that language is absorbed. During this period, if there has been systematic exposure to music, perfect pitch may develop (Sergeant, 1969). The process of musical enculturation continues throughout the individual's life. What is learned depends on the musical experiences to which the individual is exposed. Parents play a crucial role in enculturation and are likely to be influential in the extent to which the child takes part in musical activities beyond the compulsory school curriculum, e.g. instrumental lessons, belonging to a choir. Active participation in music not only contributes to the enculturation process but also promotes the development of a wide range of musical skills increasing the individual's level of expertise. Because much exposure to and learning in music occurs outside school, children can acquire very high levels of expertise at a very early age. Active involvement in music increases scores on traditional musical ability tests so what has historically been perceived as musical ability may in fact represent the extent of enculturation, i.e. what has already been learned. Because of differential musical enculturation children bring to the school learning environment a very wide range of prior experience, much greater than in other school subjects. As learning in any domain builds on prior knowledge and new material is more easily integrated into existing knowledge structures, these differences in levels of expertise are likely to widen over time.

Gender

Almost twice as many girls learn to play musical instruments as boys, this despite the fact that there are more male role models in the music profession (ABRSM, 1994). Girls also do better in school music examinations (DES, 1991). There are no obvious reasons for these differences. While gender clearly constitutes a significant factor in learner characteristics, measured musical ability is similar in boys and girls (Shuter-Dyson and Gabriel, 1981).

Learning approaches and styles

Individuals have preferred ways of learning and processing information which are known as approaches to learning or cognitive or learning styles (Riding and Raynor,

1998). There is considerable debate about the extent to which these are fixed characteristics of the individual or are adopted in response to particular learning situations. However, individuals do appear to have preferences for working in particular ways. Table 5.1 lists some of the most common approaches and styles, their characteristics and their relevance to music education. When methods of teaching and materials are matched to learning styles, learners are more effective in their work. This principle applies to each of the styles described in Table 5.1 and has clear implications for teaching. While it is not possible to tailor teaching to the individual needs of every learner, the teacher can adopt a range of teaching methods and utilise materials to enable each individual to work from their strengths, while also improving their areas of weakness.

Metacognition

Metacognition refers to the learner's ability to manage, plan and evaluate his or her own learning. This includes having strategies for assessing task requirements, being aware of personal strengths and weaknesses, selecting appropriate strategies for particular tasks, planning and monitoring progress towards a goal, developing problem-solving skills, and evaluating the final outcome reflectively. In music, learners need to acquire a range of strategies for composing, improvising or performing which they can utilise when necessary. Having a range of available strategies on its own is not sufficient to ensure task completion. The strategies need to be embedded within a substantial knowledge base. For instance, it is impossible to evaluate progress in learning to play a piece of music unless you have considerable knowledge about the nature of what you wish to achieve.

Metacognition also includes strategies which are 'person' rather than 'task' oriented. Learners need to be aware of the conditions necessary for working effectively and how to bring these about. Such strategies might include optimising concentration, coping with distractions and ensuring work is completed on time. These support strategies are a part of the discipline of learning in any subject domain, but in music, where a great deal of independent work is required, they may be even more important. In the long term it is just as important that the student masters them as well as the skills of performing, composing, listening and appraising.

Teachers can assist pupils in developing their metacognitive skills by modelling particular learning processes, encouraging discussion of process and available strategies, encouraging the development of problem-solving skills, and providing opportunities for open evaluation of composition and performance of both student and professional work.

Motivation and self-esteem

Motivation is crucial to learning in any field. Music is no exception. Motivation in any individual depends on complex interactions between the characteristics of the individual and the environment that they find themselves in and how

Table 5.1 Approaches to learning and learning styles

Learning style	Characteristics	Musical application
approaches to learning	deep approach – intention to understand, interest in what is to be learned, learner makes links with other knowledge.	interested in music for its own sake, focus on the music itself, interpretation, meaning, less emphasis on technique.
	surface approach – motivated by external factors (needing to complete a particular module, pass a particular examination), feeling that task has been externally imposed, strategies adopted are often superficial, e.g. rote learning.	concentration on technical aspects of performance and playing 'correctly', limited in conceptions of what can be achieved.
	achieving approach – desire to get high marks, win prizes, likelihood of this is maximised by identifying marking schemes, guessing examination questions, making effective use of time and effort.	desire to be better than peers, get the best music exam mark, perform best in the school concert, etc. If adopted with a deep approach can be very effective.
convergent/ divergent thinking	convergent thinker – demonstrates ability to deal with problems requiring one correct answer.	convergent thinking is appropriate for analysis of music, some listening skills, technical aspects of performing.
	divergent thinker – highly adept at solving problems requiring the generation of several and varied answers.	divergent thinking is essential for composing, improvisation, developing interpretation.
	all rounders – can adopt convergent or divergent style as necessary.	music requires individuals to be all rounders.
impulsive/reflective style	impulsive learners make decisions very quickly, often wrongly. Speed of processing is required in some musical tasks.	impulsiveness can lead to mistakes being learned into a piece of music.
	reflective learners take time, consider, reflect. Because of this they are likely to come to the appropriate conclusions.	careful, slow work often underlies high quality performance.
verbalisers/imagers	verbalisers – prefer working with words.	this distinction in music may be more related to working with notation or aurally. It is really a visual/aural distinction.
	imagers – prefer working with images.	see above.
serialist/holist/ versatile	serialists – adopt a step-by-step approach to their learning, focus narrowly on the elements of the task, examine immediate logical connections.	in music serialists are usually intuitive. This means that they develop interpretation intuitively as they learn to play the music.
	holists – take a wide view of what is to be learned, look for connections between disparate ideas, make wide use of analogy.	in music holists tend to develop interpretation from listening to a wide range of music and then planning their ideas before they begin to learn to play the music.
	versatile learners – can adopt both styles interchangeably.	ideally musicians will adopt both strategies interchangeably.

rewarding that environment is (Hallam, 1998a). Students can be motivated by combinations of external rewards, social motivation (wanting to please others), intrinsic motivation (enjoying completing the task for its own sake), and achievement motivation (wanting to do well). To sustain motivation over time intrinsic motivation is the key. If undertaking a task is enjoyable and it is then successfully completed, the learners' self-esteem will be enhanced. This increases motivation which will be carried forward to subsequent learning tasks. When learning outcomes are negative, motivation is usually impaired. However, negative learning outcomes can be mediated by the way the individual explains them. If we do poorly on a task and explain our failure through lack of effort, our self-esteem can remain high.

Teachers are clearly important in determining the attributions which are made and need to try to ensure that they are made in the most effective direction. This is not always easy. We may encourage pupils to attribute failure to lack of effort and success to ability but there are dangers in this. Attributing success to ability can be interpreted as telling pupils not to work hard. On the other hand, attributing success to effort can be interpreted to mean that a pupil lacks ability. If a pupil has worked hard and still failed, this can be very demotivating. An alternative is to try to use strategy attributions. Here failure is explained by a lack of specific skills rather than effort or general ability. This offers a way of explaining failure without demotivating the pupil.

In music education where students are faced with considerable choice in the extent to which they engage with music, the links between self-esteem and motivation are crucial. While some of these factors are beyond the control of the teacher, the teacher can do the following:

- help create appropriate expectancies for the student;
- encourage pupils to take responsibility for their learning by helping them set a range of goals over different time spans, which are clear, specific and achievable;
- try to ensure that pupils are successful but without setting tasks which are so simple that they offer no challenge.

Teachers can also facilitate explanations of success and failure being made in ways that will enable pupils to maintain a positive view of their ability in music and offer positive prospects for the future by suggesting new methods and strategies.

This section has outlined the characteristics of the learner and how these affect the way that individuals respond to teaching. In the next section we will consider how the learning environment affects learning outcomes.

The learning environment

What do we mean by the learning environment? It refers to the cultural climate at the time, the place of learning, and the people who are in it, including teachers, family and peers. Crucial to engendering motivation to learn is the value placed on music by society, institutions within it, teachers, family and friends. If music is highly valued in a school both within the classroom and as an extra-curricula activity, then students will be more motivated to participate. If music is not valued, then the class music teacher and visiting teachers will have an uphill battle. The value placed on music is also reflected in the resources made available for its use.

The teacher

No matter how positive the overall learning environment, the role of the teacher is central. Teachers have different conceptions of the nature of the teaching and learning process which affect the way that they teach. At one end of the continuum are those who view teaching as the transmission of knowledge and at the other those who see teaching as the facilitation of learning (Pratt, 1992). In addition, teaching methods are mediated by the nature of the task being taught, the available resources, the particular group of learners, the nature of the assessment procedures and other factors which may have an immediate bearing on the current classroom situation, e.g. the timing of the lesson.

Research exploring the personal characteristics of 'good' teachers has been inconclusive but a study attempting to identify what made a 'great' teacher concluded that great teachers:

- enthuse pupils (this is the most important);
- treat pupils as individuals;
- know the subject;
- are loving and warm;
- teach how to learn;
- relate to others (everybody);
- are firm, fair and flexible (pupils know where they are with them);
- are organised (in their thinking);
- prepare pupils for life (look beyond the immediate teaching materials);
- manage the classroom;
- have high self-esteem;
- have a sense of humour (are able to laugh at themselves);
- need to be a complete person.

(Boag, 1989)

While this is a daunting list, what it provides is an ideal to aim for. Within this framework, the expectations that pupils have of their teachers changes as they get older. Evidence from instrumental music studies suggests that early teachers need to be supportive and relatively uncritical while later it is more important for the teacher to have the respect of the students as they become more discriminating in their musical knowledge (Sosniak, 1985). This is equally likely to apply to class music.

Pupil–teacher relationships

Relationships between teachers and pupils are central to learning. There is considerable evidence that improving the quality of human relations in an institution improves the quality and amount of academic work produced and the attendance of the students (Greenhalgh, 1994). Pupils also like teachers to be fair, have a sense of humour and be able to maintain discipline. Sometimes interpersonal dynamics may come into operation between teachers and pupils which teachers may not be aware of consciously. Defence mechanisms where past problems related to their own learning are projected on to the pupils may be adopted by teachers to ward off unpleasant memories relating to their own experiences. The nature of the interactions between pupils and teachers are particularly influenced by the extent to which pupils are successful in their learning. This will be discussed later.

Learning requirements

As was demonstrated earlier, music offers a very wide range of learning opportunities. Tasks can be found that will provide reward and fulfilment for everybody. The diversity of tasks is sufficient to match the diversity of skills which the pupils may have and provide opportunities for their further development. Because of this possible diversity, to ensure a sense of coherence, teachers need to identify their overall aims in teaching music and develop a curriculum which will satisfy these aims. Within the framework of the National Curriculum there is scope to do this.

The processes of learning in music

Enculturation

Learning in music can be broadly conceptualised as involving enculturation and generative skills, although the development of the two is irrevocably intertwined. Enculturation refers to the ways in which individuals come to know the musical structures which underpin the music of different cultures, principally their own. This can take many forms and while it may include knowledge about music it principally involves internalising the ways that music is constructed and its characteristic sounds. Much of this is learnt without conscious awareness as we absorb the music which is being played around us. Much of this learning occurs outside school. Currently, most pupils spend in the region of 38 hours a year engaged in classroom music. In some cases it may be less. When we consider that secondary school pupils are likely to spend more time than this each month listening to popular music, we begin to see the extent to which enculturation occurs outside school. This influences musical preferences as we tend to like best the music with which we are most familiar (Zajonc, 1968), although over-familiarisation tends to breed contempt as we can become bored with what we hear (North and Hargreaves, 1997). Most enculturation occurs without any attempt to focus on particular aspects of the music, identify its structure, the instruments involved, etc. This requires active listening, concentration and effort, although repeatedly listening to music does change a listener's perceptions of it, leading to a greater understanding of the structure of the music, the relationships of the themes in it and a greater likelihood of remembering it. Experience of music of any kind is valuable in developing musical expertise. Even if it does not appear to be developing intellectual appraisal skills, it is developing the internal aural structures necessary for deep understanding of music.

Generative processes

Generative processes include the skills involved in creating music through performance, improvisation or composition. They rely to a great extent on the development of increasing automaticity of skills which are then controlled by conscious cognitive processing. For instance, novice composers exploring how they can make particular sounds and learning the technical skills to achieve them need to concentrate very hard. But as they practise performing their composition their skills become more fluent, and if they are rehearsed sufficiently they will become automated. Over time the technical aspects of the performance will become more and more automatic so that no conscious concentration is required to execute them at all. This enables more attention to be given to musical considerations. Similarly, when we first learn to read music, decoding every note will require a conscious cognitive effort, but after several years of playing we can read at sight with relative ease. A great deal of musical performance, improvisation and composition depends on the development of these automated processes. As we become expert in these skills we free up our cognitive processing system for higher level activities, for instance, concentrating on communicating with the audience or fellow performers, putting across a particular musical interpretation, developing new musical structures or sounds. In the same way when we are writing we concentrate on our message or the way that we communicate it rather than on spelling particular words or ensuring that our handwriting is neat, which are processes that become relatively automatic. Once skills are automated, their execution becomes quicker and the learning of new material more efficient. To develop automaticity requires practice. Some researchers have claimed that practice is the *sole determinant* of how expert we become in performing music (Sloboda et al., 1996). Not all the evidence supports this (Hallam, 1998b). However, there is consensus that no one will become a proficient musician without devoting some time to practice.

In addition to drawing on relevant automated skills, the process of creativity requires engagement with the task, the implementation of appropriate strategies and the utilisation of a body of musical knowledge. The more extensive our musical knowledge, the easier it is to learn and integrate new material – there are more opportunities for making connections and the more connections we can make, the more likely it is that we will remember. While having a repertoire of strategies is useful, strategies cannot substitute for knowledge within a domain. Imagine trying to solve a problem in an unfamiliar domain. How would you be able to monitor your progress towards a goal? How would you know whether you had found an acceptable solution without knowledge of what such a solution might look like? Even within the same domain difficulties can be experienced in working in an unfamiliar genre. With my Western classical music training I would be completely at sea performing most world musics, although I spent many years of my life as a professional musician. What is difficult to achieve in class music lessons is the necessary development of knowledge and automated skills in the relatively short time available. When pupils have instrumental music lessons they are expected to practise daily throughout the week. The time they spend learning is therefore much greater than the time spent in the lesson. This tends not to happen in class music lessons. In most subject domains, the automated skills required, e.g. reading and writing are common and are therefore 'practised' in most lessons. In music this is not the case. This constitutes a major problem.

One of the major issues for music education is the relationship between enculturation and generative skills. Opportunities for musical enculturation abound in society. Opportunities for developing generative skills are restricted to class music (which operates within a very limited time frame and is unable to provide sufficient opportunities for the development of automaticity in skill development); instrumental lessons (which increasingly have cost implications); opportunities for learning music in the community (which depend on local resources) and self-help (which usually requires, at a minimum, investment in equipment). For the class music teacher the mismatch between what the learner wishes to attain based on his or her well-developed musical schemata and his or her generative skills, particularly those relating to technical skills, can create problems. A possible way forward, where learners lack the necessary technical skills on an instrument, may be to make use of increasingly sophisticated technology.

Learning outcomes

The final element of the model is concerned with the outcomes of learning. These can be thought of in many different ways. They may be viewed in relation to formal assessment, e.g. the National Curriculum; external examinations; the development of increasing musical expertise; a change in the quality of work; an increase in the quantity of what is known; and in relation to affective outcomes, i.e. how we feel, our attitudes towards it or even towards learning itself. Whatever the outcomes of learning, they feed back to influence the characteristics of pupils as learners which then influence the next learning experience. The model as a whole can be conceptualised as part of an ongoing cycle. The outcomes of learning also affect the teacher. If learners have been successful, the teacher will feel that they too have been successful and will approach their teaching in the future with increased self-efficacy. Teachers' self-efficacy has been found to be one of the best predictors of the success of pupils (Tschannen-Moran et al., 1998). This is perhaps not surprising. Teachers who feel confident about their ability to teach successfully are likely to have positive relationships with their classes, creating an environment which is conducive to learning. Teacher and class become part of an interactive positive feedback system, each rewarding the other's behaviour which goes on and on and improving. Of course, the reverse can happen. If the outcomes of learning are poor, the cycle of blame can lead to deteriorating relationships which may ultimately break down completely. It is often these outcomes of learning, i.e. how learners and teachers feel which in the long term are the most important. We neglect them at our peril.

The formal assessment of learning outcomes, particularly through national and international systems of examinations, drives what is learnt and what is taught. These are the external measures by which the success of teachers and pupils is assessed. Teachers want to do the best they can for their pupils and will tailor their teaching to maximise examination performance. This leads to 'teaching to the test' which is an inevitable consequence of a formal examination structure. For this reason, the choice of examination syllabus is very important in determining the nature of what is learnt and how it is taught.

Conclusion

What we have explored in the preceding sections is the complexity and diversity of learning in music. Figure 5.3 illustrates the model in its entirety. The outcomes of learning, which are themselves multi-faceted, depend on a range of factors, many of which are beyond the control of the teacher and many of which are determined before the pupil begins formal music lessons. Even at the point of starting nursery school the nature of the musical enculturation experienced by individual children is very different. Some may have a vast knowledge of popular music, others will be familiar with different world musics, others may have experience of the classical repertoire. They will already have internalised musical structures relating to different genres, and the extent to which this has been accomplished will vary. As they progress through school, those taking part in musical activities outside of the classroom, e.g. instrumental lessons, music schools, extra-curricular activities, will spend more time engaged with music, and as a result of this they will develop a range of technical and musical skills which will become increasingly automated over time. As musical skills are not practised in other subject domains, unlike more general literacy skills, once differences in skills have developed there are few opportunities for those left behind to catch up. This may have important consequences.

Those with strongly internalised representations of music which they wish to generate in their own compositions or performances may become increasingly frustrated when they lack the necessary technical skills to achieve them. This is likely to impact on their perceived self-efficacy and their motivation. They are then unlikely to continue their musical education within school when the time comes to make choices about subject options. To overcome this teachers need to try to ensure that there is a close match between pupils' aspirations and their technical skills. Inevitably, there will be wide variation in the overall level of musical expertise within any one class. Music teachers therefore have to develop schemes of work and ways of teaching which can accommodate this. Fortunately,

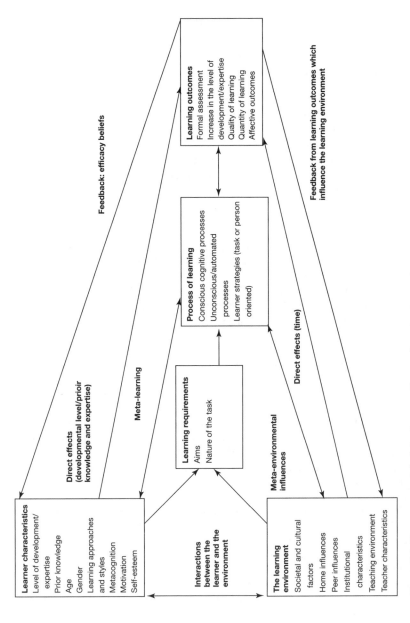

Figure 5.3 Dynamic model of the factors affecting learning in music

music offers many different kinds of learning opportunities; more than any other domain. It can satisfy physically, intellectually, emotionally and spiritually and provides opportunities for developing a very wide range of skills which may be transferred to other domains. Very few subjects offer this range of opportunities for personal development. The broad framework provided by the National Curriculum enables imaginative and creative teachers to address them all.

Questions for discussion

1   What can music educators do to bridge the gap between music in the everyday lives of their pupils and school music?
2   How can music educators harness our natural facility to learn music to best effect in the classroom?
3   How can music educators overcome the difficulties presented by the need to acquire considerable technical skills in order to perform well on a musical instrument when class time for music is restricted?

References

Associated Board of the Royal Schools of Music (1994) *Making Music: The Associated Board Review of the Teaching, Learning and Playing of Musical Instruments in the United Kingdom*, London: ABRSM.

Boag, C. (1989) 'What makes a great teacher?', *The Bulletin*, 18 July.

Department for Education and Science (1991) *Music for Ages 5 to 14: Proposals of the Secretary of State for Education and Science and Secretary of State for Wales*, London: HMSO.

Greenhalgh, P. (1994) *Emotional Growth and Learning*, London: Routledge.

Hallam, S. (1998a) *Instrumental Teaching: A Practical Guide to Better Teaching and Learning*, Oxford: Heinemann.

Hallam, S. (1998b) 'Predictors of achievement and drop out in instrumental tuition', *Psychology of Music* 26, 2, 116–32.

Hallam, S. and Price, J. (1998) 'Can the use of background music improve the behaviour and academic performance of children with emotional and behavioural difficulties?', *British Journal of Special Education* 25, 2, 88–91.

Lecanuet, J.P. (1996) 'Prenatal auditory experience', in I. Deliege and J.A. Sloboda (eds) *Musical Beginnings: Origins and Development of Musical Competence*, Oxford: Oxford University Press.

Newell, A. (1990) *Unified Theories of Cognition*, Cambridge: Cambridge University Press.

North, A.C. and Hargreaves, D. (1997) 'Experimental aesthetics and everyday music listening', in D.J. Hargreaves and A.C. North (eds) *The Social Psychology of Music*, Oxford: Oxford University Press.

Pratt, D. (1992) 'Conceptions of teaching', *Adult Education Quarterly* 42, 203–20.

Rauscher, F.H., Shaw, G.L., Levine, L.J., Wright, E.L., Dennis, W.R. and Newcomb, R.L. (1997) 'Music training causes long-term enhancement of pre-school children's spatial-temporal reasoning', *Neurological Research* 19, 2–8.

Rauscher, F., Spychiger, M., Lamont, A., Mills, J., Waters, A. and Gruhn, W. (1998) 'Responses to Katie Overy's paper, "Can music really 'improve' the mind?"' (*Psychology of Music*, 26, 97–99)', *Psychology of Music* 26, 2, 197–210.

Riding, R. and Raynor, S. (1998) *Cognitive Styles and Learning Strategies: Understanding Styles Differences in Learning and Behaviour*, London: David Fulton.

Sergeant, D. (1969) 'Experimental investigation of absolute pitch', *Journal of Research in Music Education* 17, 135–43.

Shuter-Dyson, R. and Gabriel, C. (1981) *The Psychology of Musical Ability*, London: Methuen.

Sloboda, J.A., Davidson, J.W., Howe, M.J.A. and Moore, D.G. (1996) 'The role of practice in the development of performing musicians', *British Journal of Psychology* 87, 287–309.

Sosniak, L.A. (1985) 'Learning to be a concert pianist', in B.S. Bloom (ed.) *Developing Talent in Young People*, New York: Ballentine.

Spychiger, M., Patry, J.-L., Lauper, G., Zimmerman, E. and Weber, E. (1995) 'Does more music teaching lead to a better social climate?', in R. Olechowski and G. Khan-Svik (eds) *Experimental Research on Teaching and Learning*, Frankfurt: Peter Lang.

Tschannen-Moran, M., Hoy, A. and Hoy, W. (1998) 'Teacher efficacy: its meaning and measure', *Review of Educational Research* 68, 2, 202–48.

Zajonc, R.B. (1968) 'Attitudinal effects of mere exposure', *Journal of Personality and Social Psychology* 9, 2, 1–21.

Further reading

Biggs, J. and Moore, P. (1993) *The Process of Learning*, London: Prentice-Hall.

Hallam, S. (1998a) *Instrumental Teaching: A Practical Guide to Better Teaching and Learning*, Oxford: Heinemann.

Part II

The content, design, implementation and development of the music curriculum

6   The body and musical literacy

Chris Philpott

Introduction

Being literate implies using, understanding, reading and writing the language as exemplified in the attainment targets of the National Curriculum for English (DfEE, 1999a). In addition to these different *dimensions* of literacy there are also different *types* of literacy, in different social situations, in different applications of language (such as advertising) and in relation to different cultures, styles, genres and traditions. Not all of the *dimensions* are equally important, or found at all, in the different *types* of literacy. For example, reading and writing are not vital to an oral tradition of joke telling. The National Curriculum for English aims to recognise the breadth of what constitutes being literate.

The National Curriculum for Music (DfEE, 1999b) programmes of study are also designed to help pupils become musically literate in this broad sense, and the orders include criteria for recognising this at different levels. For example, at level 6:

> Pupils identify and explore the different processes and contexts of selected musical genres and styles . . . They improvise and compose in different genres and styles . . . sustaining and developing musical ideas and achieving different intended effects . . . They use relevant notations to plan, revise and refine material. They analyse, compare and evaluate how music reflects the contexts in which it is created, performed and heard.
>
> (ibid.: 37)

The National Curriculum (NC) for music assumes that being musically literate has similar *dimensions* and *types* to the English language with children being able to compose, perform and understand music in a wide range of styles, traditions and genres. However, concepts of literacy are problematic and there have been many celebrated debates on both the English and Music curriculum over the relative importance of the *dimensions* and *types*. For example, what emphasis should there be on 'standard' English, and should a jazz musician be considered 'illiterate' if unable to read or write notation?

This chapter focuses on how musical literacy is achieved, although it will be argued that the principles outlined below have implications for good practice which transcend the different dimensions and types. Musical literacy is here interpreted in the broad sense of using, understanding, reading and writing in a wide range of traditions. It will be argued that the route to musical literacy is through musical learning and cognitive development. Key questions are: what are the basics of musical literacy, and how do we become musically literate?

It is assumed in the National Curriculum that pupils will become musically literate through developing the skills of performing, composing and appraising. For example, it is interesting to note how the NC plots the development of responding, reviewing and appraising music through the Key Stages in the programmes of study.

> Key Stage 1 – pupils should be taught how to explore and express their ideas and feelings about music using movement, dance and expressive and musical language.

> Key Stage 2 – pupils should be taught how to explore and explain their own ideas and feelings about music using movement, dance, expressive language and musical vocabulary.

> Key Stage 3 – pupils should be taught to communicate ideas and feelings about music using expressive language and musical language to justify their own opinions.

These statements are notable for the 'disappearance' of movement and dance at Key Stage 3 as part of the process of learning to become musically literate. Does this mean that pupils should have gone beyond this mode of learning at Key Stage 3? Is it unreasonable to expect pupils to dance in the secondary classroom? Are music and movement only for primary school children? The model of musical development enshrined within the NC suggests that we progress from learning with our bodies to learning with our minds. The rudiments of musical literacy can be found in bodily understandings, at least at first. However, this chapter will argue that the body, and its dynamic relationship with the world, are a fundamental component of musical literacy at *all* levels of development and musical cognition (including Key Stage 3 and beyond!). The importance of the dynamic body is not only crucial to all learning (musical or otherwise), but is also wrapped up in the very nature of music itself as a medium for knowledge, expression and under-standing. What are the links between the body, music, cognitive development and a broad notion of musical literacy?

The dynamic body as a basis for consciousness, cognition and learning

For the purposes of the following analysis a group of themes will be treated as fundamentally related; these are: *the body, the physical, sensory motor experience, movement and play.*

The body is a dynamic organism and movement is the essence of our bodily experience in the world. This assertion derives from the assumption that being alive is a dynamic experience. Movement is central to our bodily experience, and our sense of self:

- the heart beats, blood flows through our veins, we move around;
- emotions are dynamic and are able to be both sensed and described in terms of relative 'ups and downs';
- ideas and thoughts are dynamic; they move in our minds, take place over time and rise and fall in our consciousness.

Our sense of being in the world is also characterised by movement:

- as a consequence of our experience of time marked by clocks, seasons, days, the weather;
- in relation to our dynamic experience of relationships with others, society and various institutions.

Experience is always dynamic and never static except in a relative sense; it 'moves' through space and time. Kant suggests that space and time are the chief characteristics of the structure of our consciousness and thus *a priori* conditions for our knowledge. Kemp characterises the Kantian philosophy of the 'transcendental aesthetic' as dynamic and one in which:

> all things as they appear to us in the human condition are in time relations. Our capacity for receiving sensations . . . is so constructed that whatever its material, it is arranged in temporal order and, as far as objects outside us are concerned, in spatial order as well.
>
> (1968: 18)

One of the chief characteristics of our experience is movement in time, i.e. the ebb and flow, tension and resolution of our existence, which is felt through our bodily experience of the world. However, our bodily sense of the world goes beyond a mere 'essence' of consciousness.

There is a great deal of educational theory and practice which suggests that the dynamic, moving body is the foundation for the development of all cognition and learning. For Piaget (Piaget and Inhelder, 1969), Vygotsky (1962) and Bruner (1966a, 1966b), the actions of the body when interacting with the world can be eventually internalised as thought. Wood describes how Piaget's sensory-motor phase of development in young children, is vital to the 'higher' learning of concepts and language:

> Sensory-motor schemes, the learned co-ordinations between actions and their sensory consequences, provide the bedrock of all knowledge, . . . the biology of human beings dictates that such sensory motor learning is *structured*

in the infant to form not only 'internalised actions' but, ultimately, mental operations.

(1988: 20)

Thus, for Piaget, there is a biological conditioning which means that our minds learn through our bodily interactions with the world. Wood identifies a similar theme in the work of Vygotsky and suggests that:

> Although . . . he did not claim that mental activities are direct 'enactments', 'copies' or 'recordings' of external activities, he did argue that their *nature and their structure* are derived from them . . . When we speak, say, of creating a 'mental model' there is a real sense in which the 'imaged' actions that we perform and their 'imagined' consequences are derived from physical actions that have previously been done to real objects.

(1988: 19)

Even the metaphors we use to describe our cognitive processes reflect the dynamic actions of the body. For example, we 'work it out', 'think things through', 'grasp an idea', such that there is a sense in which the body is in the mind, a theme which will be revisited later.

There is an important notion of sequence and readiness for further learning in much developmental theory, in which the role of bodily learning is logically prior to higher cognitive processes. Wood draws out the similarities between Piaget and Bruner in this regard:

> Both place emphasis on the importance of *action* and problem solving in learning. They also adopted a similar position with regard to the different ways in which knowledge can be 'represented' or embodied . . . Abstract thinking, in both accounts, should grow out of, be abstracted *from*, material actions.

(1988: 9)

For Piaget, Vygotsky and Bruner the rudiments of learning and cognition can be found in dynamic sensory experiences and physical actions of the body. The work of these authors has influenced many primary school educators to emphasise play and the development of kinaesthetic awareness as the foundation for the development of learning. Readiness for further learning and development can only be assumed if the 'bodily' phase has been successfully negotiated.

Music and the dynamic body

Thus far it has been argued that human bodily experience is characterised by movement in space and time, and that this is the foundation of cognitive development. We also sense and understand music as movement; we *feel* it, both bodily and cognitively as movement. It is a common assumption among many philosophers of music that music symbolises the shapes of our conscious experience, i.e. it symbolises the felt world of bodily experience and consciousness through taking on similar dynamic shapes. For example, just as our felt world is characterised by the dualisms of growth–decay, birth–death, ebb–flow, intensity–resolution, excitement–calm, struggle–fulfilment, so music can be described in similar terms. Scruton suggests that 'our experience of music involves an elaborate system of metaphors – metaphors of space, movement, and animation' (1997: 80). Susanne Langer in a chapter on music maintained that the rhythms of life 'are the prototypes of musical structures' (1942: 227). Indeed, Langer's arguments are seminal in making the philosophical link between movement–feeling–consciousness–music. Music, she says, 'logically resemble[s] certain patterns of human experience' (ibid.: 226), it 'reflect[s] . . . the morphology of feeling' (ibid.: 238) and as such music is a tonal version of our felt life. Music, for Langer is a metaphor for movement; virtual movement.

Swanwick illustrates the music–movement relationship through the following description of a piece of music by Elgar (the opening of *In the South*):

> Without warning or preliminaries, *In the South* launches off into musical space. With a flourish and a striding fanfare figure over three simple chords – each in turn – triumphantly and with massive energy, the orchestra pushes forward and upward. Out of this explosion of sound the strings and upper wind float easily yet confidently downward while a pulsing drum marks the time against a background texture of fanfares.
>
> (Swanwick, 1994: 11)

This writing is full of rich descriptions of 'movement' in the music and uses words which convey weight, energy and impulse. What is important in the writing is the *quality* of the movement being described as embodied in the music. The music is about movement and it uses movement to construct this meaning.

Indeed, Swanwick (1979, 1988, 1994) has developed the relationship between music and the dynamic body (characterised by qualities of movement) in much of his writing and research. A definition of music derived from his work is that 'expressive gestures' are related in time as 'musical structures'. The 'gesture' is important for Swanwick and he feels that music draws on, and can be described in terms of the essentially human experiences of plasticity of gestures, posture, stiffness, weight, size, space, activity, manner of movement, tension, outward–inward direction. Clearly, much of this points to the idea that music is *about* movement.

Body, musical learning and development

The dynamic body is important to learning and is embodied in music. It should not therefore be surprising that music educators have made explicit links between the body and musical learning. Emile Jaques-Dalcroze felt that the connections between the physical and musical learning are very close, if not synonymous. He became frustrated that his conservatoire students could not play their music fluently, expressively or technically correct to his satisfaction.

He saw feet tapping, heads nodding, bodies responding to the nuances of the music, following a crescendo, marking an accent. They were allowing the music literally to penetrate them through and through, they were responding to it *in movement*. Here lay the answer! these pupils of his, *they* were the instrument he needed, they *were* the instrument. He realised that to music and rhythm he must add movement, thereby acknowledging the body as man's first instrument of self expression.

(Dutoit, 1971: 9)

For Jaques-Dalcroze all types of rhythmic movement (actual, harmonic, dynamic, tonal, expressive, structural) were the most potent elements in music and the most closely related to life itself. Hence his argument that rhythm is movement, is essentially physical and that musical understanding is the result of a physical experience. Furthermore, every movement involves time and space, and the perfection of physical resources in time and space results in clarity of musical perception.

Rhythm, like dynamics, depends entirely on movement, and finds its nearest prototype in our muscular system. All the nuances of time – allegro, andante, accelerando, ritenuto – all the nuances of energy – forte, piano, crescendo, diminuendo – can be 'realised' by our bodies, and the acuteness of our musical feeling will depend on the acuteness of our bodily sensations.

(Jaques-Dalcroze, 1921: 60)

It is not possible to do justice to his system of 'eurhythmics' here. In short, he encouraged musical learning through a series of exercises, when moving to music and assuming the expressive quality of the music in actions, e.g. pupils might be asked to take on the shape of the music. While Jaques-Dalcroze felt that rhythmic movement was *the* common and unifying factor in music, i.e. the physical and the cognitive, he also saw music as being capable not only of integrating but ultimately transcending these in a holistic vision of education.

More than ever [children] should be enlightened as to the relations existing between soul and mind, between the conscious and the subconscious, between imagination and the processes of action. Thoughts should be brought into immediate contact with behaviour – the new education aiming at regulating the interaction between our nervous and our intellectual forces.

(ibid.: x)

Research by Taylor (1989) seems to suggest that moving to music can indeed promote musical learning. She used two groups of children in their early years at secondary school (experiment and control) to listen to a wide variety of short extracts of music, and then asked to them convey 'how the music goes' to a deaf boy or girl. The control group were to jot ideas down while the experimental group were asked to move or use physical gestures to help the deaf child understand the music. The results supported the hypothesis that children using the kinaesthetic strategy would perform better on recognition tests delivered some time later. Taylor's work supplies significant evidence for the important realisation that all understanding is enhanced when the physical and cognitive dimensions are recognised.

The developmental spiral proposed by Swanwick and Tillman (1986) has been heavily influenced by the developmental models of Piaget and Bruner. It is therefore not surprising to find that the first and fundamental 'turn' of *Mastery* is characterised as a phase of development which is dominated by a sensory and manipulative engagement with music. Children are impressed at this level with the physical sensation of sound and with the gross exploration of instruments.

> In the compositions of our very young children . . . we observed a keen interest in very soft and very loud sounds . . . The 'mechanical' impulse can be seen at work when the physical aspects of instruments themselves determine the organisation of the music.
>
> (Swanwick, 1988: 64)

From this early 'bodily' engagement with music children progress to the higher cognitive levels of Expression, Form and Value. However, while this is not the place for a full exposition of the spiral, an important implication of Swanwick and Tillman's work is that the sensory aspects of music are never left behind. Thus, the spiral operates in at least three different senses (see Figure 6.1):

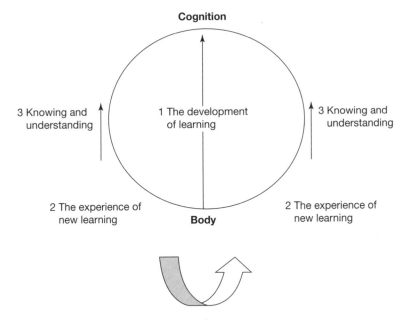

Figure 6.1 Body and cognition in musical experience and development

1   The musical development of children begins with bodily sense which is then internalised as thought in the higher turns (this is very Piagetian).
2   The spiral is experiential in that it is 'reactivated each time [new] music is encountered' and the 'first and most striking impression of music is always its sensory surface' (Swanwick, 1988: 82).
3   The spiral is also experiential in that the lower turns never leave us in our engagement with music and 'we never lose the need to respond to sound materials, re-entering the spiral repeatedly, no matter what age we happen to be' (ibid.: 67).

While children move on to other cognitive levels, the lowest and most 'physical' turn is always a part of higher understanding. Perhaps this is peculiar to higher levels of musical cognition. Piaget argues that the sensory/active phase is an important stage in development but there is also the suggestion that the phase is then somehow left behind. Once we are able to use abstract conceptual tools, we do not need to engage with the lower levels of development in order to learn. Indeed, the 'body in the mind' at all levels of cognition is often given scant attention, i.e. it has been considered important in early development but is then somehow transcended in higher cognition. However, the notion of the 'body in the mind' can be seen as common to all forms of cognition and this can be explored through the concept of metaphor which is an important vehicle for the transference of bodily understanding into higher cognitive processes.

The body in the mind and metaphor

Polanyi (1958) has suggested that all human activity, which normally might be considered as specifically mental or physical, lies on a theoretical continuum between the bodily and the conceptual. It is only theoretically possible to imagine any human experience which lies *entirely* at one end or the other.

Johnson has argued that the link between body and mind is metaphor. Metaphor is a device of transference 'by which we project patterns from one domain of experience in order to structure another domain of a different kind' (1987: xv). Furthermore, metaphor is a device through which our bodily understandings are both held in and part of cognition: 'Through metaphor, we make use of patterns that obtain in our physical experience to organise our more abstract understanding' (ibid.). Thus our experience of the world through our sensuous bodily experience structures the very nature of our cognition, i.e. metaphor is rooted in our bodily experience:

> Our bodily movements and interactions in various physical domains of experience are structured . . . and that structure can be projected by metaphor onto abstract domains . . . concrete bodily experience not only constrains the 'input' to the metaphorical projections but also the nature of the projections themselves.
>
> (ibid.)

Johnson gives the example of a typical metaphorical understanding of *more is up*. It is no accident that we understand quantity in terms of 'verticality', for example 'the volume kept on going up'. Our common everyday experiences of adding more involve upward movement such as adding liquid to a container, and this provides a physical correlate for our abstract understanding.

There is another sense in which metaphor is a *moving* experience in that the transference that occurs when one thing is seen in terms of another is a dynamic process where meaning involves a shift. Metaphor induces a cognitive shift and there is a 'play' in the construction of meaning when seeing one thing in terms of another. In this definition cognition relies on metaphorical processes and metaphor is dynamic; it 'moves' us to understand. There is play in the construction of meaning when seeing one thing in terms of another and this mirrors the very nature of our bodily experience. Indeed, some writers have argued that all symbolic discourse is essentially metaphorical, and that metaphor is the defining feature of all higher levels of cognition. From this analysis it can be argued that the body is always in the mind as a part of all types of cognitive activity. As with Swanwick's analysis of music, bodily understanding is a constant feature of all higher levels of understanding and can always be found in the higher cognitive processes of all forms of symbolic discourse.

Music, metaphor and cognition

It is common for music to be regarded as metaphor, and it is commonly regarded as a metaphor for movement. However, a further implication of Johnson's work is that music has a rather special status as metaphor. Johnson notes that metaphor is born out of our bodily experience of the world; when meaning in one domain is applied to another. However, it is clear that music:

- has its experiential roots in the body (as identified by Swanwick);
- is also metaphor for the dynamic moving body itself (Langer and Scruton);
- uses movement itself in the very construction of metaphorical meaning.

By thematising movement itself there is a sense in which music is a metaphor for the metaphorical processes of cognition themselves; it is a double metaphor! Music seems to 'play' with the dynamism of metaphor for its own sake, and it actually uses movement in order to construct its own (dynamic) metaphorical meanings. This double engagement with metaphor makes a case for music having a very special relationship with the 'body in the mind'. What are the implications of this analysis for music education?

Implications for music education

What are the rudiments of musical literacy? It is clear that the following themes are important foundations to musical learning and cognition: *the dynamic body, sensory-motor experience, the physical, movement, dance, active learning, play*.

These themes are important in at least three ways as identified earlier. First, as the basics of musical development in keeping with much other developmental theory. Second, as the basics in any new learning when children (or adults) re-engage with the sensory layers of experience. Third, the themes are constantly present with cognition at all levels; the body is always in the mind.

Following on from this analysis it seems obvious to state that dynamic bodily understanding needs to be a part of musical learning, and that pupils develop best by doing and making music in a programme of active learning. However, many music educators have forgotten the lessons offered by Dalcroze. He knew that the body is the very foundation of mind, and that through movement and dance, musicians can come to a higher cognitive understanding. For him the body was important at all levels of musical learning, and certainly beyond Key Stage 2! The implications for music teachers are that the 'rudiments' of musical literacy demand that they construct opportunities for pupils to respond and learn through their bodies. This is quite natural when teachers use active learning strategies for singing, playing and composing at all ages, but might also involve moving and dancing to music. It is important to recognise that such work is prior to higher and more abstract learning and that the correct sequence is vital for effective development. For example, concepts of pulse and groupings of pulse need to be felt as part of the body if they are to make any real sense. In order to understand 3 time pupils could usefully move to 3 time, dance to 3 time, compose in 3 time, play in 3 time; by 'becoming' 3 time, pupils understand 3 time. The same principles can be applied to expressive and structural features of music, where pupils can respond to the 'shape' of the music with their bodies.

Models of musical learning from other cultures, in which movement is ever present and not merely a starting point, have much to teach us here. Kwami's rationalisation for his approach to teaching African music is based on 'the underlying practice of music making in communal contexts in Black African societies, in which there is an integration of various aspects of the arts – of drumming, dancing, singing, dramatisation' (1998: 6).

There are also important implications here for music teachers when considering 'readiness', especially in relation to the notational dimension of musical literacy. There are many music theory books which claim to be the 'rudiments of music', and yet many pupils have become disenchanted when studying these in music lessons, especially in secondary schools (see Ross, 1992). One important reason for this is that pupils are often asked to learn musical notation with little sense of readiness, or of what constitutes a good sequence for learning. Again, Jaques-Dalcroze suggests that:

> The trouble with most educational practice is that children are not made to experience things for themselves until the very point at which they are expected to learn from what they do, instead of having active experience encouraged right at the start of their studies, when body and brain are developing in parallel and are constantly communicating their impressions and feelings to each other.

(1921: 5)

This adds weight to the adage in music education of the 'sound before the sign', which is not only important with the very youngest pupils, but also in the secondary school. The further implication is that we need to live, do, act out, become part of musical concepts if they are ever to make sense to us when written down as notation or in analysis. Part of the reason for alienation of some older pupils is that the needs of the body are severed from the mind when trying to understand notation and the technical structure of 'musical concepts'. Pupils often 'know' but cannot 'name' the content of their experience. That is to say, they have an intuitive understanding but cannot always give the correct technical term or appropriate analytical category. However, pupils can feel the sheer 'physical' sensation of fugue, for example. Whether or not pupils 'move' to the music, the structure and nature of fugue will impinge upon them as a physical presence. It is unwise to ignore such vital intuitive understanding for it is the forerunner of naming, formal analysis and philosophising about music. It is also the case that, given their foundation in our bodily sense, intuitive understandings are a constant presence in all musical experience and cognition.

The use of active learning, in its broadest sense, is perhaps less common when older pupils and students are engaged in 'academic' learning. The implications of this chapter are that the body is always in the mind and that connections need to be constantly reinforced between cognition and our bodily sense. For this reason it is appropriate that A level students are set active problem-solving tasks such as composition and improvisation, whether or not these are actually part of the syllabus. It is also why students at all levels should be asked to sing, for it can be argued that the voice is the most direct conduit between the various layers of musical cognition. To be 'part' of harmonic dissonance and to feel the expressive qualities of tension and resolution through the voice are an important foundation for recognition and dictation during an aural test. It is also appropriate that A level and degree students of all ages move to music as a basis for developing their musical literacy and understanding.

The rudiments of musical literacy, of all dimensions and of all types, are grounded in particular bodily understandings which are chiefly characterised by the dynamic qualities of movement. Bachmann summarises the position argued in this chapter, again in relation to Jaques-Dalcroze:

> Music, says Dalcroze (1921: 43), 'is composed of sound and movement, and sound . . . is a form of movement'. The body, for its part, is composed of bones and organs and muscles – and 'muscles were made for movement' ([ibid.:] 39). As to *mind*, whether taken to imply emotions (which literally mean movements), or whether it refers to the mobility of thought itself – mind is also movement, and capable of being moved.
>
> (1991: 13)

Conclusion

The implications of the body in the musical mind go beyond pedagogy, and can also contribute to a justification for music in the curriculum. Given that music is literally a moving and bodily experience it would be surprising if it were not important in general cognitive development, given Piaget's premise that 'intelligence starts off in a practical or sensory-motor form, only little by little internalising itself into thought' (1969: 231). In this very general sense music is good for child development! However, music is also a unique symbolic mode which happens to exemplify the very process of cognition through its double relationship with metaphor. For this reason it is not only unique, but also a paradigm of human knowledge, meaning and understanding. More speculatively, if music is a double metaphor, then it is perhaps doubly efficient in terms of cognitive development. Indeed, here may lie the reasons for the much documented gains which music can bring about in other cognitive realms. Music has a special role in placing the body in the mind.

Questions for discussion

1   How do you feel about the notion that the body is fundamental to musical literacy and cognition?
2   What are the implications of this notion for classroom practice at all levels?
3   Can and should the body play a part in musical learning in the secondary classroom?
4   Does music have a special role to play in placing the 'body in the mind'?

References

Bachmann, M.-L. (1991) *Dalcroze Today: An Education Through and Into Music*, Oxford: Oxford University Press.

Bruner, J.S. (1966a) *The Process of Education*, Cambridge, MA: Harvard University Press.

Bruner, J.S. (1966b) *Toward a Theory of Instruction*, Cambridge, MA: Harvard University Press.

Department for Education and Employment/Qualifications and Curriculum Authority (1999a) *The National Curriculum for England: English*, London: DfEE/QCA.

Department for Education and Employment/Qualifications and Curriculum Authority (1999b) *The National Curriculum for England: Music*, London: DfEE/QCA.

Dutoit, C.-L. (1971) *Music Movement Therapy*, Croydon: Dalcroze Society.

Jaques-Dalcroze, E. (1921, 1965, 1980) *Rhythm, Music and Education*, Croydon: Dalcroze Society.

Johnson, M. (1987) *The Body in the Mind*, Chicago: University of Chicago Press.

Kemp, J. (1968) *The Philosophy of Kant*, Oxford: Oxford University Press.

Kwami, R. (1998) 'From words, to rhythm, to movement, and to MUSIC', *Primary Music Today*, 10, 3–6.

Langer, S.K. (1942, 1957) *Philosophy in a New Key*, Cambridge, MA: Harvard University Press.

Piaget, J. and Inhelder, B. (1969) *The Psychology of the Child*, London: Routledge and Kegan Paul.

Polanyi, M. (1958) *Personal Knowledge*, London: Routledge and Kegan Paul.

Ross, M. (1992) (ed.) 'Wasteland wonderland, the arts in the National Curriculum', *Perspectives 49*, Exeter: University of Exeter.

Scruton, R. (1997) *The Aesthetics of Music*, Oxford: Oxford University Press.

Swanwick, K. (1979) *A Basis for Music Education*, London: Routledge.

Swanwick, K. (1988) *Music, Mind and Education*, London: Routledge.

Swanwick, K. (1994) *Musical Knowledge: Intuition, Analysis and Music Education*, London: Routledge.

Swanwick, K. (1999) *Teaching Music Musically*, London: Routledge.

Swanwick, K. and Tillman, J. (1986) 'The sequence of musical development: a study of children's composition', *British Journal of Music Education*, 3, 3, 305–39.

Taylor, D. (1989) 'Physical movement and memory for music', *British Journal of Music Education* 6, 3, 251–60.

Vygotsky, L.S. (1962, 1986) *Thought and Language* (revised edition), translated by A. Kozulin, Cambridge, MA: The MIT Press.

Wood, D. (1988) *How Children Think and Learn*, Oxford: Blackwell.

Further reading

Bachmann, M.-L. (1991) *Dalcroze Today: An Education Through and Into Music*, Oxford: Oxford University Press.

Johnson, M. (1987) *The Body in the Mind*, Chicago: University of Chicago Press.

Taylor, D. (1989) 'Physical movement and memory for music', *British Journal of Music Education* 6, 3, 251–60.

7 Creativity and composition in music

Jonathan M. Barnes

> The marvels of the creative spirit are the offspring of the marriage between play and discipline, purpose, and mastery.
>
> (Okri, 1997)

Music is essentially a creative discipline in all its aspects. For many music educators, however, creativity is at its strongest in the act of composition where knowledge, imagination, intellect and skill come together in one pursuit. Composition is a central activity in the National Curriculum. Indeed, even before the age at which the National Curriculum becomes compulsory, 3 and 4 year olds are expected to be able to 'express their creativity' (DfEE/QCA, 2000b), 'recognise and explore how sounds can be changed' and 'use their imagination in art and design, music, dance' (DfEE/QCA, 1999a). Between the ages of 5 and 7 children should 'create short compositions with increasing confidence, imagination and control (and) explore . . . how sounds and silence can create different moods and effects', and by Key Stage 2 'they improvise, and develop their own musical compositions, in response to a variety of different stimuli with increasing personal involvement, independence and creativity' (DfEE/QCA, 1999b: 16). These simple words from the National Curriculum are neither aspiration nor example. They are the law of the land; all children in our primary schools *must* have experience of composing music as part of their broad and balanced education. Indeed, in the recent Qualifications and Curriculum Authority (QCA) *Music: A Scheme of Work for Key Stages 1 and 2* (DfEE/QCA, 2000a), fourteen of the twenty-one suggested units expect pupils to compose. The words create, creative, choose, combine, compose, improvise or make up, are prominent in the *expectations* for children in most of the units. This chapter will briefly examine music teaching in primary schools and stress the importance of composing musical ideas in the classroom. It will also discuss notions of creativity applicable to the music curriculum, and offer case studies for consideration.

The state of music in primary schools

It is clear that if composition and improvisation are to be taught in our primary schools, then there is a need for suitably qualified and confident practitioners.

However, experience of present reality would suggest that we are far from a situation in which all children are thinking and acting as proto-composers. The Royal Society of Arts (RSA, 1999) records that in 1998, 30 per cent of primary teacher training students from two universities did not teach music in their second teaching practice and 40 per cent failed to teach it in their third and final practice. Some 63 per cent of the same students considered they had not learned how to teach music in their second practice from their mentor or class teacher, and 81 per cent said the same of their final practice. In a separate study of third year students from another university, the RSA found that 82 per cent were only 'slightly' confident about teaching music as a result of their *college* training. In my own institution up to half of the first and second year trainees returning from teaching practice during 1999 and 2000, considered they had neither seen nor been asked to teach any music during their block school experience. Almost 30 per cent of teacher training institutions now do not offer specialist courses in music to primary teacher trainees (RSA, 1999: 24).

In-service music courses both within schools and those offered by other providers have also suffered. Kent, England's largest education authority, offered a total of only eleven music courses in 1999–2000 for its 623 schools and 11,500 primary, special and secondary teachers. Eight of these courses were cancelled through lack of support and none of the three remaining were full. If good practice is not being observed in many schools, not being taught in a third of colleges and not being disseminated through in-service training, then one must question how developments in music teaching are to take place.

This is not a new problem. Twenty years ago the Gulbenkian Foundation reported a lack of confidence and 'woefully inadequate' training among teachers across the arts (Gulbenkian Foundation, 1982: 8) and the *Arts in Schools Project* (1985–89) (NCC, 1990) was launched to address this. Less than seven years later, however, a major School Curriculum and Assessment Authority conference on the arts again raised the same concerns (SCAA, 1997: 31).

Prominent figures in the arts (Sir Simon Rattle, *TES* 22 May 1998; Sir Peter Hall, *The Guardian*, 2 November 1999) have argued that the most rapid decline in status and standards of music came when requirements for the inspection of foundation subjects were lifted between 1998 and 2000. At the same time the Qualifications and Curriculum Authority publication *Maintaining Breadth and Balance* (QCA, 1998) may have added to the 'disappearance' of classroom composition by advising primary teachers to: 'teach singing regularly but provide opportunities for composing less frequently . . . [and to] . . . reduce the amount of music selected for performing . . . [and] . . . revisit the same music to increase the quality of performance' (ibid.: 17).

Schools also report the squeezing of time available for music in the primary school resulting from the Literacy and Numeracy strategies. A survey for *The Times Educational Supplement* (*TES*, 24 April 1998) found that 20 per cent of primary schools planned to cut time for music because of timetable pressure from the 'Literacy Hour'. The picture in 1999 and 2000 is likely to have been worse as other core curriculum strategies such as National Numeracy Strategy, 'booster lessons' for literacy, SATs target setting and ICT development plans were implemented.

The government took note of fears for the arts and creativity in general by setting up the National Advisory Committee on Creative and Cultural Education (NACCCE) in February 1998. Their report *All Our Futures* summarised the concerns:

> Many of those who contributed to our enquiry believe that current priorities and pressures in education inhibit the creative abilities of young people and of those who teach them. There is a particular concern about the place and status of the arts and humanities . . . There are deep concerns about the supply of teachers and the extent to which current training takes account of the importance of creative and cultural education.
>
> (Robinson, 1999: Para vi)

Inspections for music and the other foundation subjects were reinstated in September 2000. Many schools now face a dilemma: should they deny children their right to a broad and balanced curriculum in order to maintain the push for target test results in English, Maths and Science and greater access to ICT, or devote their resources to the restoration of standards in subjects which have been neglected over the previous three years?

Apart from fighting for more time and renewed status in the curriculum along with other foundation subjects, music has had to re-mount its own special battle for public understanding. Music in England continues to be seen by the public and many teachers as a passive and not an active, creative subject for all children (RSA, 1998: 2). Indeed, many see creativity in music as being reserved for the prodigies. Unlike art, where creative and imaginative aspects continue to be accepted as central, school music often seems to contain little music *making* (apart from singing) and still less composition (Barnes, 2000).

Happily, the revised National Curriculum provides useful clarification on the importance of creativity in the music classroom with a new rationale. It also includes helpful, general guidelines on Inclusion, PHSE and Citizenship and a Statement of Values. In each context the notion of building self-esteem, teaching self-respect, respect for difference, developing confidence and co-operation are central. These skills are particularly exercised by teaching which asks pupils to behave creatively in music lessons (Ross, 1984; Hancox, 1982, 1988; Mills, 1995). Although much research and philosophy argues that music is vitally important, recent trends in school curricula and Initial Teacher Training (ITT) suggest that this is not always transferred into practice.

However, some hope can be taken from a revised National Curriculum which values music and makes the requirement for pupils to engage *creatively* quite specific. But, how can we teach for the development of creativity in our schools from such an apparently low base, with so few confident teachers and often against a background of little public understanding? The issues related to teaching for creativity in music in the primary classroom can be summarised in the following questions:

- What do we mean by creativity when applied to composition?
- Why is creativity important?
- What conditions need to be in place to teach for musical creativity and imagination in the classroom?

The rest of this chapter will be concerned with answering these questions.

What do we mean by creativity when applied to composition?

A working definition of creativity was suggested by the report *All Our Futures*. For the NACCCE Creativity is: 'Imaginative activity fashioned so as to produce outcomes that are both original and of value' (Robinson, 1999: 29). This definition attempts to find the balance between process and product, and between individuality and a wider value system. Creativity, according to this definition, involves imagination, originality, activity, product and value. Creativity can also be seen as a way of 'being' and Read (1943) felt that helping children to behave as creative artists is *the* main aim of education.

Plato, Dewey, Steiner, Jaques-Dalcroze and Freud all recognised a strong link between play and creativity. As with play, creativity in music is an activity only truly meaningful if entered into for its own sake. The connection between play and creativity can be seen in our language, where we *do* a play, are involved in role-*play*, *play* music, *play* with words. When we improvise musically, essentially we play with sounds and for most children composition starts with allowing them such musical play. In the transition from improvisation to composition we begin to play with structures, patterns and combinations of sound.

Creativity usually involves some kind of performance. Performance demonstrates the degree of understanding and mastery achieved through the creative process (Perkins, 1998: 51–4), and brings about completion through sharing. In both play and performance, creativity can be seen as *making* meaning in a personal and social sense. Creative activity gives *organisation* to our physical, emotional and spiritual experience. Sound, silence, shape, space, movement, stillness, line or colour are arranged and rearranged as metaphors for our sensuous experience (see also Abbs, 1989).

Bronowski (1976) saw the creative mind as one which looked for unexpected likenesses between disparate domains and all arts can be seen as using metaphor in this way (Hawkins, 1991). In the process of inventing musical metaphors (such as using quiet, downward moving, slow, chromatic tones for a sense of falling) and organising these into structures, we are solving genuine musical problems using both cognition and imagination (Plummeridge, 1991: 123). Indeed, many have argued that imaginative and practical processes of creativity in the arts are more valuable than the product; *making* music is where the learning happens.

To summarise, creativity may be seen as part of our intelligence, a way of thinking or making sense of life, or even linking ourselves with the eternal (Taverner, 1999). It can also be seen as synonymous with play. Creativity engages us in the bringing out of new ideas from the imagination and gives us the power to break away from the expected. However, it always involves managing originality within a cultural, social or personal context.

If music is a creative discipline and if we can teach for creativity, then composing in class should involve organising sound with some originality through the following:

- the use of imagination;
- activity (including play);
- making;
- sharing;
- reflection.

Consider the following familiar example: When on a 'sound journey' around the school building, a class of Year 2 children are asked to translate the sound of birds singing, the secretary typing or children talking, into metaphors of those sounds using classroom instruments. They are applying imagination even before they pick up an instrument. They are involved in musical activity as soon as they begin to listen and think about the sounds they hear. This is refined as they remember, translate, experiment with, choose, and play with the sounds which represent their journey. Children are making music when they select the most appropriate sounds and improvise or organise them into structures. They are also making sense of the music when they reassess, refine and rehearse these sounds before committing them to a performance. Pupils are sharing through a demonstration of their work and their understanding to an audience (usually the rest of the group or class). While making and performing music, individuals, ensembles and audience will inevitably be involved in reflection when appraising either completed work or work in progress.

Each part of the process involves creating something original which can be appreciated within the culture of the class or school. Sounds are played with, invented, translated into abstractions and grouped into structures. Structures are arranged and combined in new ways to make musical pieces and first performances are opened up to the critics. The establishment of this type of activity within a school is dependent upon teacher confidence and imagination, but not necessarily on high levels of musical skill. Creative thinking or problem solving, applied to music, can be handled by creative teachers thinking and behaving creatively themselves. The implication for teachers and the message given to pupils is that *all* humans have the potential for being creative.

Why is creativity in music important?

It has been argued that creativity requires that we operate on several cognitive levels simultaneously, for example, using skills and knowledge, the imagination and reflection – the very characteristics which Perkins and many other researchers have argued are necessary for transferable learning:

All too often teaching in the subject matters involves a very artificial version of disciplines that emphasises facts and routines but neglects enquiry . . . Real learning that builds good retention of knowledge, genuine understanding of it and the active use of knowledge in other situations, emerges from active thoughtful engagement with the content being learned.

(Goodrich-Andrade and Perkins, 1998: 73)

The encouragement of creativity in any subject is more likely to engage our individual learning styles, different intelligences, imaginations and bodies. I have found that including a range of creative learning experiences within a school curriculum where the brain is simultaneously working on many levels most effectively produces the atmosphere of high challenge and results in learning (Barnes, 1994, 1998, 1999).

Jensen (1996: 7–10) and Gardner (1999a: 81–2) quote studies which show that when the brain operates at several levels at once, it is at its optimum level for understanding. In the 'sound journey' example above, composition involved bringing together parts of the brain which handle image, intellect, imagination, sound, metaphor, movement, emotion and reflection in a challenging process. In encouraging creative music making in schools we are providing challenge without the crushing and educationally limiting effects of stress which can result from embarrassment, competition or feelings of inadequacy.

We are not only all potentially creative, we are also all musical. Blacking (1967, 1976) and Trehub *et al.* (1989) among many others, have attempted to demonstrate an innate musicality in us all, but Gardner has gone further by suggesting the existence of an independent 'musical intelligence' among a range of eight or more intelligences (Gardner, 1984, 1993, 1999a). He has, for example, shown that brain damage in the sub-cortex (the feeling, motivational, emotional part of the brain) results in the loss of interest in the creative aspects of music even if the intellectual capacity for reading, playing and knowing about music is undamaged (Gardner, 1999b: 82). This recent understanding of the brain might suggest that to be properly 'musical' we *must* also be creative.

Sachs (1995: 230–1) suggests that creativity is vital to our making of meaning. For Swanwick, all music making, whether composition or performing the works of others, imparts a 'strong sense of significance . . . an almost magical quality of experience' (1999: 17). Experience surely strong and magical because when we engage in the creative we reach deeply into our personal and cultural histories through the emotional power of metaphor. Through creativity we invest emotionally in both the process and product of our work and in this sense creativity can be an important tool in the management of our emotional health and the development of 'emotional intelligence' (Goleman, 1996). Furthermore, Robertson (1999: 166) suggests that education for emotional literacy is a key challenge to the schools and education systems of the twenty-first century. A music education which is founded upon the creative response develops emotional literacy not only in the ways it helps to express and understand emotion, but also in that it involves handling relationships, emotional self-awareness, harnessing and managing emotions. The most personalised activities, I believe, are creative activities such as composition and music making. In the context of teaching children to think, Bonnett suggests that:

> The arts have much to offer, if treated in the right spirit, i.e. not as things to be learnt or evaluated in a rational/critical mode, but as things to be entered into and felt. Free, though not undisciplined, participation in poetry, literature, art, music, drama are vital forms of poetic thought . . . uninhibited and wholehearted involvement in which a person is inspired by, and carried along by, their engagement.
>
> (1994: 140)

If creativity is an effective way to stimulate meaningful, emotionally engaged, thinking in children, then composition is a particularly strong case in point. For example, of the list of thinking skills offered by Jensen (1996: 164), *all* have immediate musical application within the National Curriculum as shown in [ ] brackets:

- the ability to identify and organise information ['choose sounds' . . . 'organise them into musical structures, NC, KS1, 2b, KS2, 2b];
- learning about something and describing it objectively [explore and explain . . . feelings about music using movement dance, expressive language and musical vocabulary, KS1, 3b, KS2, 3b];
- sequencing [combined musical elements can be organised within musical structures, KS2, 4b, or simple structures (like beginning, middle and end) KS1, 2b];
- problem solving [combined musical elements are used to communicate different moods and effects, KS2, 4b];
- understanding themes and categories [time and place can influence the way music is created, KS2, 4d, pupils should be taught . . . a range of live and recorded music from different times and cultures, KS2, 5e];
- thinking for creativity [create musical patterns, KS1, 2a, explore and express ideas and feelings . . . using movement, dance and expressive and musical language, KS1, 3a, improvise, KS2, 2a, respond to a range of musical and non-musical starting points, KS2, 5b];
- the ability to step outside your role or culture [respond physically, intellectually and emotionally to a variety of music from different times and cultures. Introductory statement to Key Stage Two];
- composing or creating new thinking [composing!].

Teaching for creativity in music is an affective and potentially the most effective way of bringing thinking together with the desirable qualities of co-operation, self-confidence, flexibility, risk-taking, and communication. Each of these contemporary arguments from widely different sources suggest that the case which *All Our Futures* makes for promoting an engaging, imaginative, active, social, reflective, creative and cultural education in our schools is well supported by psychology, neurology, philosophy as well as many practising teachers and parents.

If music creates meaning in our lives, forms an essential part of our humanity, helps us think more deeply and effectively and enhances our emotional literacy, then it seems highly negligent to give it such a lowly place in the curricula of our schools. The lack of music-making opportunities is particularly serious for primary education since it now looks probable that attitudes to many key aspects of life are set in most of us by the time we are 12. If we have not won children's hearts for music by the end of the primary school, there is very little chance of changing them in secondary school. Neurological research into the development of the adolescent brain (Geidd, 1999; Thompson *et al.*, 2000) strongly suggests that if we do not take advantage of the temporary surge of growth in the human brain between the ages of 9 and 13, then the significantly increased potential for taking on new attitudes, making new connections, developing new skills, language and knowledge is wasted.

What conditions need to be in place to teach musical creativity and imagination in the classroom?

Teaching for creativity in music is not only desirable but very possible in the primary classroom *even for the non-specialist student or class teacher*. In some local schools I have seen encouraging examples of non-specialist composition lessons in the best creative tradition, as the following case studies show:

- As a Year 1 class study science, a sound table contains classroom instruments, 'home-made' instruments and other sound sources for children to experiment with. They explore the sounds and incorporate them into class stories and descriptions. Throughout the afternoon small groups of children visit the table and play with sound, classifying their observations on a simple laminated tick sheet attached to the table.
- As part of a cross-curricular Millennium project on new life, each class in a junior school near Deal took the subject of an egg and made music connected with it. Year 3 chose the theme of growth and used un-tuned percussion instruments to describe in sound the growing and hatching chick, then brought together three linked compositions. Year 4 took on Easter Eggs and illustrated a dramatised story about a lost and found egg with musical sound effects. Year 5 concentrated on the structure of eggs and made a class composition to reflect their shape and internal structure; the whole piece was surrounded by a 'shell' of dry scratching sounds made by an egg-shaped ovoid of onlookers. Year 6 made the most effective scrambled egg music accompanied by a dance!
- Before starting a local history study unit on houses and homes, in Dover Castle's cavernous and echoing medieval keep, twenty-eight 7-year-olds stand with recorders and un-tuned percussion. Each child is hidden from the other

throughout the second floor (behind doors, in fireplaces, in the bedrooms, on the spiral staircases, in the passageways between rooms). At a signal from the class teacher on the staircase, a sound 'message' (to the rhythm 'A strang-er is com-ing') is passed from child to child up the stairs, along the passageways from room to room. All the children listen to the echoes and the effects of stone walls and different spaces on the familiar sounds of their instruments. They then break into four groups and are sent with their instruments and an adult to four different spaces, a hall, a passageway, a staircase and a small bedroom to compose an atmospheric 'story in sound' to accompany a tale read to them by an adult. Their music uses the unique timbres available from the stone interiors.

- After visiting a steam train as part of work on the Victorians, half a class stand in a circle, each child in turn adding his or her own 'train' sound to a group representation of the steam train just heard. A Learning Support Assistant keeps the pulse on claves and children invent their rhythmic sounds. The teacher chooses four contrasting rhythms and asks children to form four 'carriages' following the originator of each different train sound. They steam around the hall in a visual demonstration of the counterpoint of train sounds.

- A planned introduction to the elements of music is incorporated into weekly composition sessions by a teacher piloting an inclusion project between two schools in Canterbury. A mainstream primary class and a class of similarly aged children with severe learning difficulties sit in a circle and play rhythm games and musical turn-taking, inventing and copying rhythms, echoing simple chants or fragments of tunes. Activities then develop into 'question and answer' exercises in pairs where children improvise rhythms, chants or tunes which are answered with related but original responses. On another day the group listens to single instrumental sounds, varying and choosing the most appropriate for a proposed composition. Having explored sounds, played with simple structures and practised musical responses to a conductor, children then begin the main composing activity in groups. After listening to recorded examples they compose music on emotive themes such as 'sadness' or 'the clock factory' or 'rain forest'. Groups are given simple grids on A3 paper to record their music so that it may be performed to the rest of the class. Children with skills in orchestral instruments work on their own Rondo theme that will eventually link the seven pieces together.

Music in each example provides the physical and emotional link with other curriculum subjects; the composition exercises are challenging for all without being reliant upon high levels of musical experience. Only a few simple things are required for creative music to bring colour to individual lives, transform a school environment and ethos and thereby enhance learning and thinking.

Time

In the light of current pressures on the curriculum it has become necessary to 'double use' experiences, as in the case studies above. Such real, purposeful and playful activity is essential as children increasingly drift into the virtual experiences of new technology in their leisure time. Music making, because it so clearly engages the body, the emotions and the intellect, can be the most effective stimulus for every subject in the primary curriculum.

A range of musical instruments

The examples above used a range of instruments. Schools had slowly accumulated typical classroom 'Orff' instruments, class guitars, recorders or ocarinas, musical instruments from other cultures and various 'found' instruments. This mix ensures a variety of exciting timbres, moods and associations. There need to be enough instruments for each child to feel there is always a choice and opportunity to master a new instrument.

Teacher understanding of the elements of music

Composition is not purely about self- or group expression. For most children it requires a progressive and scaffolded introduction, leading to a gradual mastery of the skills and discipline of music. The National Curriculum suggests this is done through the building blocks of duration, structure, tempo, dynamics, timbre, texture, silence and pitch. These are not specialist understandings, and while they remain intuitive for many teachers, the challenge is to instil confidence in working with the 'elements'. We are a long way from such generalised musical competence at the moment and this is where the role of the teacher training institutions is so crucial.

Musically confident generalists

None of the case studies above were conducted by specialists; none needed specialist skills or knowledge on the part of the class teacher. Indeed, none of them even referred to the 'elements' of music. Each, however, was led by a teacher with what Mills (1995) calls 'musical self-esteem', the quality which indicates that their musical confidence had not been embarrassed out of them. Teachers used real experience as the springboard for truly creative thought. Each used a limited range of instruments or voices in a controlled situation with a clear musical objective in mind. Later activities built upon these objectives by adding more complex demands but none beyond the level of the enthusiastic but generalist class teacher. Yet every lesson, because the class teacher led it, gave powerful messages to the participating children: music is for all, music is active, music making does not necessarily require high levels of technical proficiency before embarking on creative projects.

Conclusion

The supply of specialist musicians and even confident generalists in primary schools is dwindling alarmingly as a result of an educational climate which has afforded music a reduced status and value. The only way therefore to raise standards, to fulfil both the requirements and the aspirations of the National Curriculum is through a renewed vision of teacher education both in ITT and in-service courses.

Bringing back musical creativity requires an annual cohort of musically confident generalists entering the profession. These class teachers need to be aware of current research on the impact of music on learning, thinking and feeling and also need to have some understanding of the musical 'elements'. Teachers need to be personally convinced of the peculiarly un-English belief that music making is for all. Chiefly, however, they need to know that *they* have the ability to make music themselves. The challenge to teacher training institutions and in-service training providers is to persuade a generation of class teachers that in the context of music *they* can think creatively, and can also help their pupils to do the same.

Questions for discussion

1 What do you see as the value of music to twenty-first-century individuals and society?
2 What conditions are required for *you* to feel creative and how can such conditions be constructed in the classroom?
3 How can the creativity inherent in music be used in the service of other curriculum subjects?

References

Abbs, P. (ed.) (1989) *The Symbolic Order*, London: Falmer.
Barnes, J. (1994) 'Meet the young city planners of St Peter's', *Heritage Learning*, 1, September, 3–6.
Barnes, J. (1998) 'Getting the balance', *Yamaha Education Supplement*, 29, autumn, 19.
Barnes, J. (1999) *Design and Technology and the Historic Environment*, London: English Heritage.
Barnes, J. (2000) Letter to *Yamaha Education Supplement*, June 2000.
Beever, S. (2000) *Learning Experience Through Music*, Newham Academy of Music, Project summary to date online e-mail, 8 May 2000.
Blacking, J. (1967) *Venda Children's Songs*, London: Chicago.
Blacking, J. (1976) *How Musical is Man?*, London: Faber.
Bonnett, M. (1994) *Children's Thinking*, London: Cassell.
Bronowski, J. (1976) *The Ascent of Man*, London: BBC.
DfEE/QCA (1998) *Maintaining Breadth and Balance*, London: QCA.
DfEE/QCA (1999a) *Early Learning Goals*, London: DfEE.
DfEE/QCA (1999b) National Curriculum, *Handbook for Key Stages 1 and 2*, London: DfEE.
DfEE/QCA (2000a) *Music: A Scheme of Work for Key Stages 1 and 2*, London: DfEE/QCA.

Creativity and composition in music 103

DfEE/QCA (2000b) *Curriculum Guidance for the Foundation Stage*, London: DfEE/QCA.

Gardner, H. (1984) *Frames of Mind*, London: Collins.

Gardner, H. (1993) *Multiple Intelligences*, New York: Basic Books.

Gardner, H. (1999a) *The Disciplined Mind*, New York: Simon and Schuster.

Gardner, H. (1999b) *Arts Education and Human Development*, New York: Simon and Schuster.

Geidd, J. (1999) 'Brain development during childhood and adolescence; a longitudinal MRI study', in *Nature: Neuroscience* 2, 10, 40–3.

Goleman, D. (1996) *Emotional Intelligence: Why it can Matter more than IQ*, New York: Bantam.

Goodrich-Andrade, H. and Perkins, D. (1998) 'Learnable intelligence and intelligent learning', in R. Sternberg and W. Williams (eds) *Intelligence, Instruction and Assessment: Theory into Practice*, New Jersey: Lawrence Erlbaum.

The Guardian (1999) 2 November.

Gulbenkian Foundation (1982) *The Arts in Schools: Principles, Practice and Provision*, London: Calouste Gulbenkian Foundation.

Hancox, G. (1982) 'Music education and industry', in J. Paynter, *Music in the Secondary School Curriculum*, Cambridge: Cambridge University Press.

Hancox, G. (1988) 'The dissemination of innovation', unpublished M.Ed. thesis, University of Wales.

Hartland, I. (1999) *Shaping the Spirit: Guidance on Spiritual Education*, Kent: KCC, SACRE.

Hawkins, B. (1991) 'Metaphor: the arts and children with special educational needs in the primary school', *Journal of the Association of Workers with Maladjusted Children*, 9, 2, 90–106.

Jensen, E. (1996) *Brain Based Learning*, Del Mar: Turning Point.

Mills, J. (1995) *Music in the Primary School*, Cambridge: Cambridge University Press.

NCC (1990) *Arts in Schools Project: Arts 5–16 Practice and Innovation*, London: Oliver and Boyd.

Okri, B. (1995) *Astonishing the Gods*, London: Phoenix.

Okri, B. (1997) *A Way of Being Free*, London: Phoenix.

Perkins, D. (1992) *Smart Schools: Better Thinking and Learning for Every Child*, New York: Free Press.

Perkins, D. (1998) 'What is understanding?', in M. Stone Wiske (ed.) *Teaching for Understanding*, San Francisco: Jossey-Bass.

Plummeridge, C. (1991) *Music Education in Theory and Practice*, London: Falmer.

Read, H. (1943) *Education through Art*, London: Faber.

Robertson, I. (1999) *Mind Sculpture*, London: Bantam.

Robinson, K. (Chairman) (1999) *All Our Futures: Report of the National Advisory Committee on Creative and Cultural Education*, London: DCMS/DfEE.

Ross, M. (1984) *The Aesthetic Impulse*, Oxford: Pergamon.

Royal Society of Arts (1998) *The Effects and Effectiveness of Arts Education in Schools* (summary and interim report), London: NFER.

Royal Society of Arts (1999) *The Disappearing Arts?*, London: RSA.

Sachs, O. (1985) *The Man who Mistook his Wife for a Hat*, London: Picador.

Sachs, O. (1995) *An Anthropologist on Mars*, London: Picador.

SCAA (1997) *The Arts in the Curriculum*, London: SCAA.

Swanwick, K. (1999) *Teaching Music Musically*, London: Routledge.

Taverner, J. (1999) *The Music of Silence*, London: Faber and Faber.

Thompson, P., Geidd, J. *et al.* (2000) 'Growth patterns in the developing brain detected by using continuum mechanical tensor maps', *Nature*, 404, 190–2.

Times Educational Supplement 24 April 1998.

Times Educational Supplement 22 May 1998.

Times Educational Supplement 12 June 1998, Issue 4276.

Trehub, S. *et al.* (1989) 'The musical infant', summarised in *Musica Research Notes* http://www.musica.uci.edu/ by N. Weinberger (accessed January 2000).

Webster, P. (1996) 'Creativity as creative thinking', in G. Spruce (ed.) *Teaching Music*, London: Routledge.

Further reading

De Bono, E. (1999) *New Thinking for the New Millennium*, London: Penguin.

Gardner, H. (1993) *Creating Minds: An Anatomy of Creativity Seen through the Lives of Freud, Einstein, Picasso, Stravinsky, Eliot, Graham and Ghandi*, New York: Basic Books.

Okri, B. (1997) *A Way of Being Free*, London: Phoenix.

8 Continuity and progression in music education

Tim Cain

Introduction

> It's a bit like taking a group of children on a sponsored walk. We start off from the car park, more or less all together. We aim for our destination, twenty miles away, with a map and compass. We all set off with enthusiasm but, as we go, some are faster than others, some lag behind and have to be chivvied along. Some are motivated by competition – they want to get there faster than their friends, and some of the parents have invested in super, lightweight boots to help them walk further, faster. Some hate the competitive aspect and others ignore it, not worrying about how many miles they have travelled and how many are still to go. We get obstacles – ploughed over paths and the like – and sometimes we have to stop and spend time consulting the map. At various stages – ten, fifteen miles – the children can choose to drop out, and a lot do. Only the really dedicated ones make it to the end.

In this chapter, I understand 'progress' as distance travelled from the starting point and 'continuity' as the fact that we try to keep going in the same direction, not wandering off and not getting side-tracked into doing other things. Mostly I shall discuss notions of progress although I shall touch on continuity when appropriate. I shall explore the notion of music education as a journey from a starting point, in a straight line, to a destination. I shall discuss the extent to which this notion appears in the National Curriculum and I shall question whether it is appropriate for all our pupils.

What's the problem?

Soon after the publication of the first Music National Curriculum, I ran an in-service day for the staff of a primary school. This school was one in which the majority of teachers did not teach music, but the Head thought that they might, if I could give them a little reassurance and a good understanding of what was expected. So I took them through a variety of musical activities which they could use with their classes. We sang, we played instruments, we composed, we listened to music and did some dance and movement. I produced some sample medium-term plans and they agreed that these accorded with what they used themselves.

We discussed differentiation and they touched on the thorny issue of resourcing. But there was something wrong – something they were unhappy about. Eventually, one of the teachers articulated it. 'We can see what to do,' she said. 'What we can't understand is, what counts as making progress?'

To do what I did, to suggest activities and to describe the learning that might take place, is simply not enough. It's like teaching people how to read a map and use a compass without telling them where they are going. If the purpose of teaching is to bring about gradually more and more learning or, in other words, to assist progress, what then counts as 'more and more learning'?

Graded exams and linear notions of progression

Especially for primary teachers, notions of progression in music are likely to be closely allied to notions of progression in other subjects. In school mathematics, it is largely true that progress happens in sequential steps. Children need to learn to count before they can add, and to add before they multiply, and so on. The line of progression goes from easy to difficult and from simple operations to complex ones. The same is true for most skill-based activities and there is a parallel with graded examinations in music, which can exert a powerful influence on teachers' understanding of progression, perhaps because many teachers have been through the grades themselves. Typically, in a Practical graded exam, the entrant is required to play three pieces or movements, usually from different musical periods. The model of progression is one in which the learner moves from music which is short and simple in both its technical and interpretive demands at Grade 1, to music which is technically and musically complex at Grade 8. Many thousands of people each year sit graded exams, sometimes at a considerable cost to the entrants and their families. Children like to say 'I'm Grade 4' or whatever; it gives them an objective measure of their growing musical ability. As Davidson and Scutt say, discussing one particular set of graded exams,

> It is well known, in the UK at least, that many teachers often use these examinations as a means of externally assessing a student's instrumental achievement. The Board attracts approximately 350,000 candidates annually . . . the exams offer a particular benchmark of achievement, and also a linear method of evaluation . . . so well known are the examinations, that music colleges and universities often expect a minimum requirement of Grade 8 from their applicants.
>
> (1999: 81)

As we might expect, the numbers entering Grade 1 are huge, and these gradually get smaller as the grades get more difficult, producing a sort of pyramid effect, with a small number at the apex and masses of people at the base. There is also a parallel between the graded exam system and certain ways of thinking about music, particularly Western classical music. According to some views, there is a hierarchy of composers. There are a small number of composers who are acknowledged as really great – Bach, Mozart and Beethoven, for instance. Then there is a larger number of others who are not quite so great – Vivaldi, Schumann and Dvorak might come into this category, and at the bottom of the pyramid come a vast number of really obscure or perhaps even unpublished composers. This hierarchical notion is embedded in books, where Beethoven will merit many more words than Hummel, and in the mass media. For instance, the long-running Radio Three programme, *This Week's Composer* typically accords a week to a single aspect of the really great composers – Beethoven's piano music, or Bach's cantatas. The less great are given one week each and the even less great are grouped together. In this way, the pyramid view is sustained and taught to new generations.

Progression in the National Curriculum

The linear view of progression with the pyramid effect pervades so many fields that it somehow seems natural. Schools, like many organisations, have a linear career path for their staff, and a hierarchical form of organisation, so a medium-sized secondary school might have one Headteacher, two Deputies, four or five Heads of Faculty, and so on. The National Curriculum, with its eight Level Descriptions, contains an explicitly linear notion of progression, which is likely to create a similar pyramid among the school population as a whole.

The Level Descriptions are presented in the form of general, holistic statements; there is an assumption that progress in performing will go hand in hand with progress in composing. Nevertheless, we can separate out certain strands, so as to see what sort of progress is intended (see Table 8.1).

If we take, for example, the statements to do with appraising, we can see a line of progression from simple actions (recognise) to complex ones (discriminate, comment on how and why). A similar sense of progression appears in what is being considered, from small things to large: sounds (Level 1), musical elements (Levels 2 and 3), kinds of music (Level 4), and so on, right up to musical styles, genres and traditions (Level 8).

The sense of progress happening in several different areas at once is heightened if we look at the range of activities encompassed within the National Curriculum. Although many of these can be tackled in tandem, others require specific planning. Twenty years ago, it was possible for a music curriculum within a school to be based on singing. More adventurous schools might include instrumental work, using Orff instruments, movement and 'music appreciation' – listening to, and learning about, the music of the Western classical tradition. These activities might be combined with a study of staff notation. The National Curriculum includes all of these and more. Singing in two parts, playing, improvising, composing, music technology, notations, analysing and dancing are all required activities at KS2, and will all require quite specific planning – they won't just happen as a result of other activities. In addition, the listening requirement has been broadened to include music from different times and cultures (including what we have come to call 'world music') and there is a requirement to provide 'a range of live music'.

Table 8.1 Some strands in the English National Curriculum

	Level 1	Level 2	Level 3	Level 4
Recognising and exploring	recognise and explore how sounds can be made and changed	recognise and explore how sounds can be organised	recognise and explore the ways sounds can be combined and used expressively	identify and explore the relationship between sounds and how music reflects different intentions
Performing	use their voices in different ways such as speaking, singing and chanting, and perform with awareness of others	sing with a sense of the shape of the melody, and perform simple patterns and accompaniments keeping to a steady pulse	sing in tune with expression and perform rhythmically simple parts that use a limited range of notes	maintain their own part with awareness of how the different parts fit together and the need to achieve an overall effect
Composing	repeat short rhythmic and melodic patterns and create and choose sounds in response to given starting points	choose carefully and order sounds within simple structures such as beginning, middle, end, and in response to given starting points	improvise repeated patterns and combine several layers of sound with awareness of the combined effect	improvise melodic and rhythmic phrases as part of a group performance and compose by developing ideas within musical structures
Appraising	recognise well-defined changes in sounds	recognise how the musical elements can be used to create different moods and effects	recognise how the different musical elements are combined and used expressively	describe, compare and evaluate different kinds of music using an appropriate musical vocabulary

Level 5	Level 6	Level 7	Level 8	Exceptional performance
identify and explore musical devices and how music reflects time and place	identify and explore the different processes and contexts of selected musical genres and styles	discriminate and explore musical conventions in, and influences on, selected genres, styles and traditions	discriminate and exploit the characteristics and expressive potential of selected musical resources, genres, styles and traditions	discriminate and develop different interpretations
perform significant parts with awareness of their own contribution such as leading others, taking a solo part and/or providing rhythmic support	select and make expressive use of tempo, dynamics, phrasing and timbre; make subtle adjustments to fit their own part within a group performance	perform in different styles, making significant contributions to the ensemble and using relevant notations	perform, improvise and compose extended compositions with a sense of direction and shape, both within melodic and rhythmic phrases and overall form	give convincing performances and demonstrate empathy with other performers
improvise melodic and rhythmic material within given structures, and compose music for different occasions using appropriate musical devices such as melody, rhythms, chords and structures	improvise and compose in different genres and styles, using harmonic and non-harmonic devices where relevant, sustaining and developing musical ideas and achieving different intended effects	create coherent compositions drawing on internalised sounds and adapt, improvise, develop, extend and discard musical ideas within given and chosen musical structures, genres, styles and traditions	improvise and compose extended compositions with a sense of direction and shape, both within melodic and rhythmic phrases and overall form	produce compositions that demonstrate a coherent development of musical ideas, consistency of style and a degree of individuality
analyse and compare musical features	analyse, compare and evaluate how music reflects the contexts in which it is created, performed and heard	evaluate, and make critical judgements about, the use of musical conventions and other characteristics and how different contexts are reflected in their own and others' work	discriminate between musical styles, genres and traditions, commenting on the relationship between the music and its cultural context, making and justifying their own judgements	discriminate and comment on how and why changes occur within selected traditions including the particular contribution of significant performers and composers

There is nothing inherently wrong with this and, after all, the curriculum is intended to be 'broad and balanced'. But it does make progression more difficult, because the time allocated for music has not noticeably increased, and may well have decreased. And there are other issues that make progression in music particularly problematic.

Some problems with linear progression

It is difficult to achieve continuity between primary schools and secondary schools, which are very different places, with very different cultures. For instance, Jo Glover, in a review of educational materials, suggests that:

> Primary pupils sing; secondary pupils play, particularly with keyboards and technology. Primary music focuses on the elements of music, often on the extreme opposites . . . secondary music focuses on popular styles, classical forms and a harmonic language somewhere between the two. Primary pupils compose programme music; secondary pupils compose blues songs. Everyone plays gamelan.
>
> (1996: 165)

Although the author admits that this picture is 'slightly exaggerated', her examination of educational materials does provide evidence that the National Curriculum has not yet achieved the seamless continuity that was hoped for. There is also evidence that secondary schools pay too little attention to the work that is done in the primary schools (Mills, 1996). Despite strenuous efforts in some places, some of which are listed in Janet Mills' article, the primary/secondary transfer is still a huge problem for continuity, and therefore, progression.

The amount of disruption to the curriculum does nothing to improve matters. From 1998 until 2000, the music curriculum, along with the other Foundation Subjects, was suspended in primary schools, in order to allow schools space and time to implement the government's new Literacy and Numeracy strategies. This will not have helped continuity. During the same period, Primary Initial Teacher Training courses cut their numbers of music specialists and, at the same time, cut the time allocated for music in the generalist curriculum (see Rogers, 1998). Although the effect of this has not yet been documented, the likely result is that there are now, and will be in the future, fewer teachers trained to teach music in primary schools than hitherto.

Both measures can make it more difficult for teachers in secondary schools to assume a level of musical competence from all, or even most, pupils at entry. Some undoubtedly have a good experience through curricular and extra-curricular music making; others haven't. On the other hand, some pupils arrive with many hours of individual or small group tuition in an instrument. Obviously this is desirable and we wouldn't have it any other way, but it does mean that a typical Year 7 class in music might have a huge ability span.

This has always been the case, of course – the National Curriculum cannot be blamed for causing this state of affairs. The same problem arose when the post-16

GCSE examination came into being. GCSE was intended for the whole ability range and the National Criteria stated that it should be possible for candidates who receive no instrumental tuition outside the course to achieve high grades in the examination. Nevertheless, a small-scale survey of 134 GCSE candidates indicated that it was extremely difficult for pupils to achieve high grades without such tuition. In this survey, the greatest number of 'U' grades went to pupils with no extra tuition and the greatest number of 'A' grades were awarded to pupils who had more than eighty hours of extra tuition (Cain, 1989). If this scenario is repeated, it is likely that the higher levels of the National Curriculum will be given almost entirely to pupils who have extra tuition outside the classroom.

To summarise, the charges against the linear model of progression are as follows:

- There are factors outside our control, which militate against linear progression.
- Linear progression inevitably leads to hierarchical pyramids: lots of people only get half way to the destination. This really isn't good: in my working life, I constantly meet prospective primary teachers who are terrified of engaging in simple musical activities because, like many other people, they think of themselves as 'unmusical'.
- Linear progression sits well with some views of music making, but is at odds with other, equally valid views.
- The higher levels appear to meet the needs of those pupils who have certain sorts of extra-curricular music, but may be too high for even successful musicians who don't have this experience. For example, despite earning huge fame and fortune from the music business, it might be considered doubtful whether all the musicians that appear on *Top of the Pops* would gain National Curriculum Level 8. (I am thinking of groups such as the 1990s' sensation the Spice Girls.)
- The notion of progression happening at the same rate in several different areas at once, seems to have no foundation, either in the world outside school or in theories of development. Most musicians simply aren't broad and balanced – they sing or play or improvise or compose or analyse or dance or use IT. The musical polymath, if he or she exists, is extremely rare.
- The emphasis on analysing and evaluating would appear to militate against those pupils who have well-developed musical skills but poorer language skills. (The same thing happens at GCSE, when the standard of pupils' commentary sheets can affect their marks for composing.)

Since linear progression is not unproblematic, we might ask whether there is another way.

Folk, rock and authenticity

We are no longer on a sponsored walk; the school trip is now in a theme park. The children are going on rides and visiting attractions. They don't ever travel far from the car park, but they do see a lot and cover a lot of ground. They tend to go on each ride once, although a small minority chooses to go on the same ride over and over again. At the end of the day, some of them go home tired and footsore, but there is a general sense of satisfaction; nobody feels let down and most want to come again.

Years ago, playing folk music, I came up against people whose musical education was very different from my own, and whose notion of progress was not measured by graded exams. Typically, they were self-taught, although they tended to admire musicians who were taught 'classically', assuming that the classically trained were necessarily better than they were. The chief attribute of a folk musician was authenticity. Ideally, to be a proper folk-singer, you should be a labourer, on a farm or down a mine or on a building site. (Most of the musicians I knew actually worked in schools or offices, but perhaps spiritually they were labourers.) Ideally, folk-singers would learn most of their repertoire at their mother's or perhaps their grandmother's knee. 'Aural tests' have no place in this tradition, but musicians would learn new material by listening carefully to recordings, imitating closely what they hear. The idea of learning simple music as a preparation for learning more difficult music is alien, as is the notion of mastering scales or other technical exercises in order to play more complicated music. The best musicians would learn a large repertoire of music by heart and would stay true to their roots, communicating directly with their audience.

On a similar theme, Nicholas Cook contrasts the apparent authenticity of rock musicians with the supposed artificiality of classical musicians:

> This goes back to the origins of rock in the blues, and specifically in the blues as they were played and sung by Black Americans in the deep South. The blues were seen as the authentic expression of an oppressed race, a music that came from the heart . . . in contrast to the starched formality of the classical 'art' tradition that had been imported from Europe.
>
> (1998: 7)

He goes on to show that this notion is still alive and, by way of illustration, he describes an episode of a television show in which Ry Cooder, the legendary blues-rock guitarist and singer, teaches a virtuoso classical performer (a pig called 'Piginini') to play, 'from the heart – letting it come naturally'. The underlying notion that allows the viewers to make sense of this episode, is that a blues performer, who does 'what comes naturally', is better equipped to play from the heart than a classically trained musician, who is required to undergo a rigorous training in order to read and play the more complex music of the classical tradition.

The fact that this is a caricature is beside the point; the idea has a hold on the popular imagination. Nevertheless, folk or blues or rock musicians will have some form of music education, or at least, self-education. Malcolm Ross describes how this can start:

> Many teenagers for instance elect to teach themselves to play a musical instrument – the drums perhaps or the guitar . . . They usually know already

the kind of sound they are interested in . . . They listen to their mentors and try to emulate them, running into problems of sound production and control, figuring their own way through them, comparing notes with fellow practitioners, following the example of preferred models.

(1995: 196)

Elsewhere, Ross describes what education might look like if it were to encourage this sort of natural approach:

Pop music is, of course, part of a multi-media experience for the young that includes movement, dance, graphics, drama, make-up, costume. Our vernacular arts curriculum would be similarly eclectic and multi-disciplinary . . . the classes would be jam sessions and the public events, community happenings.

(1984: 46)

I find this vision very attractive. The rich and diverse range of activities Ross describes, the crossing of boundaries between art forms so that ideas explored in one art form can feed into work in another, the emphasis on the contemporary, on democratic processes involving individual choice – all these sound authentic; congruent with what music is. How can we get progression within this mode of working?

John Paynter, writing some six years before the imposition of the National Curriculum, suggests some answers. He starts with the point I made earlier, about notions of progression being borrowed from other disciplines:

Part of our dilemma may spring from being too strongly influenced by what we see of other subjects . . . Subjects which rely on a steady intake of information, with relatively little time devoted to interpreting or generating ideas, create a powerful model for the whole curriculum. As a result the arts – which do not operate extensively upon received information – have to . . . try to bring themselves in line with the 'sequential information' view of a syllabus.

(1982: 57)

He points out that this can be achieved if teachers concentrate on 'ancillary skills' such as notation, but that this is 'missing the point'. He believes that:

musical insight is not the sum of an agreed series of theoretical points. The true rudiments of music are sensitivity to and delight in sound and its expressive qualities, and the progression we create must be within this mode of understanding and derived from musical experience itself.

(ibid.: 59)

He goes on to consider what sort of progress might be made by a painter or sculptor:

A retrospective exhibition of his work would undoubtedly reveal progression but not necessarily a growing complexity or even evidence of the artist having acquired more theoretical knowledge than he had in his early years. Instead we would most likely notice the way in which the artist followed various lines of thought, responding afresh to stimuli, exploring new ways of working with his materials and developing techniques to meet new problems . . . The key to progress in an art is the connection between exploration and construction (and in music 'construction' includes interpretation and performance of existing music).

(ibid.: 59)

Paynter considers what this might mean for schools:

In the classroom the teacher's task is to help pupils make the all-important evaluations of their work so that they are aware of the successes and the miscalculations. Obviously we should expect them to learn new techniques and acquire points of information that will assist them in further work, but the real progress will be measured by the extent to which they are able to use an increasing diversity of musical ideas with confidence.

(ibid.: 60)

We might ask to what extent it is appropriate to base our notions of progression in the classroom on that of adult artists. Although 'the true rudiments of music' might be 'sensitivity to and delight in sound', would a pupil get very far without, for instance, a sense of pulse? And if this is the case, surely it is the job of the teacher to do everything possible to impart this? The answer would undoubtedly be yes, but only in a context in which the student needed it. Work on pulse would be done, but only because it arose from a specific need, not because it happened to be the next thing on the syllabus. This approach might allow the realisation of the vision articulated by the Music Advisers' National Association:

The first step must be to cease attempting to frame syllabuses in terms of predetermined products. Instead, a series of experiences should be planned which have a clear developmental thrust, but which leave room for the unpredictable, the original, and even the idiosyncratic as far as pupils' products are concerned.

(Preston *et al.*, 1986: 19)

A theory of musical development

The notion of progression being linked to specific contexts is so obvious that we might wonder why it was not adopted in the National Curriculum. Part of the answer will have to do with political pressures and the need to match the music National Curriculum with that of other subjects. Perhaps, also, part of the answer is because the linear model of progression has been given a boost from an unexpected quarter, from developmental psychology. There are a handful of stage theories of musical development, including Malcolm Ross's theory (Ross, 1984). Perhaps the fullest and most detailed of these includes and expands Ross's theory and has become known as the Swanwick–Tillman spiral (Swanwick and Tillman, 1986; Swanwick, 1988, 1991, 1994, 1998). This well-known theory is based on an investigation into compositions by several hundred children of different ages. It describes eight stages, each qualitatively different from the others. According to the theory, the child starts with a concern for the materials of music, proceeds to a concern with its expressive qualities, then to its structural properties and finally to a personal commitment based on an understanding of music's value. These stages are cumulative in nature, each stage building on and containing the stages that precede it. The authors suggest that, although different children reach the stages at different times, it is most common for a child who reaches the higher stages to do so in the latter part of their secondary schooling. Swanwick has, on a number of occasions, shown that this research can be used to generate assessment criteria in performing and listening as well as composing. There are some similarities between the criteria he offers and the levels now enshrined in the National Curriculum. Here are some of his criteria, in the version he describes as 'condensed to the briefest possible format', compared to similar statements in the English National Curriculum (see Table 8.2).

If, as I am suggesting, the National Curriculum has been influenced by Swanwick's work, then we should be grateful: examples of research influencing policy are few enough. But there are problems. First, it is not obvious that a pattern

Table 8.2 A comparison between National Curriculum statements and Swanwick's criteria

National Curriculum Levels	Swanwick's criteria
recognise and explore how sounds can be made and changed . . . recognise well-defined changes in sounds (Level 1)	recognises (explores) sonorities, for example, loudness levels, wide pitch differences, well-defined changes of tone colour and texture (Layer 1)
recognise and explore the ways sounds can be combined and used expressively (Level 3)	(communicates) expressive character in music – atmosphere or gesture – or can interpret in words, visual images or movement (Layer 3)
select and make expressive use of tempo, dynamics, phrasing and structure (Level 6)	analyses (produces) expressive effects by attention to timbre, pitch, duration, pace, loudness, texture and silence (Layer 4)
improvise and compose in different genres and styles (Level 6)	(makes) or can place music within a particular stylistic context (Layer 6)

Source: Swanwick (1998)

that has been observed in the development of children's musicianship should be used to assess classroom work. In an earlier work, Swanwick states that, 'It is not intended to suggest that one layer is somehow better or worse than another one' (1994: 91). And, although we do want our pupils to develop, it is perhaps more important that they have musically and personally enriching experiences at all stages, than that they move quickly up the levels. Second, although Swanwick's criteria seem to have left their mark on the National Curriculum, there has been no attempt to adopt the whole theory, just parts of it. This seems to miss the point – Swanwick's criteria are generated from careful inquiry into what children actually do, and they have been tested (Hentschke, 1993; Swanwick, 1991, 1994). The theory is a whole, not just a collection of parts, and to separate out some parts and adapt them to the format of the National Curriculum does not make the curriculum any more valid. Third, and perhaps most importantly, the parts of the descriptions which deal with musical ability have been interwoven with parts which refer to critical analysis and the impression given, that the two will go hand in hand, is, at best, dubious.

The triumph of the straight line

However, the linear model of progression is in the ascendancy, and we are obliged by law to use it. Of course, the charges I have levelled against it might or might not stick. It is possible that we will come to recognise the introduction of these level descriptions as the single most useful thing to happen to music education in schools. Alternatively, it might turn out that the levels are, in practice, sufficiently flexible to meet my objections. In the meantime, it would be helpful to set up large- or small-scale investigations into the effect that the levels have on the curriculum and the motivation of pupils, so as to inform the next National Curriculum revision. Case studies that show how individual children develop musically might help us better to understand the differences, as well as the similarities, among young musicians. Such information might help us to steer clear of linear models, or at least to adapt them to the young performer who is not also a good composer, or the young musician of any sort who is not also an articulate critic.

My 'school trip' metaphor is inadequate – music is far more important than this. Nevertheless, if we want our pupils to emerge from their music education with a curiosity for, and a lively interest in music, we might need a system that is different from the one currently imposed. Otherwise, we risk turning what could be a visit to the theme park into a 20-mile hike.

Questions for discussion

1   When you consider the differences in musical ability between the youngest pupils you teach and the oldest, you will see that children improve simply because they mature. To what extent do you think teachers can, and should, accelerate this process? What are the dangers in teachers accelerating the natural processes of maturation?

2   National Curriculum levels impose stages of progression on teachers and the curricula they teach. What are the advantages and disadvantages of this? What are the advantages and disadvantages of these particular level statements?
3   Examine two or three resources for music teaching (see Further reading). In what sorts of ways is progression built into these resources?

References

Cain, T. (1989) 'Supporting evidence: the GCSE results considered in retrospect', *Times Educational Supplement*, 6 January.

Cook, N. (1998) *Music: A Very Short Introduction*, Oxford: Oxford University Press.

Davidson, J. and Scutt, S. (1999) 'Instrumental learning with exams in mind', *British Journal of Music Education* 16, 1, 79–93.

Glover, J. (1996) 'Review', *British Journal of Music Education* 13, 2, 165–8.

Hentschke, L. (1993) *Musical Development: Testing a Model in the Audience-listening Setting*, London: University of London Institute of Education.

Mills, J. (1996) 'Starting at secondary school', *British Journal of Music Education* 13, 1, 5–14.

Paynter, J. (1982) *Music in the Secondary School Curriculum*, Cambridge: Cambridge University Press.

Preston, H. *et al.* (1986) *Assessment and Progression in Music Education*, London: Music Advisers' National Association.

QCA (1999) *Music: The National Curriculum for England*, London: DfEE and QCA.

Rogers, R. (1998) *The Disappearing Arts? The Current State of the Arts in Initial Teacher Training and Professional Development*, London: RSA.

Ross, M. (1984) *The Aesthetic Impulse*, Oxford: Pergamon.

Ross, M. (1995) 'What's wrong with school music?', *British Journal of Music Education* 12, 3, 185–201.

Swanwick, K. (1988) *Music, Mind and Education*, London: Routledge.

Swanwick, K. (1991) 'Musical criticism and musical development', *British Journal of Music Education* 8, 2, 139–48.

Swanwick, K. (1994) *Musical Knowledge: Intuition, Analysis and Music Education*, London: Routledge.

Swanwick, K. (1998) 'The perils and possibilities of assessment', *Research Studies in Music Education*, Toowoomba: University of South Queensland Press.

Swanwick, K. and Tillman, J. (1986) 'The sequence of musical development: a study of children's compositions', *British Journal of Music Education* 3, 3, 305–39.

Further reading

Allen, P. (1997) *Singing Matters*, Oxford: Heinemann.

Bowman, D. and Cole, B. (1989) *Sound Matters*, London: Schott.

Cain, T. (1988) *Keynote*, Cambridge: Cambridge University Press.

Campbell, L. (1985) *Sketching at the Keyboard*, London: Stainer and Bell.

Hiscox, C. and Metcalfe, M. (1998) *Music Matters*, Oxford: Heinemann.

Howard, J. (1990) *Learning to Compose*, Cambridge: Cambridge University Press.

9 Music assessment and the hegemony of musical heritage

Gary Spruce

Introduction

This chapter is predicated upon two fundamental beliefs. The first is that the manner in which musical achievement is defined and assessed inevitably articulates a set of philosophical and political principles about the nature and purpose of learning, the subject being assessed and the relationship between school and society. In other words, that assessment

> [is] always saying something about the assessors and the assessed, and about the world that the assessor is seeking to bring about. It has behind it a view of learning, of the place of the child in the larger world and of what counts as worthwhile learning.
>
> (D. Allen, Preface to Barrs, 1990)

Second, that assessment can be understood only in the context of curriculum and pedagogy. In other words, what we teach and how we teach it impact upon *what* and *how* we assess. There will be times therefore when this chapter will be as much about the music curriculum and music pedagogy as about the assessment of musical learning.

In relation to the first of these beliefs, this chapter will argue that the bourgeois aesthetic articulated through the cultural hegemony of Western art music exercises an influence on the music curriculum, pedagogy and assessment resulting in a way of thinking about music which, in the words of Nicholas Cook 'cannot do justice to the diversity of practices which that small word "music" signifies in today's world' (1998: 14). It will argue that a consequence of a restricted definition of 'music' and the *implicit* claims to superiority articulated by the bourgeois aesthetic subverts, particularly through assessment practice, the *explicit* principles of good practice in much music pedagogy and curriculum content. Good practice that seeks to put children at the centre of the educational experience, engaging with music from the inside, rather than music 'as an adult phenomenon into which children [are] to be initiated' (Pitts, 1998: 32).

The rise of the bourgeois aesthetic

Prior to the eighteenth century, music was an essentially collective, social activity. Music's existence was defined and legitimised by its contribution to the rites and rituals of church, state, court, streets, taverns and market places. Composers were fully integrated members of society producing music for specific social occasions.

In the late eighteenth and early nineteenth centuries, however, there occurred a fundamental restructuring of Western society. The Industrial Revolution created a new and affluent middle class eager to identify with the established aristocracy, while the aristocracy were keen to retain some of their social dominance. Peter Martin (1995), drawing on the work of William Weber, describes how the consumption of 'art music' and particularly concert going became 'an expression of the emerging pattern of social stratification, and in particular a demonstration of the merger of the aristocracy and the upper middle class into a single upper class' (William Weber, 1975, in Martin, 1995: 228).

If music was to act as a tool of social stratification it needed to conform to three conditions. First, that physical access be restricted to members of the bourgeoisie by means of the removal of art music to places designed for its performance (concert halls) with the cost of entry prohibitive to all but the wealthy. Second, that art music should be understood as reflecting the inherent superiority of its consumers. Third, that its inherent superiority was capable of being appreciated only by those of the refined sensitivity and sensibilities of the bourgeoisie.

This notion of art music as transcending human experience (and thus as inherently superior to other musics) was articulated primarily through the ideology of musical autonomy. Unlike the music of the streets and taverns which, it was argued, depended upon social and cultural contexts in order to communicate its message, art music is autonomous. Musical meaning is articulated exclusively through the relationship of musical elements to each other. It does not need to refer outside of itself to communicate its message. The consumer (performer or listener) simply needs to be able to decode the meaning inherent in the music; to understand how musical materials relate to each other within an autonomous musical structure.

It is upon this premise that Hanslick (among others) argues that the greater the 'learning' of the listener the greater will be their understanding and appreciation of the music: 'the "qualified" hearer, whose aesthetic judgement rests on adequate factual judgement' (Dalhaus, 1983: 25, in Cook, 1992: 170). There is thus created a hierarchy of listeners from the trained musicologist down to the ordinary listener 'firmly at the bottom of the musical hierarchy' (Cook, 1998: 27). However, the definition of a qualified hearer is bourgeois-defined, predicated upon Western art music as a tool of social stratification and, as we shall see later, not necessarily appropriate to all musical styles or contexts

From the ideology of musical autonomy emerged the notion of musical 'completeness'. Unlike other musics that are in a state of constant change and development due to the improvisatory nature of their performance and/or the oral nature of their transmission, art music is perceived as complete and self-contained. The notion of completeness is then interpreted as a further aspect of art music's superior nature and emphasised by objectification through notation. Notation results in the commoditisation of music which consequentially supports the notion of music-as-object.

The significance attached to the notation of art music resulted in the delineation and realignment of musical roles. The performer's role had been an actively creative one – realising figured basses, adding ornamentation, extemporising. However, now that meaning was perceived as being embodied in notation, the performer's role became primarily one of realising as accurately (literally) as possible the score. The status of the composer rose at the expense of the performer. The concept of the composer 'genius' and musical 'masterpiece' was born and with it the creation of a hierarchy of composer as the producer of these masterpieces, the performer as a conduit for the composer and the listener as the receiver of the musical 'message'.

The bourgeois aesthetic and the music curriculum

Christopher Small describes how Western musicians (and by implication music teachers) have a 'strong tendency to work more or less exclusively within the assumption of the western high-art tradition and to accept them without questions as universals of music' (1999: 10). Of the 'universals' to which Small refers, the primary one is the notion of art music's shaping itself 'in accordance with self-constrained abstract principles that are unrelated to the outside world' (Leppert and McClary, 1987: xii). The notion of autonomy results in the ideology of the Western musical heritage being defined by musical 'works' and the pre-eminence of the composer (over that of the performer and listener) as the producer of such 'works'. The clear distinction drawn between the roles of composer, performer and listener is explicit in most music curriculum models. Its most recent manifestation being the attainment targets – Performing and Composing, Listening and Appraising – of the first Music National Curriculum (1995). Consequently, the demarcation of roles is also to be found in most summative assessment where performing, composing and listening skills are typically assessed separately.

However, there is nothing self-evidently appropriate about mapping this strict demarcation of roles onto contemporary music curricular and assessment, particularly when one of the principal aims of the music curriculum is avowedly to introduce children to a wide range of musical styles and cultures. As Christopher Small says, in many societies, musical activity is fundamentally a communal activity 'where it is assumed that all are musical' (1987: 26). Chernoff, writing of African music, describes how music 'serves a crucially integrative function and musicians perform a complex social role' (1985, in Haydon and Marks, 1985: 101). In this type of musical and social context, delineation of roles would work against the social nature of the musical interaction. Similarly, there is little clear distinction between composer and performer in much rock music, while the development of music technology (particularly sequencing software) means that the discrete role of the performer is no longer a given.

I am therefore aware that in going on to write about performing, composing and listening as discrete activities I, too, am reflecting and perpetuating fundamentally arbitrary and often inappropriate distinctions.

The listener and the bourgeois aesthetic

I suggested earlier that the notion of art music as a tool of social stratification is predicated upon a belief that such music can be appreciated only by those of refined (bourgeois) sensitivity and bourgeois-defined education. However, even from the bourgeois perspective, such a rationale is insufficient in itself to sustain the notion of the inherent superiority of art music. There needs to be an objective measurement of a musical work's value other than 'the fluctuating assurance of the senses' (Hanslick, 1854/1891: 17). Thus, for Hanslick, an ideal listener is one who is able to understand music's meaning through a developed awareness of the relationship of musical elements both simultaneously and structurally as they occur over time. For others, 'those who cannot or will not make efforts of the right kind, however completely [they hear] the sounds that fill the room in which [they are] sitting' (Hanslick, in Cook, 1992: 16), music's meaning remains ever inaccessible. Importantly, Hanslick is not here suggesting that the listener plays a part in *constructing* meaning but only in *understanding* it. In Hanslick's terms what is important is to 'consider the beautiful *object* and not the perceiving *subject*' (Hanslick, 1854/1891: 17, in Martin, 1995: 43). The musical object is pre-eminent.

The notion of the primacy of the musical object over the 'perceiving' subject (the listener) is challenged by Adorno. A central theme of his 'materialist aesthetics' is the contention that 'the truth of a musical work [does] not depend on the composer's conscious beliefs or intentions' (Martin, 1995: 85) but, by implication, upon listeners' cognitive and affective engagement with music through time. With the caveat that these mental operations are inevitably socially and culturally mediated, Adorno's view seems (to me) to be convincing. It allows 'meaning' to be constructed by the listener rather than the musical object 'floating through history, untouched by time or social change, waiting for the ideal listener to draw its meaning out, by a process that Emmanuel Kant calls disinterested contemplation' (Small, 1999: 10).

However, the emphasis on the musical 'object', combined with the notion of the 'knowledgeable' and essentially passive role of the listener as the receiver of meaning rather than a constructor of it, continues to exert a significant influence upon music education and, particularly, musical assessment.

In this model of aesthetic listening, where the role of the listener is to gain understanding of musical meaning as enshrined in the musical object, there is an implied 'distancing' of the object from the listener in order that it can be experienced with 'disinterested contemplation' (Hanslick, 1854/1891). However, the distancing from the musical object implied by aesthetic listening is not, necessarily, an 'authentic' way of listening to all musical styles. Dance music, jazz, folk, 'pop' when performed in the social context for which they are intended, articulate a different, and much less clearly delineated relationship between performer, listener and composer than that implied by distanced, aesthetic listening.

Listening is as much a socially constructed experience as performing or composing. Consequently, listening to the same music in a different social context will be a fundamentally different experience. The issue with listening in the classroom is that whatever style of music is being listened to, it has, by definition been removed from its original social context – it has been decontextualised. The vacuum that such decontextualisation creates provides an opportunity for the assertion of the bourgeois, 'self-evident universal' of aesthetic listening. Listening in the curriculum comes to mean exclusively 'aesthetic listening' – distanced, objective listening – irrespective of its appropriateness to the style of music being encountered.

Writing of African choral singing, Small describes how:

> even if not formally involved in the performance, listeners . . . are never silent and static, but respond with what J.H.K. Nketia calls 'outward dramatic expression of feeling . . . Individuals may shout in appreciation when something in the performance strikes them, or indicate at a particular point their satisfaction with what they have heard or seen.'
>
> (1987: 26–7)

However, when such music appears in the 'music curriculum', it is 'schooled' – made respectable – by being listened to 'aesthetically' as though it were a Schubert song. The classroom becomes a surrogate concert hall where pupils sit behind desks, in silence, listening attentively, demonstrating none of the involvement described by Nketia.

It can be argued that listening to all music 'aesthetically' as though it were a piece of art music, leads to an emancipation of musical styles – all music being treated equally. However, such an idea is predicated upon an assumption of aesthetic listening as the self-evidently best or only way of perceiving music. But, as Cook says: 'To approach music aesthetically – to interpret it in terms of a specific interest in its perceptual experience – is not . . . to transcend Western cultural values, but rather to express them' (1992: 7).

If one is truly to develop children's understanding of 'music from different times and places' as well as the range of musics within their own culture, then developing an awareness of the many ways of *thinking of* and *engaging with*, music is fundamental. The problem is, that in assessing listening as a discrete activity – separate from composing and performing – one is, by definition, assessing aesthetic listening. It matters little whether the object of that listening is a Brahms symphony or a song by Bob Marley, similar skills are being assessed.

For, in the aesthetic model of listening all music comes to be understood as an object constructed of 'bits' – much in the way that a house is constructed of bricks. The assessment of listening therefore becomes the deconstruction and reconstruction of the musical object. The listener is assessed according to how well they can 'rationalise the sounds of our musical productions' (Cook, 1992: 6), through an understanding of how the discrete elements of music 'fit together' to form musical structures. Typically assessment is through ear training tests and tests of analytical listening: both appropriate to Western art music but less so for other musical styles. Unfortunately, in attempting to create a 'knowledgeable listener' through assessment that focuses exclusively upon the musical object and the elements that contribute to it, the listener is distracted from holistic engagement with the musical work as a constructor of meaning. For as Cook points out, an exclusive focus on analytical listening results in it becoming:

> increasingly difficult to conceive that music might work in other ways, or to hear it properly if it does; the harder you listen, the more you hear it in terms of the notes and chords and formal types of Western tradition, and the less you can understand music that works primarily in terms of timbre and texture.

> (1998: 107–8)

Performing and the bourgeois aesthetic

The concept of meaning as being contained entirely and autonomously within the musical object also impacts significantly upon the way in which performing is taught and assessed. This is particularly the case in the way in which pre-eminent importance is attached to the notated score as an objectification and embodiment of musical meaning. In Western art music the printed score is often considered to *be* the music with particular kudos accorded to those who profess a preference for reading a score over attending a performance or listening to a recording.

If musical meaning is perceived as being embodied within the score, then it follows that what is paramount is that the performer's realisation of the score should be as accurate (literal) as possible. Wrong notes and incorrect rhythms will all obscure musical meaning for the listener and therefore assessment of such aspects of performance is appropriate. However, in music where there is no definitive version, no defining score where meaning resides, the notion of 'wrong notes' is much more problematic.

In response to an obituary of the jazz trumpeter, Kenny Baker, a correspondent to *The Guardian* wrote: 'A tale about Kenny Baker indicates his flawless trumpet technique and sheer professionalism. Someone once asked him if he ever played a wrong note. Kenny looked puzzled. "What for?" he said' (*The Guardian*, 30 December 1999: 18). Now it may be that the correspondent's interpretation of this anecdote is true. That Baker was taking the opportunity posed by the question to bring attention to what he perceived to be his infallible technique. However, another interpretation – lent weight, perhaps, by the description of Baker's puzzled expression – is that the concept of 'wrong notes' in terms of there being fixed 'correct' ones, is inappropriate to the musical culture in which he operated. The definition of 'right' and 'wrong' notes in jazz is much more complex than through reference to a fixed score.

Consequently, assessing the performance of music that does not have a fixed, objectified form through notation is problematic. Objective assessment, which is perceived as being of such importance to the legitimacy of an assessment process and thereby the status of music within the curriculum (see Spruce, 1996: 168–85) is much more difficult. However, the common reaction is typical: the cultural context is ignored and the music is decontextualised and schooled (reinterpreted) in aesthetic terms.

This reinterpretation commonly occurs in one of two ways. Either the music is notated – objectified into a fixed form – and then the criteria for assessing art music applied as though it were a Beethoven sonata. A hierarchy of performer and composer is imposed where it had not existed and the direct creative input of the performer that once lay at the heart of the performance is removed.

The second, ostensibly more enlightened approach, is to apply a form of 'improvisation criteria' to the performance. The problem here is that the qualities by which improvisation is typically assessed are equally as embedded in the Western art music aesthetic as those for performing and listening. For the ultimate accolade for an improvisation is that it has tricked the listener into believing that it is fully notated (objectified) music (the I-can't-believe-it's-not-butter school of improvisation). Rather than improvisation being an opportunity to break the bounds of objectified notation, to challenge the *perceptual* notion of musical experience, it is judged by the extent to which it sounds as though it has emerged from a score as objectified music.

Examination Boards' and schools' desire to embrace a wide range of musical styles and cultures while their thinking about music remains rooted in a Western art aesthetic, result in assessment reflecting and further articulating the low art–high art hierarchy. A consequence of the tension created by mapping a bourgeois aesthetic, cultural hegemony on to a multi-style multicultural content, is that in assessing musical achievement, those whose skills are not of the Western art tradition are inevitably disadvantaged. Here are two examples of what I mean.

The rock guitarist

When preparing a performance of pre-existing rock music, guitarists and drummers commonly learn music from a recording of someone else's performance. This performance will rarely lay claim to being definitive even when the composer and performer are one and the same. The recording is simply a record of one performance, not an objectification of a definitive version. Consequently, for rock performers learning the music from the CD simply provides a foundation for their creative realisation of the piece. A score of the music may be used as a reminder of the structure of the music, but it almost always *follows on* from learning the music aurally via a CD or collaboratively in rehearsal. This is not just because the guitarist/drummer's natural learning mode is an aural one but also because staff notation is not capable of codifying the subtleties and complexity of much rock music. The notation of rock music (and, indeed, much pop) is almost always *post facto* to its composition and recording, unlike in art music where notation mediates with the creative process.

When rock performers are assessed, however, the assessment criteria will often be the same as for the assessment of art music – basically the accurate realisation of the score. However, this presumes that the score (if it exists) is an accurate and definitive objectification of the music – which in the case of rock music it manifestly is not. The examiner is presented with a notated version of the music of Byzantine complexity. The candidate dutifully sits behind another copy of the music (because this is what 'real' musicians do) trying to give the impression that without it the performance would grind to a halt. Meanwhile, the examiner, who is beginning to realise what it must have been like to be a member of the orchestra at the first rehearsal of *The Rite of Spring*, prepares to be taken on a roller-coaster ride of triplets, quintuplets, sextuplets, Dal Segnos, Da capos, first, second, third and fourth time bars, and bars labelled 'improvise over these chords', hoping that when the performance ends he will be looking at the final page. 'Does she realise that I gave up halfway through?' thinks the examiner: 'Does he realise that I don't play exactly what's written?' thinks the candidate.

The jazz singer

This candidate sings regularly in local jazz clubs as a member of a band. She has recently starred in a highly successful student production of *Cabaret* which is to be taken to the Edinburgh Festival fringe the following summer. She exudes confidence and delivers a mesmerising performance of a jazz standard that demonstrates secure intonation, excellent dynamic control, clear diction, a secure vocal technique across a wide range, and a real sense of performance occasion.

So what happens next? Does she leave the examination room secure in the knowledge that she has performed well against all the criteria by which she and the music are usually judged? Absolutely not. This is the world of music examinations and she has not yet demonstrated she can perform from notation. It is time for sight-reading! The draining away of confidence is almost palpable. She is given a notated copy of a song and a starting note. Over the course of the next few minutes the candidate attempts the test, the line of the melody is broadly followed, a few rhythmic fragments observed, but it is altogether a dispiriting experience for both performer and examiner.

I shall return briefly to these two examples later in the chapter.

Composing and the bourgeois aesthetic

Teachers' oft expressed unease with teaching and assessing composing is arguably symptomatic of a notion of composing rooted in the bourgeois aesthetic. A belief that composing is exclusively about the production of complete and autonomous works which are, in their perceived highest form (art music), representative and expressive of genius and of refined, bourgeois sensitivity. For it has long been understood that music of worth is composed by only those to whom the epithet of 'genius' can be attached. The role of the rest of us is to appreciate and ideally appreciate 'knowledgeably'.

Consequently, composing in the curriculum has traditionally fulfilled the same role as performing and listening: a means of educating more knowledgeable listeners capable of perceiving the meaning which resides in 'great' music. Composing pedagogy has thus focused upon the musical object and how the musical elements constitute that object. From such a philosophy emerges a model of composition teaching and assessment based upon species counterpoint and musical pastiche. In the former the musical task is totally abstracted from a musical context, while in the latter the student imitates the styles of Bach chorales, renaissance polyphony and classical harmony, thus emphasising the status of Western art music as the ideal model to be aspired to. Part of the process of 'schooling' Western art music is extrapolating from it 'rules' of harmony and counterpoint which can then form the basis for what will be perceived as objective assessment. Composition can now be assessed as confidently as performing, listening and music theory. Furthermore, by assigning 'rules' of harmony and counterpoint to composition, teachers maintain responsibility for defining what is and what is not, legitimate composition and music's potential for articulating an independent (non-bourgeois) social meaning is contained.

It can be claimed that none of this any longer holds true for contemporary music education. However, as with listening and performing, I suggest that there is a confusion and tension between the multi-stylistic curriculum and a monotheistic assessment and pedagogy. For, it can be argued that there is little difference in effect between asking pupils to compose using a blues chord sequence and asking them to do the same using a 'classical' structure. More particularly, is there fundamentally any difference between species counterpoint and a pedagogical approach to, say, 'teaching the blues', where children are asked to select notes from notated chords and write them down away from an instrument and therefore with little idea what their 'composing' sounds like? This is just as much abstracted teaching and learning as species counterpoint. However, it gives music teachers an object that can be assessed objectively, which is perhaps what matters.

The problem, of course, is that composing in the curriculum is still fundamentally locked in to the notion of music as object and as an object defined in adult terms. As Walker says: 'We accept "childish drawings" . . . but childish musical actions are rejected as such' (Walker, 1988, in Spruce, 1996: 74).

Composing is perceived as the preserve of special people (dead, white and male), the purpose of which is the production of complete and autonomous musical objects. Moreover, that composing must be mediated with notation. Children's composing is assessed according to how close it reflects this one model – how it serves to perpetuate a cultural hegemony rather than the extent to which it challenges it.

Musical assessment and musical emancipation

I have tried to demonstrate that the main problem with contemporary musical assessment is that it continues to articulate the musical values and beliefs of Western art music. In doing so, it creates a potentially unresolvable tension between a curriculum that is philosophically multi-stylistic and a way of assessing which is monotheistic. This frequently results in assessment predicated upon inappropriate criteria and consequently unfair to those whose musical skills are not rooted in Western art music.

The rationale put forward for assessing all musical styles by a single set of criteria is, ironically, one of objectivity, uniformity and above all, musical emancipation: all musics are being treated equally. However, this is manifestly not the case when the values articulated by the assessment process are exclusively those of Western art music. For by doing so, the cultural hegemony of Western art music is simply perpetuated by creating a context in which music of other styles – whether through performance, listening or composition – is perceived of as inferior. If there is to be true emancipation of musical styles (and, by implication, emancipation of musical skills), then the assessment process needs to be 'fit for purpose' and reflective of what is being learnt *musically*. Assessment will focus not exclusively upon the notion of end product which in many cultures is a spurious one but will take account of the range of contexts and many ways in which music evolves and is understood.

There is perhaps a need to acknowledge that thinking of music exclusively as 'object' – complete and autonomous with a clear delineation of composer, performer and listener – is often inappropriate. Assessment practice will recognise that whereas European art music is about 'structure' other music 'moves like a river, open ended' (Fox in Haydon and Marks, 1985: 100).

A consequence of such a reconceptualisation will be that musical learning objectives cannot so easily be predicated upon the musical object as an articulation of a predetermined standard. As Butterfield (1995) points out, a distinction will need to be drawn between predetermined objectives and emergent ones and between the 'application of a standard and the making of a judgement'. This has political implications in the context of a standards-driven educational climate, and where music's ability to demonstrate that learning has taken place through objective testing is often linked to its status within the curriculum (Spruce, 1996). I am not arguing here against standards *per se*, but rather against the assumption that objectives must always be linked to standards. For, as Butterfield says, emergent objectives 'are almost a defining characteristic of creativity' (1995: 16) while always linking standards to objectives 'implies obedience, orderliness and rationality' (ibid.: 17) resulting, in a musical context, in the further articulation of the values of Western art music.

The notion of emergent objectives provide music educators with the opportunity to add breadth both to the way we think about music and consequently the range of musical skills that are taught, learned and assessed. Teaching, learning and assessment are no longer focused on a narrow predetermined goal as an articulation of a standard: the 'polished' performance of a piece of music or a 'completed' composition or knowledge of a particular 'body' of musical works. Rather, what matters is the range of musical skills that can be developed and assessed and the range of musical contexts in which assessment can take place. Given that a reconceptualisation of what music is and how it operates will lead to an understanding that the roles of listener, performer and composer cannot always be clearly delineated, a much more integrated and holistic assessment model might emerge. For, as we have seen, the traditional focus upon the musical object and the discrete musical elements that constitute the object, have typically resulted in pedagogy and assessment based on predetermined and hierarchical musical roles and consequent fragmentation of musical experience.

A shift in perspective from the notion of music as a complete, autonomous object possessing inherent meaning to that of music as open-ended and socially constructed, can move the pedagogical focus onto the process by which music – particularly of other cultures and styles – is created. This is not to suggest that teachers or pupils will come to understand, say, Indian or African music as the indigenous population understand it. For, Cook says: 'In so far as we listen to Indian music or Machaut's music, we are bound to misinterpret it, because our concept of "music" is a contemporary Western one' (1992: 151). However, what it will do is provide children with opportunities to understand how music operates socially and, more importantly, develop their awareness of the different ways in which music can be perceived, experienced and thought about.

For example, a lesson focusing on African drumming, given by a teacher whose focus is on the musical object(ive) as an indicator of a standard, may result in a pedagogical approach that provides the most expediential route to its achievement: a polished performance of the 'work'. The teacher might construct a score of the music – will objectify it. Pupils will then learn the music from the score, perhaps going on to compose music and notating it in similar form. However, it is arguable that the skills being learnt, the understanding of music being inculcated and the relationship of the person to the music, are fundamentally the same as if the musical focus were a Mozart minuet: music-as-object with the performer and listener distanced from it.

An alternative, maybe, is for the lesson to reflect some of the process by which the music is created and performed in its original social context. So, in the case of the African drumming, the teacher might learn the various musical parts aurally and teach it to the children aurally. They will go on to compose in groups, perhaps recording their music using technology in order to work on it further in future lessons. However, what will be maintained is the aural nature of the musical learning as a fundamental characteristic of this particular music style and culture. This will possibly (though not inevitably), take longer than presenting the children with a musical score, but the musical skills developed and thereby open to assessment are much greater and much more authentic. Moreover, the musical activities of performing, listening and composing are integrated and, given the formulation of appropriate criteria, can be assessed together as part of a holistic musical experience.

In the cases of the rock drummer and jazz singer that we discussed earlier, an authentic assessment of their 'sight reading' (quick learning) skills might focus upon aural learning as well as, or instead of, performing from notation. The singer might be given a recording of a song that she would learn and interpret within a short space of time. By the same token the classical violinist might be asked to learn music aurally and to improvise. In all cases the focus of assessment has moved from an inappropriate fixation on musical object to the person as central to the making of the music. The result is a wider range of skills assessed and greater musical learning.

None of the above is meant as an attack on the principles of teaching and assessing notation or suggesting that children should not perform or listen to Western art music. It is simply arguing for consistency. We cannot on the one hand espouse the virtues of a curriculum that: 'develops understanding of music from different times and places' (DFE, 1995), while at the same time operating a philosophy of assessment predicated exclusively upon one way of perceiving music. The beliefs that are articulated through curricular and examination syllabuses *must* be reflected in assessment systems.

If the curriculum and examination syllabuses articulate an emancipation of musical styles, then so must assessment systems. Otherwise, assessment simply becomes a means of perpetuating the hegemony of Western art music at the expense of other musical styles, and most importantly, those pupils who gain their most valuable musical experiences through them. Musical achievement and its assessment should not just reflect 'content' as defined by musical objects, but should also develop children's understanding of the rich variety of ways in which music can be understood and the range of contexts in which it takes place.

Questions for discussion

1   Think back over your own music education in school. To what extent did the model of music education you experienced, and the assessment models embedded within it, effectively identify and support the range of musical attainments and skills within the class or school?
2   Thinking about your own assessment practice, to what extent does it reflect musical diversity and the many ways in which music is experienced and conceived?
3   Consider specific ways in which your own assessment practice might be developed in order to recognise a greater diversity of musical attainment and musical contexts.

References

Barrs, M. (1990) *Words Not Numbers*, London: National Association of Advisers in English.
Butterfield, S. (1995) *Education Objectives and National Assessment*, Buckingham: Open University Press.
Chernoff, J.M. (1985) 'The drums of Dagbon', in G. Haydon and M. Marks (eds) *Repercussions: A Celebration of African-American Music*, London: Century Publishing Co. Ltd.
Cook, N. (1992) *Music, Imagination and Culture*, Oxford: Oxford University Press.
Cook, N. (1998) *Music: A Very Short Introduction*, Oxford: Oxford University Press.
Dalhaus, C. (1983) *Analysis and Value Judgement*, New York: Pendragon Press.

Department for Education (1995) *Music in the National Curriculum*, London: HMSO.

Fox, C. (1985) 'Sit down and listen', in G. Haydon and M. Marks (eds) *Repercussions: A Celebration of African-American Music*, London: Century Publishing Co. Ltd.

The Guardian, 30 December 1999.

Hanslick, E. (1854/1891) *The Beautiful in Music*, London: Novello.

Haydon, G. and Marks, M. (1985) *Repercussions: A Celebration of African-American Music*, London: Century Publishing Co. Ltd.

Leppert, R. and McClary, S. (1987) *Music and Society: The Politics of Composition, Performance and Reception*, Cambridge: Cambridge University Press.

Martin, P. (1995) *Sounds and Society*, Manchester: Manchester University Press.

Pitts, S. (1998) 'Looking for inspiration: recapturing an enthusiasm for music education from innovatory writings', *British Journal of Music Education* 15, 1, 25–36.

Small, C. (1987) *Music of the Common Tongue*, London: Calder Riverrun Prentice Hall.

Small, C. (1999) 'Musicking: the means of performing and listening: A lecture', *Music Education Research* 1, 1, 1–25.

Spruce, G. (1996) 'Assessment in the arts: issues of objectivity', in G. Spruce (ed.) *Teaching Music*, London: Routledge.

Walker, R. (1988) 'In search of a child's musical imagination', in G. Spruce (ed.) *Teaching Music*, London: Routledge.

Further reading

Ross, M. and Mitchell, A. (1993) 'Assessing achievement in the arts', *British Journal of Aesthetics* 33, 2, 110–20.

Spruce, G. (1996) 'Assessment in the arts: issues of objectivity', in G. Spruce (ed.) *Teaching Music*, London: Routledge.

Swanwick, K. (1999) 'The why and how of musical assessment', in *Teaching Music Musically*, London: Routledge.

10 Music and combined arts

Charles Plummeridge

Introduction

The 1970s and early 1980s were years of rapid curriculum development when many educators advocated forms of teaching that would provide opportunities for children to experience the arts not only within the separate disciplines but also through more holistic activities. In a series of initiatives there was frequent reference to terms such as *integrated* arts, *interdisciplinary inquiry* in the arts, and *inter-related* arts, and curriculum innovators recommended strategies designed to bring teachers together in the implementation of new and broader programmes of artistic activity. These proposals were often based on the assumption that the arts disciplines share certain common unifying features, and to recognise this in curriculum planning and practice would be to deepen and enrich children's experiences. Of course, the idea of integrated or interdisciplinary studies was by no means new to many teachers; neither were suggestions for this type of work confined to one area of the curriculum. In a number of national projects integration was applied across the curriculum and often associated with a progressive tendency to break down subject barriers and thereby overcome what was regarded by some educationists as the unacceptable and restrictive compartmentalisation of knowledge.

Since the introduction of the National Curriculum, in which there is no sense of the arts forming a unified group, there has been less concern for integrated programmes although it is still common for the arts disciplines to be considered together in general discussions on educational policy, planning and development. A recent report from the School Curriculum and Assessment Authority (SCAA, 1997) and the findings of research carried out by John Harland and others (1998) on behalf of the Royal Society of Arts, both exemplify current thinking: it is recognised that there are links between the disciplines but each art form can and should make a distinctive contribution to children's education. This attitude may be contrasted with the view expressed in the present Scottish Office curriculum document *Expressive Arts 5–14* (SOED, 1992) where art and design, music, drama and physical education are described as constituting a 'generic field in education'; yet even here there is emphasis on the individuality of the subjects and only limited mention of integrated work. Nevertheless, there are educators throughout Britain who remain committed to what are nowadays referred to as *combined* (rather than *integrated*) programmes, and well-established GCSE, GNVQ and A level courses in performing arts continue to involve integrative approaches.

The term combined arts has acquired a range of meanings and is used to refer to a number of different kinds of curriculum organisation and practice. It is also one of those terms that is associated with divided opinion among members of the music education community. This is perhaps not altogether surprising since proposals for combined programmes almost inevitably lead to discussions of some controversial philosophical and pedagogical issues. Furthermore, it sometimes happens that the arts subjects are nowadays grouped together in schools for largely managerial purposes with perhaps little or no thought to pedagogical strategies. In these cases, attention is likely to focus more on the sociological and professional dimensions of schooling which again are often contentious areas.

The intention in this chapter is to review critically, from a music education perspective, some of the philosophical, pedagogical and professional issues surrounding combined arts teaching. This raises fundamental questions about the aims of music education, the content and design of the curriculum, the role and professional development of teachers, and the uneasy relationship between theory and practice. The discussion is mainly with reference to the secondary school curriculum although many of the issues have a more general applicability.

The unity of the arts

There is a long history of the arts being regarded as a group of disciplines united by the fact that they are all concerned in some way with capacities such as imaginativeness, creativity and self-expressiveness; these are taken to be the characteristic features of the aesthetic realm of experience and meaning. In the educational context the thesis emerges in a number of forms and can be traced back to the Hadow and Spens reports; contemporary versions owe much to writings of well-known philosophers and educationists including John Dewey (1958), Suzanne Langer (1957), Philip Phenix (1964) and Paul Hirst (1974). Over the past thirty years several educators and professional bodies stand out as being particularly influential in promoting the idea of the unity of the arts as a basis for curriculum design and practice. In the Schools Council project *Arts and the Adolescent*, Malcolm Ross (1975) and Robert Witkin (1974) formulated an impressive 'conceptual framework' for arts education derived from the theories of Dewey and Piaget. They argued that while the sciences relate to objective knowledge of the world 'out there', the arts contribute to the growth of students' 'inner world' of subjective knowledge or the life of feeling; together, the arts have a vital role in healthy emotional development as part of a balanced liberal education. Although the views of Ross and Witkin did not initially appeal to all music educators, they were to have a major impact on future thinking about arts education; subsequently, the Calouste Gulbenkian Foundation (1982) produced a famous report, *The Arts in Schools*, in which there was much emphasis on what the arts and artists have in common and how artistic activity represents a 'form of intelligence'. And the formation, in the early 1980s, of the National Association for Education in the

Arts (NAEA) was a further sign of arts educators' intention to share their collective interests through professional discourse and co-operative action. It was at an early NAEA conference that Richard Addison (1986) postulated the idea of artists being united by a 'common functional language' which itself could be seen as an indicator of an 'art-mode-of-thinking'. However, at the same conference it soon became clear that Addison's enthusiasm for unity was not shared by everybody. There were dissenting voices; while happy to acknowledge similarities between the disciplines, some delegates sought to reaffirm their differences and maintain the essential autonomy of the individual arts.

A more recent conception of the unity theory is to be found in the writings of Peter Abbs (1994) who views music, drama, literature, dance, film studies and visual art as components of a 'generic community'. For Abbs, the arts are a distinct category of aesthetic understanding in which cognitive, perceptual and affective operations are combined in a unique form of 'sensuous knowing'. Additionally, the disciplines have common procedural principles: all are concerned with making, presenting, responding and evaluating. The notion of the generic community also informs the work of Ken Robinson (1992) and the national project *The Arts 5–16* (National Curriculum Council, 1990a). These views of the arts are in keeping with the principle of *aesthetic education*. This is another disputed term which carries several meanings; in the present context it is taken to refer to a form of arts education that is devoted primarily to the development of an aesthetic awareness and not merely the acquisition of 'know-how' and propositional knowledge.

While the concepts of the generic community and aesthetic education have received much approval, they have also been subjected to a strong philosophical critique. David Best (1992) is one of a number of outspoken educationists who argues that there is no philosophical basis for the generic community. He is extremely scornful of the view that the arts disciplines have a common 'essence' that unites them and regards it as nothing more than an 'expedient myth' promoted by those who want to support arts and aesthetic education for ideological reasons. It is obvious, he maintains, that there is no one essential characteristic under-lying Handel's 'Messiah', a Constable painting, a Dickens novel and the ballet *Romeo and Juliet*. People who think otherwise are simply in the grip of the essentialist fallacy. David Elliott (1995) is another strident critic of those writers, and particularly Bennett Reimer (1989), who have portrayed music education as a form of aesthetic education. He argues partly from a psychological perspective and maintains that modern theories of intelligence, and especially Howard Gardner's theory of multiple intelligences, indicate that it is quite inappropriate to think in terms of an artistic or aesthetic operational mode; in fact, to do so is to undermine the distinctiveness of musical thinking and knowing.

It should be noted that Best is not arguing against combined arts teaching. He is actually favourably disposed towards arts educators working closely together. However, the reasons for doing so will be practical and circumstantial; such action cannot be justified on philosophical grounds. It is also the case that those who subscribe to the unity of the arts are not *necessarily* saying that the disciplines should always be grouped together for pedagogical purposes. Differences of opinion regarding the unity issue are essentially of a theoretical nature and represent alternative aesthetic and epistemological viewpoints; as such, they are at the very heart of philosophical discourse. Nevertheless they are seen as having implications for practice. The critical issue, which goes far beyond the question of combined arts teaching, is to do with just how this discourse might relate to what happens in classrooms. There is often a temptation to oversimplify the relationship between theory and practice and I shall return to this point later.

Combined arts in practice

The design and operation of school curricula are subject to many forces and influences and it would seem most unlikely that proposals for, or opposition to, forms of combined arts teaching would ever be based on philosophical considerations alone. Schemes and projects will naturally have some sort of theoretical underpinning regarding the nature of the arts, but as Bert Gill (1992) has pointed out, they usually result from a commitment on the part of staff to engage in collaborative work for the benefit of students; programmes seem to evolve in a fairly pragmatic fashion. There are, of course, many types of collaborative teaching in schools and in one of the reports of the project *The Arts 5–16* (NCC, 1990b) the team outline three main approaches. The term *multidisciplinary* is used to describe a strategy where teachers of the separate disciplines pursue an agreed theme; students will be encouraged to compare how the theme is explored through the different subjects and make appropriate connections. *Interdisciplinary* work is likely to involve some team teaching in order to demonstrate how disciplines can inform each other through a focus on their inter-relationships. A third possible approach described as *integration* suggests the fusing of the disciplines into an alternative art form and is best understood with reference to practices beyond Western traditions. The project team provide interesting examples of observed practices together with some very illuminating descriptions and comments from the teachers.

Most combined arts work in schools is likely to be of a multidisciplinary or interdisciplinary nature and will almost certainly receive more support in schools where staff are inclined to a 'progressive' rather than a 'traditional' orientation. Ideas such as cross-curricular themes, topic work, projects and interdisciplinary inquiry are firmly rooted in the progressive ideology and a child-centred approach to education. Consequently, it is not unusual to find that teachers who favour this type of curriculum practice are mainly concerned with how artistic experience contributes to the growth of agreeable dispositions and qualities of mind; they attach rather less importance to the acquisition of subject competencies. For example, David Adkins and Charlie Bell (1987) who introduced combined music and drama projects in their school make little reference to subject-based skills. They emphasise the development of their students' creativity, problem-solving strategies, divergent thinking, self-expression and self-esteem. This kind of progressive thinking leads to the well-known criticism that combined work can militate against the development of students' subject knowledge. In the final report of the Subject

Working Group for Music (DES, 1991) the point is made that students need to have acquired a secure base in music before embarking on any interdisciplinary programmes; in fact, there is a strong recommendation that combined work should not be considered until Key Stage 4. A similar reservation is frequently expressed about thematic approaches; it is said that students spend time on exploring a theme but do not learn very much music.

From a pedagogical point of view there is something slightly disingenuous and unconvincing about the above arguments. They seem to stem from the assumption that there exists a body of musical skills and knowledge to be acquired in a continuous manner over a period of time; progression is a matter of developing a certain assessable competence. Such a view reflects a conventional conception of musicianship in which technical proficiency is of central importance. However, to what extent large numbers of students can ever acquire this type of 'general musicianship' in one lesson each week is highly questionable. The 'theory' of musical achievement as set out in numerous curriculum schemes and guidelines (including the National Curriculum) and espoused by music educators for many years is often far removed from the reality of achievement. But progression does not have to be understood as a linear process which is based on the logical order of subject matter. Children can and do progress not simply by getting 'better' in a technical sense but by broadening their musical understanding through a variety of encounters that are made meaningful through the quality of experience. What does seem likely is that in combined programmes students will have different sorts of experiences and develop different types of skills from those that are said to be acquired in the single-subject programmes.

Reports of multidisciplinary and interdisciplinary schemes indicate that teachers (in accordance with progressive principles) assume a facilitating as well as an instructional role. Selection of content, in terms of activities and materials, becomes less prescribed and much more the joint responsibility of students and teachers. In many ways, the teacher is also required to be more versatile. Adkins and Bell maintain that drama and music teachers can successfully exchange roles and teach each other's subjects. These two very talented and imaginative teachers are perhaps over-optimistic and inclined to generalise too easily from their own experience. Nevertheless, through team teaching many teachers report that they do develop new insights and expertise and an alternative perspective on their own specialisms. They also draw attention to the need for systematic planning and organisation. Carol Slater (1992), in a very extensive and detailed evaluation of projects in her own school involving visual art, drama and music, stresses the importance of proper timetabling and accommodation arrangements as necessary prerequisites to the implementation of programmes. She also observes that the mounting of combined approaches has become more difficult since the introduction of the National Curriculum because of the obligation to follow the statutory programmes of study; there is far less opportunity for flexible organisation and experimentation.

The most important factor emerging from evaluations of combined arts teaching is that the vast majority of children enjoy working across the disciplines. Students' response to curriculum styles is obviously an issue which is of concern to all teachers. In his sharp critique of school music teaching, Malcolm Ross (1995, 1998) refers to the research of Derry Hannon (1992) who concludes that students have more positive attitudes to music when the subject is taught as part of a combined programme. According to Ross, there is overwhelming evidence to show that music, as presently taught, is not a popular curriculum subject and he paints a very dismal picture of class lessons. It may be that he is inclined to make rather sweeping generalisations from small samples and no doubt many music teachers will be of the opinion that the problem of music's unpopularity is somewhat exaggerated. Nevertheless, anybody working in the field of music education will acknowledge that Ross's observations are not without some foundation. There is undoubtedly much good practice but it may well be that in some circumstances combined programmes would prove to be a better way of motivating those students for whom music as a separate subject is lacking in appeal. There is no reason why music teaching involving much closer links with other arts subjects should not be implemented within the context of the National Curriculum although, as already suggested, a prescribed subject-based curriculum does militate, to some extent, against interdisciplinary and multidisciplinary forms of teaching. Ultimately, teachers have to make decisions about the most appropriate types of arts curricula for students in their own schools; what 'works' in one situation may be entirely unsuitable (or even disastrous) in another.

A further point arising from accounts of combined programmes is that they frequently lead to some form of public presentation. Like concerts and productions, such events generate an enthusiasm and excitement; they become celebratory occasions which can enhance the cultural and social life of the school community. The value of presentations in terms of artistic, personal and social education is widely recognised and, of course, they are always welcomed by parents who probably learn more about their children's arts education from attending these events than they do from formal reports. In *The Arts 5–16* there are also references to community arts projects arising from combined programmes within the curriculum, and some inspiring accounts of activities involving large numbers of staff and students.

Nowadays, there is much talk about the importance of the arts and governments are anxious to publicise their supportive policies. For example, a report from the Department of National Heritage (1996) sets out statements about the significance of the arts in education and society and refers to instances of commended practices. But all the points made in the document would be so much better illustrated and reach a far wider audience through arts presentations. This observation is in no way intended to be derisive of official reports and policy statements. Publicity for the arts in education is always to be welcomed; in the end, however, the most effective way of demonstrating their educational value is for people to see children engaged in artistic pursuits. These do not always have to be on a grand scale. Presentations which grow out of combined programmes within the regular curriculum can make a major contribution to raising awareness of the significance of the arts in education.

Some professional issues

A review of the literature on music and combined arts reveals that although much careful thought has been given to the organisation of schemes and projects in terms of content and pedagogy, there has been less consideration of how curricula are related to, and determined by, the culture of the school. Indeed, many writers on music and arts education seem to overlook, or even ignore, the numerous institutional 'messages' that exert a strong influence on the design and operation of curricula. Success and failure in any curriculum area, but especially in the arts, cannot simply be equated with good or bad teaching.

One of Professor Best's concerns about the promotion of the principles of the generic community and aesthetic education is that although both are essentially misconceived, they could, in fact, lead to further marginalisation of the arts disciplines. Unsympathetic decision-makers might (so he claims) seize upon the concept of aesthetic education and proceed to argue that since the arts contain a common element, then this type of education can be achieved through any one of the disciplines. With the present structure of the National Curriculum this is unlikely since the subjects are in a sense 'protected', but Best's observation cannot be dismissed lightly. Even if the subjects are retained, it is still possible to use the argument for the purpose of giving less overall time to the individual arts, and it is well known that this is already happening in some schools. In contrast, some teachers maintain that the formation of arts teams has actually strengthened the position of the individual disciplines in their schools. It is argued that a strong combined arts department improves the status of the separate subjects and staff will exert more influence in the wider decision-making process. However, generalisations are difficult since how subjects are viewed will depend very much on the culture of the school and its dominant ideology. There are schools where the arts receive a great deal of support while in others they are not regarded as being of particular importance. The point was made earlier that combined arts will probably be viewed more favourably in a progressively inclined environment. This is not simply because interdisciplinary or multidisciplinary teaching is part of the progressive ideal but because the arts themselves are valued as curriculum components. In a more traditional school the arts are often appreciated as cultural and extra-curricular pursuits but they may not be regarded as highly as curriculum subjects. Consequently, any decisions about the organisation of the arts has to be evaluated and responded to with reference to the attitudes, assumptions and customs that constitute the culture of the school.

As schools seek to become more efficient and financially secure it would seem probable that more attention will be given to organisational patterns. This in turn might well lead to the further grouping of arts subjects but for managerial rather than pedagogical reasons. However, school curricula are social as well as academic systems and the organisation of subjects will, to some extent, reflect the social structure of the institution. Consequently, any moves to change curriculum organisation are likely to be supported or rejected by staff partly in terms of how they might, or might not, affect the individual and the status quo. In those traditional schools where there is a strong division of subjects and closed departmental structures there may well be a reluctance to introduce forms of organisation that might appear to alter the academic structure of the school and thereby the professional status of teachers. Attempts to set up arts departments have often foundered because of opposition from staff who feel that they are losing their professional identity. To move from being head of, say, a music department to membership of a larger arts grouping can often be seen as a threat to an individual's standing within a school. In discussions on music and arts education these social aspects of schooling are rarely given much attention but they are factors in the shaping of curriculum policy and practice and perhaps rather more significant than is often supposed.

Theory and practice

The type of philosophical critique outlined by David Best relating to the principles of the generic community and aesthetic education arises from his conviction that unsound theory can lead to unsatisfactory practices. No doubt there is much to be said for this position. It is generally recognised that there have been many popular movements in education (and especially arts education) which have resulted in confused practice simply because ideas have been too readily accepted and not subjected to any proper analysis. However, it would be unwise to assume that the theory has got to be completely 'right' before any practice can begin; education, as a practical enterprise, simply does not function in that way. And in any case, with issues like the unity of the arts there will inevitably be differences of opinion among philosophers and aestheticians. For many practitioners, the views put forward by Best will possibly be no more persuasive than those of Abbs and others who subscribe to the unity position. Consequently, there are people who conclude that the seemingly complex arguments about the connections between the arts are only of interest to academics; the debate has little bearing on practice. This would be a mistaken and cynical view although it is one that is often supported by certain critics of the educational establishment.

All practice rests on certain values and assumptions about the structure of subject matter, how children learn, the effectiveness of instructional approaches, and many other matters. In other words, theory always determines practice to some extent and it is hard to see how things could be otherwise. Nevertheless, this underlying theory is never fixed and beyond dispute; on the contrary, it is for ever open to modification and development. Part of being a music educator is to be involved in the debate about the nature of the arts: their similarities, differences, connections, common substances, and so on. In spite of the present language of educational policy it is quite wrong to think of teachers as simply 'delivering' a curriculum. As professional educators they constantly make decisions on their own and with their colleagues, and in so doing they are bound to consider topics like the unity of the arts. The debate conducted in the academic journals is but one part of a much wider conversation that goes on at conferences, at teachers' meetings and in school staffrooms; it is of interest not only to educationists but all members of the music and arts communities. In a most important sense critical discussions about the arts is the lifeblood of arts education; it not only influences and informs practice in a variety of ways but provides one of the many sources for reflection on practice. Unfortunately, there is nowadays so much concern over the efficient delivery of the official specification that consideration of aesthetic issues in arts tends to be regarded as diversions. The music curriculum is the 'given' theory and people worry about minute and trivial details of the Orders; little attention is given to the problematic relationship between theory and practice. Conversations about combined arts lead to the questioning and challenging of accepted doctrines and policies which can, in turn, open up possibilities for alternative practices. Consequently, the conversation may be seen as a disruptive or even subversive activity and one that gets in the way of that officially ordered practice that will raise those all important 'standards'. However, the real cause for concern is that without debate and the exchange of ideas education becomes a mechanical and sterile process in which there is no place for experimentation, risk-taking and imaginative innovation; this can only be to the detriment of future educational practice in the arts. The same principle applies to all areas of the curriculum.

Conclusion

Since the introduction of the National Curriculum the mildly progressive views of content and methods that underpin combined arts teaching have been largely rejected as romantic notions that inhibit efficient teaching and learning. Furthermore, there has been a major shift in music education from wide diversity of practice to a controlled uniformity. These trends are regrettable and anybody experienced in teaching will know that there can be no formula or one approach to the construction and implementation of arts curricula. There are many variables and teachers have to decide not on 'right' decisions but on what they judge to be the 'best' course of action in particular circumstances. Few people would want to recommend the complete abandonment of subject teaching but there is plenty of evidence to suggest that combined arts programmes can be an effective context for meaningful education in music. However, since curricula are now 'strongly classified', bringing subjects together may well be seen as a challenge to established structures and the control of knowledge. Nevertheless, for some children arts projects might prove more suitable than single subject studies. And with the availability of the new technology there will be increasing opportunities for multimedia projects and new forms of combined practice which could extend and enhance children's experiences in any number of ways.

Whatever view one might hold regarding the unity of the arts, it is obvious that there are close connections between the various disciplines. Consequently, there is much to be said in favour of arts teachers working closely together in curriculum planning in order to make those connections more explicit; this can only be to the benefit of class programmes. It is certainly the case that schemes of music education have often been formulated without due consideration of other art forms and music teachers have sometimes been accused of being isolationist.

This may be an unfair judgement but it is interesting to observe that music educators do not stand out as particular supporters of combined programmes; the majority of proposals seem to have come from arts teachers in other fields. There are, of course, notable exceptions.

Questions for discussion

1   To what extent can the arts subjects be regarded as a 'generic community'?
2   Why have combined arts declined in popularity in recent years?
3   What are the practical advantages of combined arts teaching?

References

Abbs, P. (1994) *The Educational Imperative*, London: Falmer Press.
Addison, R. (1986) *The Arts in Education: Arts Initiative 1*, London: National Association for Education in the Arts.
Adkins, D. and Bell, C. (1987) 'A look at combined music and drama teaching', *Music Teacher* 66, 6, 21–3.
Best, D. (1992) 'Generic arts: an expedient myth', *Journal of Art and Design Education* 11, 1, 27–44.
Calouste Gulbenkian Foundation (1982) *The Arts in Schools*, London: Calouste Gulbenkian Foundation.
Department of Education and Science (DES) (1991) *Music for Ages 5 to 14*. London: HMSO.
Department of National Heritage (1996) *Setting the Scene: The Arts and Young People*, London: Department of National Heritage.
Dewey, J. ([1934] 1958) *Arts as Experience*, New York: Capricorn Books.
Elliott, D. (1995) *Music Matters: A New Philosophy of Music Education*, New York: Oxford University Press.
Gill, B. (1992) *Not What I Expected: An Introduction to Combining the Arts*, Northampton: Northamptonshire County Council.
Hannon, D. (1992) 'Arts and the adolescent revisited', in M. Ross (ed.) *Wasteland Wonderland: The Arts in the National Curriculum*, Exeter: University of Exeter School of Education.
Harland, J., Kinder, K., Haynes, J. and Shagen, I. (1998) *The Effects and Effectiveness of Arts Education in Schools*, Slough: NFER.
Hirst, P. (1974) 'Literature and the fine arts as a unique form of knowledge', in *Knowledge and the Curriculum*, London: Routledge, pp. 30–53.
Langer, S. (1957) *Philosophy in a New Key*, 3rd edn, Cambridge, MA: Harvard University Press.
National Curriculum Council (NCC) (1990a) *The Arts 5–16: A Curriculum Framework*, London: Oliver and Boyd.
National Curriculum Council (NCC) (1990b) *The Arts 5–16: Practice and Innovation*, London: Oliver and Boyd.
Phenix, P. (1964) *Realms of Meaning: A Philosophy of the Curriculum for General Education*, New York: McGraw-Hill.
Reimer, B. (1989) *A Philosophy of Music Education*, 2nd edn, Englewood Cliffs, NJ: Prentice-Hall.

Robinson, K. (1992) 'The arts as a generic area of the curriculum', *Journal of Art and Design Education* 11, 1, 9–25.

Ross, M. (1975) *Arts and the Adolescent*, London: Evans.

Ross, M. (1995) 'What's wrong with school music?', *British Journal of Music Education* 12, 3, 185–201.

Ross, M. (1998) 'Missing solemnis: reforming music in schools', *British Journal of Music Education*, 15, 3, 255–62.

School Curriculum and Assessment Authority (SCAA) (1997) *The Arts in the Curriculum Conference*, London: SCAA.

Scottish Office Education Department (SOED) (1992) *Curriculum and Assessment in Scotland: National Guidelines: Expressive Arts 5–14*, Edinburgh: SOED.

Slater, C. (1992) 'The place of combined arts in the curriculum', unpublished MA dissertation, Institute of Education, University of London.

Witkin, R. (1974) *The Intelligence of Feeling*, London: Heinemann.

Further reading

Abbs, P. (1994) *The Educational Imperative*, London: Falmer Press.

Elliott, D. (1995) *Music Matters: A New Philosophy of Music Education*, New York: Oxford University Press.

Harland, J., Kinder, K., Haynes, J. and Shagen, I. (1998) *The Effects and Effectiveness of Arts Education in Schools*, Slough: NFER.

Ross, M. (1998) 'Missing solemnis: reforming music in schools', *British Journal of Music Education*, 15, 3, 255–62.

11 Music education in and for a pluralist society

Robert Mawuena Kwami

Introduction

Divergence, diversity and minority interests are three issues that are relevant to the promotion of pluralism in formal education contexts in Western societies. In Britain, attention has been focused particularly on such areas as race, culture, and equal opportunities. During the last quarter of the twentieth century, politicians and teachers, among others, made efforts to address the difficult and sensitive areas of religion, special educational needs and gender issues within mainstream education. In the music curriculum the inclusion of popular music, music technology and 'world musics' have been some of the most significant developments of the period. Nevertheless, as I have argued elsewhere (Kwami, 1998a), the dominant or prevailing paradigm for musical transactions is still that of the Western classical music tradition. For this reason alone, the musical and cultural 'voices' located on the periphery may feel stifled. Indeed, it could be argued that it is unrealistic to 'listen' to every 'voice' in the curriculum and that some musics are best dealt with outside of the formal educational system.

It is expected that practical activities will be a common aspect of music lessons in British schools, with group 'performing' and 'composing' being the norm especially at the pre-GCSE stage. The 'creativity' movement championed by John Paynter, Bernard Rands and George Self has been influential in promoting classroom composition, often using experimental techniques, and this is one area where British students may be more advanced than their counterparts elsewhere. At the primary level, a more integrative and holistic approach is more commonly taken whereby music is sometimes combined within topic and project work.

In compositional activities, many teachers tend to focus on tonality or modality and students are taught to improvise, perhaps, using criteria based on modes, scales or chord clusters. Graphic and other notational systems are introduced as a part of the National Curriculum (cf. DES, 1992; DfEE, 1995; DfEE/QCA, 1999) while more traditional teaching involves listening to music and the so-called 'rudiments of music'; the teaching of conventional Western music notation. As a result of statutory and examination requirements since 1987, popular and non-Western musics have gained more status compared to the pre-GCSE and pre-National Curriculum eras.

The above portrait (cf. Salaman, 1985–86) of institutionalised music education practice, can be constricting so far as some non-Western, 'traditional' and 'popular' musical traditions and practices are concerned. For example, such musics appear to be tagged on, rather than being carefully integrated into a National Curriculum that purports to be comprehensive. For a start, it is not clear where aural–oral musics and methods of transmission fit. Indeed, it can be argued that the search for comprehensiveness, inclusivity and equal opportunities in the formal education system are ideals and that a more realistic but sensitive approach needs to be adopted. In this chapter, it will be argued first that the foremost focus in music education should be on music making which involves the acquisition of musical knowledge and understanding, skills and attitudes by engaging students 'musically' (cf. Swanwick, 1999). Second, it will be argued that a divergent, rather than convergent, approach is needed in dealing with different musical traditions in formal education contexts. And, allied to this, it is crucial that there is recognition and acceptance of a diversity of perspectives in coping with, and understanding, the different musical traditions and cultures. This is a *sine qua non* if the future of music education in schools as a distinct academic discipline and endeavour is to be guaranteed in the present millennium.

Different musics, different parameters

The various musical traditions around the world may be united in qualifying as a distinctive means of human discourse. They constitute a global phenomenon of communication and expression linked to cultural practices, and operate in different ways in different contexts. The fact that the term 'music' may not have a specific equivalence in some cultures is problematic and limiting when an attempt is made to accommodate some non-Western music perspectives into Western music. As I have argued (cf. Kwami, 1998a), the term is conceptually flawed in curricular contexts, especially where the aim is to achieve comprehensiveness through breadth, balance and depth. And, it can be argued this is not helped by the prevailing paradigm, the Western classical music tradition, even though a common ground may, in future, be provided by jazz, perhaps the most significant emergent paradigm of the twentieth century (Kwami, 1998b).

Not only is the admission of different musical practices and traditions into the school curriculum fraught with difficulties; care and sensitivity are also required in the ways that different musics are apprehended and used in creative activities. Indeed, creative activities can allow for things to be looked at in a new light, with synthesis and divergence being cultivated. However, there may be a tension between the need to transmit cultural mores, conventions and traditions, and the need to foster creativity; both are necessary in a search for new ways of looking at life and experiences. If music education is at one and the same time concerned with transmission and reproduction, on the one hand, and creativity and production, on the other, then teachers need to be careful about how to reconcile and balance the two aspects in their work.

Practical activities, particularly those of a creative kind, should involve music making which calls upon pupils and students to draw fully on their own experiences. These experiences may be entirely outside the control of teachers and include musics that are absorbed from the media – from the radio, television, and from watching videos and various kinds of films. Games, whether played via electronic means or with other people in the playground, at home or on the streets, also provide legitimate educational and musical experiences. Such experiences may depend on the socialisation process, involve holistic learning and relate to formalised education, which requires the ability to read and write music. The problematic issues raised by the use of different musics in the classroom can be illustrated through an examination of the concepts of musical literacy and temporality.

Musical literacy

In black African musical cultures known to me, there is no written form of notation; however, musical literacy is manifested through the communal performances that most people are able to (and do) take part in. Indeed, black Africans believe that all human beings are inherently musical; they also believe that musicality is a basic human attribute (cf. Blacking, 1976; Kwami, 1993, 1996). The musical literacy that operates in black African communities is transmitted and propagated through aural–oral means; it does not employ any form of writing. An example is the degree of sophistication and specificity in the mnemonics or vocables used in Anlo-Ewe drumming. This may be greater than exists in many other African cultures and ethnic groups as it has over thirty mnemonics (Kwami, 1989, 1998b). The mnemonics tell a player exactly what to do: to use one hand or both, a stick or the bare hand. The mnemonics specify whether to use the whole hand or part of it and whether the sound should be bounced, muted or slapped; they also indicate which part of the drum to play – in the centre, the middle, near the edge of the vellum or on the wood at the sides (Kwami, 1998b).

For the majority of the world's people, musical literacy does not involve the ability to read and write music, or to play music using conventional Western or other written notation. For many, musical literacy operates as the ability to communicate with others through music making in a practical way. One factor, internalisation, is a process that characterises this type of musical literacy. Applied over a longer time frame, this internalisation contributes to the enculturation or socialisation process. A second factor is improvisation – the ability to communicate musically, as it were, on the spot, on the spur of the moment. Other facets of this musical literacy involve dance, movement and language, which feature to a greater extent elsewhere than in the Western classical tradition, the main currency of the school curriculum.

According to Merriam (1964), enculturation is a natural process of getting to know a particular music. Ideally, enculturation should take place in the music's original or intended context. However, because enculturation is a time-consuming part of the growing up process (Sloboda, 1985), it may be unreasonable to expect teachers and students to become 'enculturated' into an unfamiliar music. Nevertheless, it should be possible for them genuinely to attempt, first, to understand the music concerned on its own grounds; and then to reinterpret it on their own terms, in a sensitive way. Both are necessary adjuncts or complements to the acquisition of an appropriate subject knowledge. From an equal opportunities angle, two issues, at least, need consideration in relation to musical literacy.

First, written systems constitute a unique and distinct form of knowing, and it could be argued that those not initiated into such systems might be disadvantaged. It is obvious that only a few of all the musicians in the world are 'musically literate' according to the criterion of being able to read and write music in staff notation. That this minority should dominate and relegate most of humanity to the musical scrap heap of the world is something that needs to be combated. Second, although popular and other musics are used in the curriculum of British schools, the main conceptual and operational mode is understandably the Western 'classical' tradition. The dominance of this mode has produced a situation where music is often regurgitated rather than created and may be seen as boring by pupils and students (cf. Ross, 1995). For some, the use of such notation may not lead them to become more musical. Rather, it might be responsible for 'turning them off'. From another angle, the capability of computer software applications to notate in staff notation helps to relegate the notation to a lower educational position or rung. The time gained from not having to teach pupils merely how to read and write music as a paper exercise could then be spent on more musical activities.

Information and communications technology (ICT) and interculturalism (Kwami, 1993, 1996, 1998a) are likely to exert a strong influence on the direction of music education early in the twenty-first century. The boundaries of 'musics' are being stretched in the wider community such as through the 'world musics' explosion, and it seems that music education would, in addition to embracing a more technological base, also have to be more culturally and socially located. It is also likely to be a more hybrid phenomenon of many parts involving aspects of design and aesthetics, demanding aural–oral and multimedia abilities rather than literary skills, improvisation rather than the ability to read from notation.

Making music through aural–oral means, including improvising, needs to feature prominently in cultivating a real or true musical literacy among students. The kind of musical literacy that we are concerned with has to do with 'getting down to' it – the music; it is not about dealing with or abstracting its essential elements. This musical literacy has to do with actually grappling with the music, engaging with it, appropriating it and internalising it. This can be done by trying to understand the music in a manner similar to that of the people from whom it originates or belongs. For any teacher, this is a necessary process that might involve using examples from one's own experience as well as through research and professional development.

If education is concerned with making new connections, of being open and seeing things in a different light, then, providing the necessary conditions are in place, the apprehension of a 'new' or unfamiliar music can create an educational experience. Such an experience is likely to combine an element of synthesis, which may produce syncretism in a resulting creative outcome. Synthesis is involved when connections are made between two different or complementary musical pieces, systems or types; while syncretism or hybridisation occurs when elements from two or more musical traditions are combined as in a composition.

Of course, where some musics are concerned, this may only be possible in a purely musical way; it would not help one iota to be 'learned', academic or theoretical. One demonstrates knowledge through 'doing'; and although some musicians may not be able to articulate what they do, their integrity comes from the act of doing. The fact that they may not be able to explain or theorise about their musical practice does not negate their musical integrity. Now, this musical integrity is informed by the enculturation process, a time span which allows people to assimilate and internalise the musical canons, vocabulary, techniques, procedures – the tools that allow them to demonstrate not only their technical proficiency and fluency, but also their musicality. And, in many cultures, this sensitive musicality is shown primarily in the practical domain. It is from these 'tools' that fluency, creativity, and improvisation take their source, although it is possible for some people to master the rules of the game without necessarily demonstrating an acute and sensitive musicality. Fluency on its own could be deficient, as its only focus might be on the technical, the instrumental, and not the musical.

In addition to musical literacy the concept of temporal organisation can serve to shed some light on the problematic issues surrounding the use of 'different' musics in the classroom.

Temporal organisation

It is perhaps simplistic to state that a linear orientation of time dominates in the West and that this conceptualisation has influenced many aspects of human endeavour. There is, in fact, an underlying cyclical movement in the operation of time, such as is obvious in the daily, weekly, monthly, and yearly cycles which are dictated by the revolutionary orbits of the moon and the earth around the sun. At the same time, each individual has his or her own biological time and clock, which are in a sense regulated by the heart. Before the advent of digital technology, time used to be represented in both a cyclical and linear manner even in the West. For example, the sundial represents a combination of linear and cyclical (or elliptical, depending on latitude) dimensions. But the precision with which time is now measured and the way in which it dictates and regulates our lives seem to emphasise the linear more than the cyclical.

Accepting that musics are intangible phenomena of human discourse, there are likely to be problems in their physical representation. It may be problematic to portray the different concepts of cyclical movement which are an inherent and core constituent of many non-Western musics. In the Western 'classical' music tradition, particularly in its visual representation through the notation of music, the linear seems to dominate. The symbolic representation of music in a two-dimensional format is problematic so far as the concept of cyclical movement concerned. As shown in Figure 11.1, it is possible to relate pitch to 'high' and 'low', and motion in terms of 'before' and 'after'. However, if one took the reference point of a music piece from its beginning, then all the other events that transpire would be in the future. In such a context, time is progressive rather than cyclical or regressive. Even if one contemplated on a piece of music just heard, the reflection takes place in the future of the event. In using two-dimensional graphical and 'symbolic' notation to represent musical cyclical movement one may have to use circles in time-cycle frames.

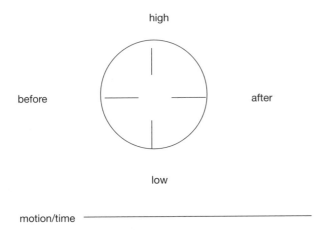

Figure 11.1 Linear representation of motion in music

Note: The musical 'motion' goes from left to right although there appears to be no logical reason why other formats – inverted, retrograde, and retrograde inversion – could not be used.

Apart from the problem of continuity in representing musical cyclical movements in notational form, whether using concentric circles or segments, there is also the problem of how individual parts are assigned. It may be that they are assigned primarily according to pitch, with the highest sounding instrument in the centre and the lowest within the biggest and outermost.

In Indian music, for example, the concept of cyclical movement may be primarily felt, heard and understood in a rhythmic way as Jhaptal tala or 10-pulse cycle (see Figure 11.2a); but it may also include the part played by the drone (instruments). However, improvisation, the formal musical structures and the exigencies of the performance are also treated in a 'cyclical' way. Furthermore, extra-musical factors such as the selection or choice of raga, which relate the cyclical movement to time (of day or night), the seasons, and moods, are also integral aspects.

In Indonesian music, there are issues to do with the various manifestations of the balugun (see Figure 11.2b), but the colotomy – the interlocking rhythmic patterns that have an ostinato-type feel to them – which is an inherent feature, has not been represented. In African drum music, it is only the supporting instrument patterns and the framework for one simple master drum phrase that can be accommodated (see Figure 11.2c). Although it would be possible to indicate

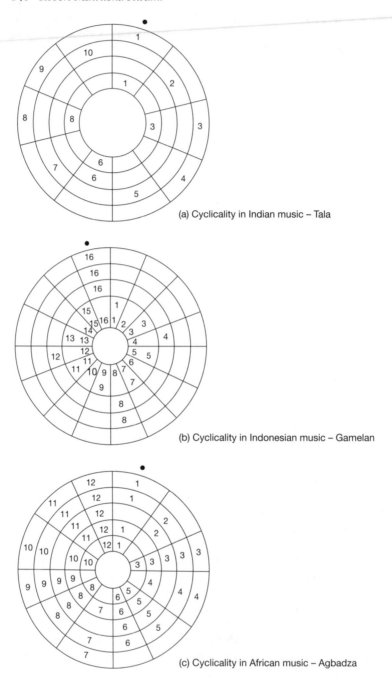

(a) Cyclicality in Indian music – Tala

(b) Cyclicality in Indonesian music – Gamelan

(c) Cyclicality in African music – Agbadza

Figure 11.2 Examples of musical cyclicality from non-Western cultures

Note: The numbers stand for pulses in a cycle, the dot represents the beginning of the cycle, and the highest pitch is in the most central circle.

open and closed strokes in the main supporting drum part, it is problematic to represent 'compound' master drum phrases and to capture the operation of the improvisational aspects of the compositional process.

Musical cyclical movement can be modelled in African musics in other ways and with detailed analytic explanation (see Anku, 1988, 1997). It is possible to argue that there is more than one type of cyclical movement present in some musics. There may be cycles within cycles, with some of the structures being more helical if the temporal aspects are to be represented more accurately. But, this is not to deny the possibility of existence of temporal duality – both linear and cyclical orientations – in the same music. In African musics, Anku (1996/1997) has aligned the repetitive parts to those that change, in a combination of linear and cyclical time that could alleviate other problems of cyclical representation. Nevertheless, it seems that the graphical representation of DNA structure in a helical format may provide a visually more accurate picture. In examining African musics with 'Western spectacles', the architectural design of, say, a West African drum ensemble music could be explained in terms of polyrhythm or polymeter. However, such a perspective fails in that it may not be an accurate tool to use in explaining the reality of the music as perceived by 'insiders' or from an emic perspective. Such a perspective also loses the holistic view – that everything is linked in the ensemble, there really is no conflict between the parts, they complement one another.

The concept of 'tension and release' does not only apply to the Western classical music tradition. However, it operates differently. In African musics, for example, this can be conceived in terms of 'in' and 'out' of phase drumming. The various parts contribute to a resultant pattern and a holistic framework which is held as a mental score. At the same time, both the linear and cyclical orientations of time are valid as the music progresses over time. There is a tension and release in the superimposition of a cyclical movement above a linear time through the way in which some instruments play a basic, unchanging pattern over which the other parts – master drumming, dancing, singing, and dramatisation – are juxtaposed.

What are the curricular implications for different musics in the classroom after an analysis of the concepts of musical literacy and temporality? To what extent is it possible or desirable to achieve authenticity?

Curricular applications

The length of time involved in performing some aural–oral musics in which improvisation plays an important part needs serious consideration in curricular contexts. A 'movement' or section of a non-Western music piece might be the length of a full-blown symphony by Mozart or Beethoven! Let us give some examples. A recording of a Balinese gamelan piece[1] is likely to be longer than 15 minutes while an excerpt of the alap of an Indian classical music piece[2] is a mere 3 minutes 45 seconds. A Ghanaian funeral ceremony at Ho in the Volta Region[3] featured Agbekor and Agbadza music performances, more or less continuously, for over two hours. By contrast, an Agbadza dance performed by the Adzido group in an Essex primary school[4] lasted a mere 5 minutes or so. Although the primary school pupils were able to get a sense of the performance, there are important factors other than the temporal and sonic aspects which are vital in understanding a music piece or performance holistically. Often, in order to appreciate the structural dimension of a performance, a deal of time may be needed for appraising or getting to know a piece of music.

It may be impossible, in the classroom, to replicate the music's traditional or original context. And, indeed, as some might argue, replication should not be an educational objective. For example, the various aspects or elements involved in a Javanese puppet performance or African dance may be difficult to incorporate into a music lesson where the focus is often on the sound dimension. Would it be possible to do justice in the classroom to such aspects as the dance, the vocal and instrumental music, the dramatisation and the role of the audience participants? And, what about the role of improvisation?

In the classroom, the tendency of music teachers is to focus on obvious elements. Teachers tend to abstract elements, which are defining qualities of a music as they understand or conceptualise it, as they 'see' it, from their own perspective. And these may be aspects that may be relatively easy to replicate. The improvisational and other more problematical areas are often ignored. So, in the case of African musics, for example, a simple responsorial song with easy-to-pronounce words, with a limited vocal range, in a major key, harmonisable with primary chords, would do just fine. Guttural and forced sounds, scooping, ululation and other such devices may be problematic. Such unusual, atypical and improvisational aspects, and untempered tuning systems, require knowledge of cultural, social and other conventions that may be alien to those teaching and using the musics. There may also be problems of socio-cultural translation and transposition, and the dangers of misrepresentation, which may contribute to lack of confidence on the part of teachers who may regard themselves as 'outsiders'.

Although there may be a validity in an etic or 'outsider's' perspective, it is the emic or 'insider's' perspective that seems more valued in the present day. From my experience, it seems that teachers and pupils are more interested in the insider's perspective and in getting to know things from first-hand, rather than second-hand, sources. If this is so, the classroom teacher may be wary of presenting 'second-hand' or 'other' musics, musics that they may not profess to know enough about or to be proficient in performing. This is counterbalanced if we accept the validity of the classroom as a cultural context in its own right. However, we might want to question whether the classroom teacher is the person best placed to teach children about all musics.

Although one may question the authenticity of the classroom transaction where non-Western musics are concerned, it is possible to describe the artificiality of the classroom as a reality in its own right. Indeed, 'school music' can be seen as having a rightful reality, an authenticity of its own, providing the skewed prevailing paradigm can be properly balanced so that it does justice to other musics outside of the sphere of influence of the Western classical tradition. A possible solution to the problem of cultural skewing might be to accept plurality, diversity, and the coexistence of divergent, sometimes diametrically opposed viewpoints: for example, as in the duality of linear and cyclical orientations regarding time and structure in music. Even in the Western classical music tradition, within a dia-chronic perspective, we may find that a particular concept, device or technique may vary. For example, concerning the concepts of 'duple' and 'triple', in the juxtaposing of tempus perfectum and imperfectum in the Ars Nova, the 'triplet' and hemiola in the Baroque, and 'three-against-two' in the Classical and Romantic.

To summarise, the following three brief points will be made. First, it needs to be noted that the curriculum transaction is a communal context in its own right, it is different from the reality of other communal contexts. Second, teachers must not kid themselves about replicating other communal musics in their work with pupils. This is especially relevant in the case of non-Western musics where due sensitivity needs to be exercised. And, finally, pupils are active participants in the process whereby they acquire their musicality, individually and on a group basis. In this, they are guided by the totality of their experiences gained from school and the wider community.

Sensitivity in curricular contexts

In searching for a solution as to how teachers can confront the issues of adequate knowledge and confidence, and the adoption of an 'open' stance, it may be helpful to focus on sensitivity on three main grounds – contextually, in the use of resources and in the employment of teaching strategies. Each of these will now be briefly discussed.

Contextual sensitivity

The fact that the classroom context is different from any music's cultural context can make it possible to ensure the application of equal opportunities in relation to such issues as gender, race, religion, and so on. For example, girls should play instruments that they would not be allowed to play in a traditional context.

In the classroom, it may be advisable to exclude musics that are too closely linked to particular religious, social and cultural conventions. Removed from their original contexts some musics lose their original referential and musical significance. In using musics, such as an Imam's call to prayers, a raga intended to be performed at night, Yeve religious music, and so on, teachers need to exercise due sensi-tivity. Such sensitivity would need to deal properly with culturally placing and explaining 'where' and 'when' the music is normally performed. Other relevant questions include 'why' and 'what'; and stereotypes have to be confronted and understood. In doing so, value judgements cannot be ignored. But the teacher can present an unbiased perspective if they remain open and present both sides of the coin.

Sensitive use of resources

Due to the unavailability of authentic instruments in their schools some teachers feel unable to introduce non-Western musics in their teaching. As I have witnessed, students are more likely to adopt a more serious attitude when authentic instruments are used. In spite of the logistical and financial issues, it is important that students are introduced practically to some of the world's most significant traditional musics such as those of Africa, China, India and Java. It might be difficult for any school to have a significant number of instruments from those cultures for class use, and it would be quite convenient to argue that such musics should be relegated to the extended curriculum or to extra-curricular activities.

We can counter the view that one needs authentic instruments in order to engage in legitimate music making from 'other' traditions as follows. First, we need to note the artificiality of the classroom context and that we are not dealing with what may be termed 'the real McCoy' (Kwami, 1998b, 1998c). Second, we need to go further than replicating or simulating a music – we need to analyse, criticise, reinterpret and re-create. However, as I have found from experience, it is sometimes difficult to accept an unrefined aesthetic; for example, when playing African drum music on Orff instruments. At the other end of the scale, sensitivity is also likely to be difficult if one is not familiar with the music being taught.

Sensitive teaching strategies

If the intention is to replicate a music, then, perhaps, the acid test of a classroom performance is whether those whose music it was originally would recognise and accept it as a version of their own. The importance of musical sensitivity on the part of teachers entails being aware of different types of musical cyclical movement as well as the combination of both linear and cyclical orientations in music. It is important that duality, both in terms of the temporal aspects and musical literacy need to be encouraged right from the earliest stages of primary education.

In playing and re-creating non-Western musics in the curriculum, an appropriate sensitivity might mean the operation of different levels of understanding, engagement and transmission. As enculturation in curricular contexts is minimal, teachers may have to resort to teaching strategies that are antithetical to, or different from, those employed in the teaching of Western classical music. Let us give some examples. First, the anatomical deconstruction of a music piece on an individual part basis may be unsuitable in contexts where a resultant rhythmic pattern is the unit. Second, it may be necessary to be able to align one's part to an internalised recurring rhythmic cycle, and this requires a holistic aesthetic. Finally, the acquisition of improvisational and creative skills in some cyclical musics may be best acquired through the informal enculturation process of the communal setting. In taking such musics into the classroom, as we have argued, lack of time is a real problem. This is particularly so if it is intended to employ authentic transmission methods, procedures and strategies used in traditional contexts in order that students can engage convincingly and meaningfully with the musics. The issue of how best to effect a formal enculturation process for non-Western musics perhaps needs further investigation. Is there, for example, a correct way for sequencing the teaching such that it includes structuring, progression, differentiation, or must it remain a muddy and mainly subjective area?

Conclusion

Teachers tend to use models and templates in much of their curricular work especially where unfamiliar musics are concerned. But, in doing so, they need to exercise due care on a number of grounds. The music in question would need to retain its essential elements so that it can be traced to its original source. This is especially important in the case of hybrid or syncretic musics where one has to contend with more than one source. But, where the aim is to 'recreate' the music as it is performed in its original setting, then it is important that the music should have an internal integrity. The integrity is possible where participants are confident and knowledgeable about the music concerned. At the same time, there has to be some flexibility, which can allow the music to grow and be enriched, without it losing its basic tenets, its source. The music should be traceable to its source in a meaningful and musical way even though it may be classifiable as a new musical product, and it could be possible for the new music to be explainable in more than one way. There might be more than superficiality in it, so that deeper levels of musical engagement can take place. In the case of many of the world's influential music cultures and traditions, this would involve the ability to engage in music making solely as an aural–oral, rather than as a primarily written, notational, transaction.

It has been argued that music teachers need to exercise sensitivity and openness with regard to curriculum context, resources and teaching strategies if they are to deal adequately with problems raised by a pluralist music education. Two of these problems, the concepts of musical literacy and temporality, have been discussed on and used as illustrative examples. Templates and models can be used as a way of understanding a music piece, tradition, or style, although this may sometimes do injustice to the particular. However, if carried out sensitively, then there is a chance that the music can be understood and creatively worked with in an appropriate way in curricular contexts. The broad cultural perspective required needs to be inclusive and global if it is to be comprehensive. Otherwise, we need not kid ourselves that the study of musics in the curriculum is not primarily a study based on the Western, with an arbitrary sprinkling of musics 'from other parts of the world'. For then, it would be a curriculum that focuses on the few, pays lip service to some and excludes the many.

Notes

1   *Gending Tembung*, cf. CMP CD 3008.
2   *Thumri: Jogia* (Jogia is an early morning raga). Cf. The Nonesuch Explorer Series, LP H7-1, Side 2.

3   Kwami, R.M. (1996) *Field Recording*, Ho, Volta Region, Ghana.
4   In which I participated and which was recorded; see British Broadcasting
    Corporation (BBC) 'Talking Drums' (Programme 2), *Music Makers*, 1994–2000.

Questions for discussion

1   To what extent are pluralism and diversity a feature of music education in
    schools and colleges?
2   The prevailing paradigm of the Western classical music tradition needs to be
    changed if music education in educational institutions is to do justice to the
    world's musics. Discuss.
3   Discuss the relevance of concepts of musical literacy and temporality for an
    intercultural music education programme.
4   In what ways can teachers be sensitive in their use of unfamiliar musical styles
    or musics from cultures other than their own?

References

Anku, W. (1988) 'Procedures in African drumming: a case of Akan/Ewe traditions
    and African drumming in Pittsburgh', unpublished PhD dissertation, University of
    Pittsburgh.
Anku, W. (1996/1997) 'Holistic consideration of West African drum music analysis: an
    assessment', *Journal of Performing Arts* 2, 2, 12–16.
Anku, W. (1997) 'Principles of rhythm integration in African drumming', *Black Music
    Research Journal* 17, 2, 211–38.
Blacking, J. (1976) *How Musical is Man?*, London: Faber and Faber.
DES (1992) *Music in the National Curriculum*, London: HMSO.
DfEE (1995) *Music in the National Curriculum*, London: HMSO.
DfEE/QCA (1999) *Music: The National Curriculum for England – Key Stages 1–3*, London:
    HMSO.
Kwami, R.M. (1989) 'African music, education and the school curriculum', 2 vols,
    unpublished PhD dissertation, Institute of Education, University of London.
Kwami, R.M. (1993) 'Music education in Britain and the school curriculum: a point
    of view', *International Journal of Music Education* 19, 2, 25–39.
Kwami, R.M. (1996) 'Music education in and for a multicultural society', in C.
    Plummeridge (ed.) *Music Education: Trends and Issues*, London: Institute of Education,
    pp. 59–76.
Kwami, R.M. (1998a) 'Non-Western musics in education: problems and possibilities',
    British Journal of Music Education 14, 2, 161–70.
Kwami, R.M. (1998b) 'Towards a standardised catalogue of Ewe drum mnemonics',
    African Cultural Studies 11, 1, 27–38.
Kwami, R.M. (1998c) *Music Education Practice in Primary and Secondary Schools in Britain:
    Inclusion of the Black Contribution to Classical Music. A Research Report for the Standing
    Conference on Studies in Education*, London: Institute of Education, University of
    London.
Merriam, A.P. (1964) *The Anthropology of Music*, Evanston, ILL: Northwestern
    University Press.

Ross, M. (1995) 'What's wrong with school music?', *British Journal of Music Education* 12, 3, 185–201.

Salaman, W. (1985–86) 'School music: a new approach', in M. Barton and J. Fowler (eds) *British Music Education Yearbook*, London: Rhinegold, pp. 3–8.

Sloboda, J. (1985) *The Musical Mind: The Cognitive Psychology of Music*, Oxford: Clarendon Press.

Swanwick, K. (1999) *Teaching Music Musically*, London: Routledge.

Audio-visual materials

1   Gamelan Semar Pegulingan Saih Pitu: *The Heavenly Orchestra of Bali, Gending Tembung*: Saih Tembung, track 2 (19:04), CMP CD 3008, 1992.

2   *The Nonesuch Explorer: Music from Distant Corners of the World* (Treasures of the Explorer Series), Side 2: India, Sarangi / The Voice of a Hundred Colors (H-72030), track 2 (3:45), Thumri: Jogia, LP record H7-11 (Stereo).

3   *Field Recording* from Ho, Volta Region, Ghana by Robert M. Kwami, 1996.

4   BBC, 'Talking Drums' (Programme 2), *Music Makers*, (20 minutes) 1994–2000.

Further reading

Elliot, D.J. (1996) 'Consciousness, culture and curriculum', *International Journal of Music Education* 28, 1–15.

Kwami, R.M. (1995) 'A framework for teaching West African musics in schools and colleges', *British Journal of Music Education* 12, 2, 225–45.

Kwami, R.M. (1998a) 'Non-Western musics in education: problems and possibilities', *British Journal of Music Education* 14, 2, 161–70.

Kwami, R.M. (1998d) *African Songs for School and Community: A Selection from Ghana*, Mainz: Schott.

Lundquist, B. and Szego, C.K. (eds) (1998) *Musics of the World's Cultures: A Source Book for Music Educators*, Nedlands, W.A.: Callaway International Resource Centre for Music Education for the International Society for Music Education.

Volk, T. (1998) *Music, Education and Multiculturalism: Foundations and Principles*, New York: Oxford University Press.

Walker, R. (1996) 'Music education freed from colonialism: a new praxis', *International Journal of Music Education* 27, 2–15.

12 Equality of opportunity and instrumental tuition

Chris Philpott

Introduction

There are two distinct strands to music education in England and Wales. On the one hand there is the general education for all pupils between the ages of 5 and 14 in the National Curriculum for Music (which is statutory), with the further option of GCSE up to 16. Alongside of this provision are various music services offering instrumental tuition for individuals and ensembles, usually paid for by parents. This double life of music education is both its glory and Achilles' heel and is shared by no other statutory subject (except perhaps PE). Certainly there is no other discipline where the extra curricular impinges so significantly on the curricular.

The *quality* of opportunity offered to youngsters by instrumental tuition is usually of a high standard, and long may this flourish and develop. However, there is a double issue of *equality* of opportunity which arises as a consequence for those who cannot afford instrumental tuition, and for the extra advantage offered to the general curriculum for those who can.

If a pupil takes part in geography classes from the age of 5 to 14, works hard, completes homework, revises and takes an interest, they have every chance (providing they are capable enough) of achieving the highest levels of the NC and top grades in GCSE examinations. There is evidence to suggest that this is not the case for music, as contact with extra-curricular tuition significantly enhances achievement at all levels. Extra tuition on a musical instrument helps pupils achieve the highest grades in the statutory curriculum to the detriment of pupils who have not participated, and this extra tuition has usually been bought by parents. This is an important issue of economic equality of opportunity which needs some attention, i.e. the ability of families to 'pay and play' impinges upon musical achievement in the statutory domain.

While many parents pay for extra tuition in, say, maths (there is an issue of equality of opportunity here too!), this does not constitute a 'service' on the same scale as that which supports instrumental tuition, and consequently does not impact as strongly on access to the highest levels of mathematical achievement. Indeed, it is likely to be the case that extra maths lessons are given to those who find the subject difficult, as opposed to those who are perceived as the most able, which is often the case with music.

Equal opportunities and music education

Equality of opportunity is an important aim of educators although the emphasis has changed with time. Capel *et al.* have identified that equal opportunities 'are about maximising the aspirations of all pupils' (1995: 181), and that 'rapid strides have been made in identifying the cultural issues which affect the academic performance of pupils . . . Cultural issues include factors such as family background, social class, gender and ethnicity' (ibid.: 165). The literature on equality of opportunity in music education has also been centred on issues such as gender, culture and learning difficulties. The rhetoric of equality of opportunity is often pathological in tone, assuming a deficit model in which pupils underachieve, or are likely to underachieve, because of a lack of access to educational resources. For example, Green suggests that the music curriculum can 'help to provide some of the missing historical links of women in music' (1996: 52), and Kwami argues that: 'the enculturation process in the British music curriculum is deficient and that minority subcultures, particularly non-Western traditions, have suffered' (1996: 72). In short, providing for equality of opportunity is a matter of differentiating for individual needs and in this way disadvantage can be compensated for.

It is no longer fashionable to suggest that the economic circumstances of parents, pupils and school can explain educational achievement. According to some writers, this has become 'almost a taboo subject in public policy debate in recent years' (Smith and Noble 1995: 133), although there was a time when such links were made more explicit by government reports:

> Quite the worst problem is the pockets of poverty, some times rural, more often urban – the slum centres of towns where too often grim housing conditions are paralleled by the worst school buildings.
>
> (Corbett, 1968: 1)

At the time of the Newsom and Plowden Reports, 'positive discrimination' was seen as an important engine for equality of opportunity. In the new millennium poverty is no longer seen as an excuse for failure. In an OFSTED report on city schools those schools studied were set in communities which 'are affected, to different degrees, by bleak surroundings and poor facilities, by poor health, by dislocation and disaffection, and by high levels of alcohol and drug abuse' (2000: 10).

However, the report cites evidence of successful institutions which 'illustrate what schools can do to improve standards within their own expertise and other resources, although there are weaknesses on which they know they need to continue to work' (ibid.: 8). Here education can compensate for the effects of society through 'good' teaching. This is not the place for a critique of such assumptions but even if the effects of economic background can be overcome by good teaching (which is dubious), it is clear that the relationship between social disadvantage and educational achievement is still problematic.

The 'new' National Curriculum (1999) does not mention economic deprivation in its huge statement on inclusion and, in a culture where 'poverty is no excuse' for educational failure, this is not surprising. Teachers of all types *are* called to account for an inclusive curriculum in many different areas of difference, e.g.

gender, cultural diversity, disability and learning difficulty. However, because of the duality of music education, this ideal is difficult to pursue in reality for having access to economic resources is a large factor in determining access to musical achievement both inside and outside the classroom. This is an issue both in terms of pupils' ability to pay and play instruments and the additional advantage that this economic privilege bestows upon them in the general music classroom. This denies the ideal of music for all enshrined within the National Curriculum.

Some writers (see Fletcher, 1987) have argued that 'music for all' is unrealistic and that music education is *essentially* elitist, requiring the additional realm of instrumental tuition to achieve its (elitist) aims. Furthermore, in a book on instrumental teaching Hallam (1998) is forced to conclude that her excellent pedagogical ideas will not be available to more than a privileged few:

> One of the criticisms which has been made regarding the provision of instrumental tuition is that it is elitist. This has been made on a number of grounds. Firstly, because the nature of tuition on offer is generally within the Western classical music tradition, although this is gradually changing. Secondly, and perhaps more importantly, because the system has been selective. Not everybody has had the opportunity to learn to play an instrument. Because provision has been limited, only those with perceived musical ability have been given the opportunity to learn . . . [and] . . . Increasingly, access to tuition will be restricted to those who can pay, denying opportunities to those who cannot.
>
> (1998: 5–6)

In the past some LEAs have promoted 'free' schemes to offer more equality of opportunity, although most of these now operate music services governed by economic forces. The delegation of funds to schools cannot guarantee that schools will spend these funds on promoting instrumental tuition, unless they 'ring fence' such money. Given the choice between mending a leaking roof or offering free, or subsidised, instrumental tuition, headteachers are often in a very difficult situation.

This chapter promotes a commitment to music for all. If the relationship between the two sides of music education denies pupils access to musical achievement, then strategies are needed to address the issue. Given the well-documented benefits of learning to play a musical instrument, we must ask ourselves whether a parent's ability to pay, or to adopt the values which prioritise such payment, is a sound basis for equality of opportunity in music education.

What is the evidence on economic access to instrumental tuition, and how does this access impinge upon musical achievement in the wider statutory curriculum?

Access to instrumental tuition

The Performing Rights Society, in conjunction with PricewaterhouseCoopers and MORI (1999), have published a comparison of instrumental provision in schools in England between 1993 and 1998. The positive news from this survey is that there are now more opportunities for pupils to learn musical instruments in schools (although demand still exceeds supply). There are also more pupils learning and they can learn on a wider range of instruments than in 1993. However, the headlines from the survey in relation to economic factors are not as optimistic and the report states that:

- parents are paying more for their children's instrumental tuition;
- more parents are having difficulty in paying for instrumental lessons;
- parents are less willing or able financially to support additional participation in performance ensembles/groups;
- fees for tuition have tended to rise more than inflation;
- the availability of remission fees for poor families is patchy and randomly distributed nationally;
- LEA contributions to music services vary widely;
- one in five schools does not spend delegated money 'buying in' the local music service.

Clearly, for certain pupils, in certain schools in certain areas equality of access to instrumental tuition is problematic. As John Lakin of PWC states in the report: 'The increase in opportunities for tuition and the range of instruments covered is good news, but the growing reliance on fees to parents raise issues of access for children of poorer families' (1999: 5.2). It may also be concluded that access to musical achievement in the statutory realm for such pupils, is similarly problematic.

What is the evidence that instrumental tuition bestows an advantage on achievement in the statutory curriculum and in the GCSE examination course?

The advantages of instrumental tuition for musical achievement in the statutory curriculum

There are two different types of evidence for the impact of learning an instrument on wider musical achievement. First, there is the *explicit* evidence of examination results and surveys. Second, there is the *implicit* evidence, which is both ephemeral and contentious, embedded in the nature of the school music curriculum itself.

Explicit evidence

In 1989 Tim Cain conducted a small survey which examined the relationship between GCSE grades and the number of hours of 'outside' tuition given to pupils during the course. The main conclusions of this survey were that:

- it *is* possible for pupils who received no instrumental tuition to achieve the top three grades (A–C);
- over 90 per cent of pupils taking GCSE in the survey did have instrumental tuition;

- outside tuition did not guarantee high grades but made them more likely;
- all pupils who were awarded a grade A had outside tuition and 90 per cent of them had had more than eighty hours.

Cain (1989) concludes that 'those pupils who did not have extra vocal or instrumental tuition may have done less well precisely because they were to some extent competing against those who did'.

There is no evidence currently available for a similar comparison with National Curriculum levels at the end of Key Stage 3, although music teachers instinctively know about these links from their work with pupils of all types. However, the Cain survey is old now and it could be that the egalitarian aims of the National Curriculum have taken effect, such that the advantage of taking instrumental tuition is no longer an issue.

Bray (2000) conducted research on GCSE uptake rates and has suggested that the situation has changed little (although his work does not deal specifically with the economic issue). He concludes that rates of uptake for GCSE music are better than those for the old O Level and CSE combined and, while this is generally considered to be a success story, the proportion of pupils in any one national cohort who take the examination is very small (around 6.8 per cent), and poor in comparison with the other arts (art around 36 per cent and drama around 14 per cent). However, within a sample of fifteen subjects the average points score and A–C pass rate for music was considerably above the average (which was also noted by Cain). There are many reasons why the uptake is still relatively low, not least the market economy surrounding subjects which are considered to be most 'useful' in the job market, which can also be reflected in GCSE options frameworks offered by schools.

Bray speculates on further reasons for low uptake and relatively high results and concludes that:

- pupils and teachers feel that expertise on a musical instrument is required to take GCSE music and only those who have had the 'good fortune' to take advantage of instrumental lessons can reasonably take part;
- many pupils are negatively orientated to music because of the 'special' status of extra-curricular work in many schools.

Bray points to the fact that pupils who have had instrumental tuition are drawn towards GCSE music and that the extra lessons bring about better grades. Given that in most cases pupils pay for their tuition, economic equality of opportunity is an issue. Indeed, from Bray's work it can be seen that around 7–10 per cent of any cohort have instrumental tuition compared with an uptake at GCSE of 6.5 per cent! These figures are too close for comfort in the context of GCSE music as an examination for all. This is clearly an important area for further up-to-date research.

Quite apart from the musical advantages bestowed on any one pupil by having extra lessons, there seem to be some *implicit* aspects of the school music curriculum which multiply the advantage in the statutory realm.

Implicit evidence

In addition to the actual and measurable effect that the taking of instrumental lessons has on musical achievement in the statutory realm, there seem to be many more implicit and hidden factors which perpetuate the situation. These factors are inherent in the statutory music curriculum, its assessment tools and the attitudes of teachers themselves.

The music curriculum

Instrumental tuition in the past has often been concerned with the linear development of technique on a musical instrument, moving from the easy to the difficult and from the simple to the complex. This is exemplified in the graded examinations which are favoured by instrumental teachers as a source of motivation and as a measure for success. Swanwick characterises this tradition as: '[one] where . . . a student can be confronted simultaneously by a complex page of notation, a bow in one hand and a violin in the other, along with exhortations to play in time, in tune, and with good tone' (1994: 142).

Furthermore, it seems that instrumental teachers have adopted a limited range of teaching styles to achieve these ends, which are often didactic and teacher-led (see Hallam, 1998). While much instrumental teaching is clearly broader and more sensitive than this cameo, it would be fair to say that 'technique' has often formed the focal point of instrumental tuition and that this bestows a considerable advantage in the current statutory curriculum. At least part of the National Curriculum for music is constructed on the assumption that there is a linear path to skilful performance. For example, pupils should be taught at:

Key Stage 1: to play tuned and untuned instruments.
Key Stage 2: to play tuned and untuned instruments with control and rhythmic accuracy.
Key Stage 3: to perform with increasing control of instrument specific techniques.

Clearly, pupils who learn a musical instrument will be better equipped to meet these targets.

That instrumental tuition has concentrated on technique, notation and limited teaching style is recognised by the work of MANA (1995), FMS (1998) and Hallam (1998), all of whom have written on the need for instrumental teaching to embrace creativity, sensitivity, improvisation and a wider range of pedagogical strategies styles. This is good news for instrumental pupils but is also liable to exacerbate their advantage in other areas of the National Curriculum for music, i.e. composing and appraising skills.

Assessment

The assessment criteria for both the National Curriculum for Music and GCSE are so constructed that pupils who have had extra instrumental tuition are in a position to benefit. Given the pattern of 'easy to difficult' noted in the National Curriculum programme of study, it is not surprising to find this notion replicated in the criteria provided for assessing the 'levels' achieved by pupils:

> level 2 = performing simple patterns and accompaniments keeping to a steady pulse.
> level 5 = performing significant parts from memory and from notations with awareness of their own contribution such as leading others, taking a solo part and/or providing rhythmic support.

At GCSE the level of 'difficulty' as a measure of musicality is even more explicit and the following marking grid is typically used (see Figure 12.1). Thus a pupil who achieves a level 4 for the performance of an intermediate piece will achieve 16 marks. In the exemplars of 'difficulty' offered by the examination boards, levels 1–4 approximate to grades 1–4 of graded examinations of the Associated Boards of the Royal Schools of Music. It is unlikely that many pupils could achieve these technical standards within normal exposure to classroom music and any 'homework' set. The assessment criteria of the NC and GCSE are by their nature 'exclusive' and not in keeping with claims that 'The highest grades are accessible by those candidates who may not receive additional instrumental tuition' (Edexcel, 2000).

Difficulty of piece Level of performance	Easy (1)	Elementary (2)	Intermediate (3)	Hard (4)
6	12	18	24	30
5	10	15	20	25
4	8	12	16	20
3	6	9	12	15
2	4	6	8	10
1	2	3	4	5

Figure 12.1 GCSE performance marking grid

There is an implicit assumption that extra tuition is necessary to achieve the highest grades and many issues arise from this style of assessment which put non-instrumentalists at a distinct disadvantage. The 'perfect' and 'musical' performance at foundation level can only receive half marks, two marks more than a 'higher' piece played relatively poorly! Swanwick is concerned that such mark schemes are obsessed with quantitative differences between the levels of difficulties and technical virtuosity. He remarks, 'This is not totally satisfactory and may make too much of relative virtuosity, as well as luring performers into water technically too deep for the good of their musical development' (1994: 106). Much of Swanwick's work has been aimed at constructing criteria which recognise the quality of musical engagement as opposed to the difficulty and technical virtuosity demanded by the examination. This is an important project for all music teachers, i.e. recognising that a simple piece can be played musically and that being musical is not necessarily a complex business.

Spruce (1999) suggests that the values implicit in the statutory curriculum are those of the Western 'bourgeois aesthetic', which has promoted the objectification of complex, 'high status' classical music through notation. In this sense Western classical music is seen as an exemplification for pupils' aspirations, i.e. music at its best. Indeed, these values are particularly implicit in the criteria for the assessment of composition in both the National Curriculum and GCSE music, where complexity, subtlety, difficulty and diversity are again rewarded. Given that much instrumental tuition takes place on Western classical instruments using 'classical' pieces, pupils receiving tuition may take advantage of assessment criteria which favour their particular skills, knowledge and understanding. This can in turn militate against musical success in those who do not take extra lessons. For example, it is interesting to note that the PRS survey found that: 'Acoustic instruments are offered in almost all responding schools . . . and although electronic instruments are less widely offered there has been a large increase in their availability as there has been in vocal tuition' (1999: 2.10). However, lessons on 'ethnic' instruments were found to be relatively rare. The picture is of Western classical instruments still dominating the uptake of instrumental lessons.

To compound the issue of equality of opportunity for those who cannot 'pay and play', teachers' attitudes can also confirm that pupils with certain types of background are most suited to study at GCSE and A Level.

Teachers' attitudes

Many writers feel that music teachers tacitly identify with the values bestowed on the instrumentalist as the basis for a sound music education, i.e. the value of technique, the ability to 'read', and an acquaintance with Western classical music. These attitudes could determine the nature of the curriculum in schools at a local level, again putting non-instrumentalists at a disadvantage:

> the large proportion of these pupils will probably listen to contemporary popular styles, which may be at odds with the more traditional, classical styles

prevalent within schools. There is an interesting potential cultural dissonance here between the interest of young people and the training and background of most teachers.

(Bray, 2000: 86)

Similarly, Ross is worried that despite the many changes in the music curriculum over the past twenty-five years or so there are deeply ingrained attitudes among teachers which have militated against change and a curriculum for all.

> As competent instrumental musicians, trained in the conventional 'academy' tradition, they were simply at sea with much of the progressive thinking initiated by the reformers . . . Despite quite elaborate strategies generated by national projects and local advisors, changing the spots on the old musical leopard has proved much more difficult than perhaps might have been imagined.
>
> (1995: 189)

While Ross's polemic fails to recognise the many genuine gains towards an eclectic music curriculum, it is also clear that there are values which militate against the non-instrumentalist deeply enshrined in statutory curricula and assessment schemes.

There is a transference of success from instrumental tuition to the classroom and this is not surprising. However, the economic issue exacerbates the problem of 'poor' children from 'poor' families getting relatively 'poor' results. The economic issue serves to perpetuate music as an elitist and to some extent exclusive subject. What, if anything, can be done to move towards a music curriculum for all, in which there is equality of access to achievement for all pupils which is not based upon economic background?

What can be done?

Clearly, the issue of access to musical achievement is part of a wider structural problem in society, i.e. wealth = access. Indeed, one solution would be to do nothing and simply accept the economic problem as a fact of life. Alternatively, one could accept the argument that music is an essentially elitist discipline and those that succeed deserve to succeed. However, given that the National Curriculum aspires to the provision of music for all and is a suitable preparation for open access to GCSE, there is a moral responsibility to address the problem. The speculative ideas below are a contribution to the debate and in need of further research and refinement.

There are three ways of looking at the problem:

1   by accepting that music is a 'special' case and that many more pupils deserve the highest grades;
2   by opening up current 'extra' opportunities to as many pupils as possible;

3 by radically rethinking what constitutes musical achievement in terms of the curriculum and what counts as success as recognised by assessment procedures.

Music is a special case

In this scenario the levels of achievement for the highest grades are set at a level which is congruent with the amount of work which can be reasonably carried out in the music timetable, plus attendant homework. Given the numbers of pupils taking instrumental lessons, this could mean a swarm of the highest levels and grades. This would not represent a lowering of standards but a realistic recognition of what can be achieved (as in other subjects) and an acceptance that music is 'special', but not to the disadvantage of those who *do not* have extra instrumental tuition.

Extending current opportunities

The more open the access to instrumental tuition, the more open the access to musical achievement in the statutory curriculum. There are initiatives in place which aim to improve access. For example, the UK government is committed to supporting music through the 'standards fund' and it will be interesting to see what impact this spending has on music services and their ability to offer cheap and freely available lessons on a wide variety of instruments, from a wide range of cultural backgrounds.

Some schools have taken the initiative themselves and have either provided free instrumental tuition for all who want it, or have provided subsidies such that the economic issue is minimised. These schools spend above and beyond their delegated funding for instrumental music and prioritise it above other funding needs. They are committed to equality of access and realise that quantity is an important engine for *quality* and *equality*. However, in most cases the delegation of funding to schools has not served music well. The choice for a headteacher between an essential repair and a subsidised instrumental lesson is a tough one.

However, some schools operating in difficult economic circumstances have developed imaginative ways of offering more open access to instrumental tuition, for example, through teaching pupils in large groups. Such large group tuition can be relatively cheap and has a sound pedagogical foundation with a strong tradition, if not fully accepted by all English music educators. The positive experiences of the Tower Hamlets String Teaching Project (closed as a consequence of the delegation of funding), are a testament to the musical quality which can emerge from large group work (see Swanwick and Jarvis, 1990). There are also models from the community such as the English brass band system where participants of all ages often work and learn together. The social benefits of learning together are clearly important and the cheaper cost allows parents and pupils time to establish whether or not playing a musical instrument is a priority for their child. However, despite the evidence, much instrumental tuition has and still does take place on an individual basis.

Both these solutions tend to skirt around a deeper problem, which centres on the very nature of musical achievement itself.

Rethinking musical achievement

By way of anecdote and as an illustration of explicit and implicit factors in musical achievement here is the story of Jason.

> Jason was in a GCSE group and played the guitar and drums. He was largely self-taught, 'worked' with his father in the evenings at pubs and clubs and could not afford (or chose not to afford) 'extra' lessons. He composed competent, uncomplicated 'pop' songs for his final examination portfolio and performed them securely and with appropriate style. Jason was finally graded as a D. His ability to notate was poor and he could not perform from a notated score. However, he was a good musician with highly developed intuitive understanding, and he could improvise with ease within certain styles. Pupils with less 'natural' ability in the group obtained C and above and deserved to do so. Jason did not develop the skills of notation and formal aural analysis (to be honest, he had no interest), and his performing and composing skills were not 'traditionally' based. These skills, many of which can be developed through extra instrumental tuition, were 'missing' in Jason.

The implications of rethinking what counts as musical achievement involves rethinking the criteria for success and progress. As has been seen, current criteria seem to be imbued with values which model progress as linear, moving from the simple to the complex, as exemplified by the Western classical tradition. Such a model denies certain types of learning and progress important to the arts in general and also to other cultures. Complexity, subtlety, difficulty and diversity are not necessarily universal aesthetic virtues:

> Complexity by itself is no virtue. Performing a wide range of complex music without evidence of understanding would definitely not count as high level of achievement. And it is certainly possible to perform, compose and enjoy a high quality of musical experience without any great complexity . . . Of course we may want to see that students extend their technical range. But not in every piece . . . *quality* in music making and musical appraisal . . . can be missing or present no matter how simple or complex the technical materials happen to be.
>
> (Swanwick, 1999: 78–9)

Swanwick suggests that qualitative criteria are of more use when recognising musical achievement than the quantitative shifts implied by the easy–complex model. The quality of engagement is more important than the difficulty of the music composed or performed. Indeed, some styles and genres champion simplicity as an aesthetic virtue. If this had been recognised by examination criteria, Jason would not have been given a D! Progress does not need to be marked by playing and composing more complex pieces, and in any case these are not the criteria we apply to professional musicians or composers. For example, for Oasis or Mark Anthony Turnage to make 'progress' from one piece to the next we do not expect their work to become more difficult. It might refine previous work or it might move on to take up different musical ground. They *might* become more complex but this is not a necessary criteria for progress. There is much work which needs to be carried out on the recognition of the quality of musical engagement and the Swanwick–Tillman spiral of musical development (1986) has broken much ground here. It is also encouraging to see that new A Level and GCSE assessment proposals are to pursue a more integrated and synoptic style of assessment where pupils can show the 'ensemble' of their skills and understanding through performing their own compositions and writing about them. Again, this would have been of some use to Jason. If a wider concept of what counts as musicality had been accepted as part of the GCSE examination, Jason could (should) have scored more highly.

The values enshrined within our current criteria are exclusive; exclusive for pupils who have come to music from more informal routes and on the back of alternative cultures and traditions, which do not share the values enshrined in current curriculum and assessment schemes. Qualitative as opposed to quantitative criteria are fairer to both the nature of music and the musical achievements of all pupils. The stakes are high for music teachers as Bray identifies:

> We need to be honest when asking ourselves whether we want more students to take GCSE music. If we do, we shall have to cater for wider ranges of ability and experience, and address the issue of just how appropriate the examination really is for those students who have not received extra instrumental or vocal tuition. Or, even more worryingly, why it is that music teaching may currently not enable and encourage all students to consider GCSE as a realistic option?
>
> (2000: 88)

Work carried out by Exeter University (Ross, 1992) found, yet again, that school music is unpopular among the majority of pupils, as it had been when last researched by the Schools Council (1968). If 'music for all' is a worthwhile aim, then the project of rehabilitation does not imply the lowering of standards but a celebration of the fact that given the special nature of music education many more can achieve the highest grades. Part of this project will also involve deconstructing the elitist tag and the mystique which often surrounds being musical. The current expectations for success perpetuate this myth by being unreasonable and prejudicial for the pupil with a normal exposure to school music.

Conclusion

This chapter is not *against* the National Curriculum for Music or GCSE. Indeed, both of these developments represent considerable steps towards a more *musical* curriculum, and the evidence here should be seen as part of the debate on further development. Furthermore, it is not intended to be resentful of the achievements of instrumental tuition. Rather, the more of it the better, for as many pupils as possible. Our instrumental tuition has an international reputation of which music education should be proud. However, it cannot be allowed to give exclusive access to success in relation to statutory requirements, especially if parents are required to pay for the privilege. This is not only an issue of equality of opportunity but also to do with the nature of music, musical achievement and musical progress. If music teachers want music to be taken seriously, then they need to open up the discipline for their pupils. Perhaps the majority of pupils recognise that they have little stake in school music. They will only invest in greater numbers if the notion can be dispelled that musical achievement is bound up with the ability to pay for and be successful in additional instrumental lessons.

Questions for discussion

1   Are there moral issues surrounding access to musical tuition and musical achievement?
2   In what ways can access to musical achievement be addressed in the context of music for all? To what extent are any solutions a realistic possibility?
3   In your experience, what are the main issues in relation to equality of opportunity in music education?

References

Bray, D. (2000) 'An examination of GCSE music uptake rates', *British Journal of Music Education* 17, 1, 79–89.
Cain, T. (1989) 'Supporting evidence: the GCSE results considered in retrospect', *TES*, 6 January.
Capel, S., Leask, M. and Turner, T. (1995) *Learning to Teach in the Secondary School: A Companion to School Experience*, London: Routledge.
Corbett, A. (1968) *Much to Do about Education*, London: Council for Educational Advance.
DfEE/QCA (1999) *The National Curriculum for England: Music*, London: QCA/DfEE.
Edexcel (2000) 'GCSE Draft Specification for 2001', http://www.edexcel.org.uk, accessed June 2000.
Fletcher, P. (1987) *Education and Music*, Oxford: Oxford University Press.
FMS/NAME (1998) *A Common Approach: A Framework for an Instrumental/Vocal Curriculum*, London: Faber Music.
Green, L. (1996) 'The emergence of gender as an issue in music education', in C. Plummeridge (ed.) *Music Education: Trends and Issues*, London: Institute of Education.
Hallam, S. (1998) *Instrumental Teaching: A Practical Guide to Better Teaching and Learning*, Oxford: Heinemann.
Kwami, R. (1996) 'Music education in and for a multi-cultural society', in C. Plummeridge (ed.) *Music Education: Trends and Issues*, London: Institute of Education.
MANA (1995) *Instrumental Teaching and Learning in Context*, London: MANA.
OFSTED (2000) *Improving City Schools*, London: OFSTED.
Packer, Y. (1996) 'Music with emotionally disturbed children', in G. Spruce (ed.) *Teaching Music*, London: Routledge.

Performing Rights Society (1999) *Musical Instrument Tuition in Schools*, London: PRS, PricewaterhouseCoopers and MORI.

Ross, M. (1992) (ed.) 'Wasteland wonderland: The arts in the National Curriculum', *Perspectives 49*, Exeter: University of Exeter.

Ross, M. (1995) 'What's wrong with school music?', *British Journal of Music Education* 12, 3, 185–201.

Schools Council (1968) *Enquiry One: The Young School Leavers*, London: HMSO.

Smith, T. and Noble, M. (1995) *Education Divides: Poverty and Schooling in the 1990s*, London: CPAG.

Spruce, G. (1999) 'Music, music education and the bourgeois aesthetic: developing a music curriculum for the new millennium', in R. McCormick and C. Paechter (eds) *Learning and Knowledge*, London: Paul Chapman and The Open University.

Swanwick, K. (1994) *Musical Knowledge: Intuition, Analysis and Musical Education*, London: Routledge.

Swanwick, K. (1999) *Teaching Music Musically*, London: Routledge.

Swanwick, K. and Jarvis, C. (1990) *The Tower Hamlets String Teaching Project: A Research Report*, London: Institute of Education, University of London.

Swanwick, K. and Tillman, J. (1986) 'The sequence of musical development: a study of children's composition', *British Journal of Music Education* 3, 3, 305–39.

Further reading

Performing Rights Society (1999) *Musical Instrument Tuition in Schools*, London: PRS, PricewaterhouseCoopers and MORI.

Ross, M. (1995) 'What's wrong with school music?', *British Journal of Music Education* 12, 3, 185–201.

Swanwick, K. (1988) *Music, Mind and Education*, London: Routledge.

13 Using ICT in music teaching

Richard Hodges

Introduction

Information and Communications Technology (ICT) embraces all developing and enabling technologies relevant to the curriculum. ICT includes all forms of computer-based learning, and recognises the importance of the Internet and associated communication technologies. The government acknowledges that both the workplace and leisure pursuits will be increasingly affected by technology. Consequently, the National Curriculum has incorporated conceptions of information and communications technology in all subjects. Effective ICT should prepare pupils to engage with technologies to discover, investigate, exchange, and present information. The general teaching requirements for the National Curriculum clearly articulate the necessity for all pupils to engage with ICT across the curriculum: 'Pupils should be given opportunities to apply and develop their ICT capability through the use of ICT tools to support their learning in all subjects (with the exception of physical education at Key Stages 1 and 2)' (DfEE, 1999a: 36).

ICT encompasses a much broader range of technologies than formerly acknowledged in National Curriculum documentation. The promotion of Information Technology capability as a tool to enhance learning across all subjects of the curriculum has been extended to embrace a wider range of technologies that are explicitly recognised as a necessary constituent of the curriculum. However, ICT capability supports subjects, rather than dictating teaching methodologies and subject content in its own right. With respect to the music curriculum, this approach has been accepted for a number of years. For example, the influential music curriculum document, *Curriculum Matters 15* (DES, 1985), outlines the need to extend and deepen pupils' understanding and appreciation of computer technology and associated applications.

An important issue for the utilisation of technologies in teaching and learning concerns the distinction between training and education. This distinction correspondingly relates to the difference between skills acquisition and conceptual understanding. In determining the success of educational encounters, it is tempting to identify and isolate the required skills that pupils need to demonstrate. This notion of skills profiling is becoming more commonplace in assessment, particularly in vocational qualifications related to competencies associated with the world of work. However, skills profiling inherently encourages a fragmented approach towards assessment, particularly with respect to artistic endeavours. For instance, it is relatively easy to isolate the essential skills that can be demonstrated in the pursuit of an activity such as composing music in an ICT environment. But there is a strong possibility that the skills themselves can be demonstrated outside the context of the activity itself. For example, using a computer mouse effectively (demonstrating the skills of grab, drag and drop, etc.) does not necessarily give an indication of a pupil's understanding of writing music with a computer sequencer, or provide a realistic point of reference by which to assess aesthetic understanding or artistry. Although skills profiling can be useful, it should not be seen as an end in itself. It is certainly the case that assessment strategies often use profiling as a means of evaluating the responses of pupils, as it is relatively easy to measure skill-based learning by direct observation. Unfortunately, undue reliance on this approach may diminish the educational value of learning experiences, particularly from a musical perspective, although the intention is to provide a closely organised learning framework linked to clear outcome descriptors.

The effectiveness of ICT is allied to its integration in the curriculum. ICT serves to provide a means to enhance and expand educational opportunities for children, and should not restrict the exploration of particular learning environments. This is particularly true in music, in which the nature of the activity sometimes precludes notions of predetermined specific outcomes. In performance-related activities, it is possible to specify learning outcomes in advance of the performance, particularly if the intention is to interpret an existing score rather than explore improvisational creativity. However, not all technology will necessarily enhance performance activities: for example, the auto-accompaniment feature of an electronic keyboard may have a detrimental effect on performance when used by a musically in-experienced pupil. The nature of composition-based activities encourages a more flexible approach than is possible in performance activities. The use of automatic technological tools in composition activities should stimulate artistic response and encourage the imaginative treatment of musical ideas. However, while ICT tools should foster an increasing independence of the learner in an educational setting, there is a danger that artistic development may be constrained by factors associated with particular technological environments.

Primary music teaching

The intention that all children should benefit from the use of ICT is qualified in the National Curriculum documentation in relation to the designation of Music as a non-core foundation subject, as there is no statutory requirement to teach the use of ICT in the programmes of study at Key Stage 1:

> At key stage 1, there are no statutory requirements to teach the use of ICT in the programmes of study for the non-core foundation subjects. Teachers should use their judgement to decide where it is appropriate to teach the use

of ICT across these subjects at key stage 1. At other key stages, there are statutory requirements to use ICT in all subjects, except physical education.

(DfEE, 1999a: 36)

As ICT music-related activities are locally defined, there is considerable potential for wide national differences in the provision of ICT-related music experiences for Key Stage 1 pupils. However, the National Curriculum documentation includes examples of ICT opportunities that provide appropriate models for determining the integration of ICT in National Curriculum subjects. A number of examples are given of ways in which ICT might be expected to contribute to the educational experiences of pupils. For example, the Key Stage 1 programme of study suggests that pupils use appropriate software to explore sounds and musical ideas (DfEE, 1999b: Music1/2b), and also promotes the use of recording equipment in recalling sounds and making improvements to their own work (DfEE, 1999b: Music1/3b). Using these approaches, pupils in Key Stage 1 can exploit ICT to create and develop musical ideas, and review and respond to their own and each other's compositions.

The establishment of the Music IT Support Project in 1995 acknowledged the importance of the use of IT resources to improve the achievement of pupils in music, rather than using music to support training in IT capability. This project was managed by the National Council for Educational Technology (NCET), which has undertaken a number of important initiatives in music related technologies. The document *Primary Music: A Pupil's Entitlement to IT* (NCET, 1996) was the principal outcome of this project, and was circulated to all maintained primary schools in 1996. This guidance encouraged a greater awareness of the potential for IT opportunities in musical activities, and was targeted specifically at the Music Co-ordinator and IT Co-ordinator in the planning and implementation of policy. The provided examples foster the development of conceptual under-standing across a number of dimensions. The KS1 examples suggest using cassette recorders, computer programs, recordings, and TV/video systems and concentrate on the conceptual development of pitch, dynamics, and timbre in particular. There is considerable emphasis on listening and appraising both sounds and music. Interestingly, the integration of musical activity with other aspects of the curriculum is promoted by the suggestion that pupils might use a computer paint program to develop a graphic score of a composition that might serve as a reference point for subsequent listening and appraising.

The exploration of graphic notation does not demand a computer-based environment: in fact, it could be argued that the desired spontaneity in responding to sounds might be hindered by engagement with some kind of computer-based notational transcription at too early a stage in the composition process. However, a transcription of a cassette recording of a composition could be used to develop both conceptual understanding and aesthetic appreciation. A tape recorder is indispensable in providing a record of children's own work, and such technology can be used to provide a basis for further related musical activities. The transient nature of musical performance and the inability to participate as both performer and audience concurrently are important reasons for using technology in this context. While active involvement is important in musical activities, listening and making judgements about music can be transformed by technology in this way.

The Key Stage 2 music IT activities which are provided as examples in *Primary Music: A Pupil's Entitlement to IT* seek to strengthen the conceptual development of timbre, tempo, and rhythm in particular. In addition, pupils are encouraged to use a sequencer to explore and arrange short musical ideas. At Key Stage 2, the National Curriculum programme of study for music clearly states that the educational experiences of pupils are informed by 'using ICT to capture, change and combine sounds' (DfEE, 1999b: Music2/5d). This approach exemplifies the methodology so often evident in IT environments in creating and saving work, editing or making changes to previously saved material, before saving work again for subsequent editing, if required. One of the problems with the activity of changing and combining sounds as specified is that the production and manipulation of sounds do not of themselves necessarily engage musical understanding. While it is evident that sounds are a constituent of music, it does not follow that all sounds constitute music. What can be understood to be musical understanding in an activity that encourages the manipulation of sounds? An activity of this kind might develop important discrimination skills related to timbre or dynamics but might not necessarily engage aesthetic awareness. Music compositional activity might be appropriately defined as combining musical sounds to engender an aesthetic response from a listener.

There is some evidence to suggest that much remains to be done to incorporate technologies into the primary music curriculum. Hennessey notes that:

> Appropriate music software for primary age children is still fairly thin on the ground. This has a lot to do with how production has developed; small companies and individuals design packages which . . . do not always reflect a particularly relevant or creative approach to the needs of the child in terms of music learning, or the needs of the teacher in terms of class teaching.
>
> (1998: 92)

There is no doubt that some of the software used in music education, especially music software used in secondary schools, has been developed for commercial contexts in serving the needs of the music industry. This has impacted on the appropriateness of adopting such software in educational contexts, particularly with younger children. There seems to be a recognition that ICT is of greater benefit to older pupils, and this is acknowledged as a general perception of primary teachers. Hennessey (1995) notes the strong arguments in favour of technology for secondary pupils and for those with learning difficulties, where it provides a link between performing abilities and creativity, while recognising that the applications for primary children are different.

Ellis (1997) has reported on the development of his Sound Technology Project with children who have special needs. Most importantly, 'traditional music skills' (ibid.: 185) are not required for children to engage with Sound Therapy, the sonic environment he has developed which utilises technology. The mode of interaction is potentially constrained by the fixed tonality of keyboards and synthesisers. Ellis is concerned that this potential limitation should not confine the nature of a child's interaction, and has exploited the nature of musical electronic instrument voices that are not tied to the fixed pitches of traditional music. Ellis suggests that engagement with the project has made children more aware of themselves and their environment. The primary focus of engagement is in exploring sounds expressively.

Glover and Young highlight the fact that much technology, available outside the school, has yet to relate to mainstream primary music teaching:

> Increasingly, outside school, children have access to computers, karaoke sets, CD players and video, keyboards, multimedia workstations which enable them to acquire self-taught proficiencies. If primary schools are to connect up with the wider culture of music beyond the primary school, technologies will play an increasingly important role in primary school music.
>
> (1999: 176)

The technological resources readily available to children outside the school environment continue to develop. It is intriguing to note that as much as one-fifth of UK spending on new musical instruments is attributable to portable electronic keyboards. A recent report commissioned by the National Music Council (NMC, 1999) reports that electronic keyboards enjoyed the greatest popularity of all instruments in terms of value in 1997, with sales of nearly £72 million set against a total national expenditure of over £378 million on all new instruments.

For some time, electronic keyboards have been acknowledged as readily available in primary schools (Hodges, 1989). Salaman (1997) has outlined the strengths and limitations of keyboards as a classroom resource, and points out that they can serve a useful function in providing musical activities for children, although the use of headphones can contribute to solitary confinement and isolation. Salaman also has misgivings about the artistic value of keyboards, as vital defining characteristics of expressive musical playing such as phrasing, tone, and intonation are often absent from keyboard performances. The principal problem with keyboards relates to the fact there is no expressed or agreed consensus regarding their use. As Salaman puts it:

> While many authors have argued passionately on behalf of singing, the percussion band, musical appreciation and much else in the past, there is an eerie silence about electronic keyboards. There is no philosophy and no Vaughan Williams or Orff has come forward to support their presence.
>
> (1997: 143)

Notwithstanding this difficulty, keyboards are seen as a useful resource when they support musical activities that engage an aesthetic response.

A further complication arising from the use of keyboards in primary education concerns the relationship between individual and group working. Manufacturers in recent years have developed keyboard instruments that serve as music work-stations, which provide an independent integrated music-making environment. Consequently, modern electronic keyboards have historically made a greater contribution to secondary education, not only as classroom performance instruments, but also in the preparation of examination coursework when used in conjunction with computers.

Secondary music teaching

It is generally acknowledged that technologically intensive activities are more suited to secondary education, particularly composition-based musical activities. Consequently, the materials developed by the National Council for Education Technology have been targeted primarily at Key Stage 3 pupils. The *Music IT Pack* (NCET, 1997), was circulated to all maintained secondary schools, and the support materials included a number of guides for teachers, exploring specific technologies related to the use of keyboards, recording and sequencing, and CD-ROM technologies. The *Music Technology in Action* support materials (BECTa, 1998) also provide guidance particularly relevant for Key Stage 3 pupils. *Music Technology in Action* includes a training guide and booklets on MIDI sequencing, electronic keyboards in the music classroom, sound processing and recording, and a guide to using CD-ROM. The pack also includes a video and a CD, and provides examples of appropriate activities for pupils engaging with IT in supporting their musical activities. The support materials recognise the importance of the professional development of teachers. Consequently, the CD includes a PowerPoint presentation that can be used for INSET sessions, as well as useful MIDI files and audio tracks.

Key Stage 3 of the National Curriculum documentation goes slightly further than Key Stage 2 in requiring pupils to use 'ICT to create, manipulate and refine sounds' (DfEE, 1999b: Music3/5d). This is an appropriate description of the many ways in which music technology can provide a basis for musical activities in secondary schools, but it is not particularly helpful in articulating the type of musical experiences in which pupils should be involved. Guidance in the use of ICT in subject teaching in relation to teacher training has been outlined by the Teacher Training Agency (TTA, 1999b). This publication makes clear that approved training providers have a responsibility to ensure that teachers are equipped to use ICT within a particular subject, rather than teaching generic uses of ICT, or seeing the employment of ICT as an end in itself. Busen-Smith (1999) has explored strategies for delivering training in music technology in the Postgraduate Certificate in Education (PGCE) secondary music course at Kingston University. She points out the need to develop the partnership between training providers and schools, so that training in music technology is located in the practical context of the classroom, rather than simply being reliant on developing skills.

There are a number of possible approaches to the teaching of composition when using ICT. The teaching methods might involve whole class work, group work, paired work, and individual work. The age range is an essential factor to consider in planning appropriate activities for computer-based work. Individual work is problematic with limited physical resources in that not all children may have access to particular facilities, but a considerable amount of composition-based activity is undertaken on an individual basis, particularly in the preparation of music examination coursework. Individual working in ICT-based musical activities does not promote social interaction, which is an important aspect of music making. Unfortunately, collaborative working can pose difficulties in assessment, in that paired or group work does not necessarily allow an evaluation of the extent to which each person has contributed to the group. It is possible to devise tasks that encourage individual contributions, even within the group context, and a collaborative composition might include particular sequenced tracks composed by individuals.

However, using a computer in particular ways may dictate operational thinking and prescribe ways of working. Some research suggests that computer-based composition can promote considerable freedom with respect to modes of working. Folkestad et al. (1998) have identified a number of different approaches that are used by pupils when composing. They investigated the compositional strategies utilised by a number of 15–16-year-old pupils by analysing the intermediate stages of the composition process, as evidenced by regularly saved MIDI-files of compositional work in progress. They found that pupils employed distinct horizontal and vertical compositional strategies. Composition and arrangement were seen as one integrated process in vertical approaches, and as separate compositional processes in horizontal approaches. Adopted strategies also related to levels of interactivity that were demonstrated by pupils. The research showed that compositional strategies varied between individuals and between different styles of music. Folkestad proposes that this study indicates that schools should provide a context for exploration with respect to computer-based composition, rather than attempting to teach any particular method of composition.

Aspects of social interaction in relation to technology in the secondary classroom have been explored by the Creative Dream research project, established in 1997. The three-year project is exploring not only pedagogical issues, but also aesthetic and cultural concerns particularly related to the use of keyboards and the teaching of composition. Odam and Walters (1998) outline the need for teaching materials that will support teachers in developing appropriate teaching strategies for incorporating electronic keyboards in composition-based activities. They lament the lack of fully researched training materials for teachers, and articulate the need to develop appropriate resources and identify good practice. The research project has investigated the effectiveness of a variety of methods of interaction, including individual work, paired work, group work and class activities. Interestingly, no single method of interaction seems most effective (Odam and Walters, 1998: 17). Nevertheless, Odam reports that the paired work context often used with electronic keyboards and headphones can lead to stylistic restriction in composition, and lack of ensemble experience.

There is some evidence to suggest that girls and boys adopt different compositional strategies when composing with computers. Colley *et al.* (1997) examined the attitudes of boys and girls in both co-educational and single sex school environments. They discovered that older girls from co-educational schools reported a lower rate of confidence in using technology than boys. The teacher interviews they conducted suggest that girls and boys adopt fundamentally different approaches to using technology:

> Some [teachers] described an important difference in the way in which boys and girls use music technology: once using it, girls treat it as a tool which helps them to produce music to the best of their ability, while boys are inclined to use the technology as an end in itself or play around.
>
> (Colley *et al.*, 1997: 125)

Colley *et al.* suggest that this may be attributable to gender differences in the classroom, but acknowledge that experience of computer games software outside the classroom may be contributing to this difference. The comments made by teachers indicate that many more boys have computers at home than girls, and accordingly, this could explain the lack of confidence demonstrated by girls in co-educational schools.

The use of ICT can lead to problems in assessment as the technology can limit the nature of interaction, and even dictate particular modes of functioning. An area of considerable concern relates to the automatic transcription function of a number of computer sequencers, which can convert a MIDI-file into a musical score. Although a pupil's composition may be aurally very effective, the errors in a score printout from a sequencer may reveal that the pupil has a very limited knowledge of staff notation. To what extent should the assessment process take account of the pupil's lack of skill in this particular area, given that it does not relate directly to the finished artistic product? This is particularly problematic, as audio processing continues to assume greater independence from MIDI.

The promotion of graphical interfacing in computer programs as a means of controlling an audio environment is another issue of concern in relation to assessment. The drag-and-drop nature of musical programs with a graphical interface is well suited to pupils who do not read conventional notation. A number of developments in recent years have encouraged the development of such music programs with a graphical interface, which are now quite sophisticated. Advances in computer hardware now allow computers to deal with real musical sounds, or samples, equivalent in audio quality to the compact disc format, which can be relatively easily manipulated. Such manipulations allow samples to be looped and combined in conjunction with sound processing to improve perceived quality, perhaps adding reverberation to simulate performance in a large hall or resonant acoustic. Effects such as reverb and delay and transformations such as flanging and chorus are readily available at the click of a button. Furthermore, pitch shifting and time stretching functions are now easily accomplished in many software packages and encourage the easy construction of dance music. Conventional music staff notation has really no part to play in the editing and manipulation of audio tracks in a computer sequencer environment, and the interface for the composer is often a graphical representation of the audio waveform. In some programs, designed to simplify the interface, iconic representation might not even resemble the musical shapes, but the icons of the drag-and-drop interface are easily combined to build the track. The audio quality of the results is not necessarily determined by the competence of the composer, as the audio samples are pre-recorded, but this creates problems in formally assessing the quality of the finished composition.

The use of pre-programmed musical ideas mimics the composition of dance music in a commercial context. Many composers of dance music, dealing almost exclusively with sampling technology, do not need to read conventional musical staff notation, and use their artistic sense in juxtaposing and modifying samples when composing. Using pre-recorded samples can promote relatively quick results, particularly with inexperienced pupils. The disadvantage of such software, when used in an educational context, is that the pupil's proficiency in using the environment can be more easily assessed than the artistic process of composition. The quantification of artistry is central to evaluation and assessment, but presents problems when pre-composed musical material is used. In music performance, technical accomplishment is easy to recognise, but musicality and imagination are more difficult to quantify. When art works are considered as artefacts, assessment encourages an evaluation of the finished product. Such assessment of the finished product may not necessarily be representative of the total learning experience of the pupil. However, this limitation may be overcome by the development of a portfolio of work that provides evidence of conceptual understanding relating to the process of composition.

At Key Stage 4 and beyond, examination courses dictate the nature of the music curriculum. The GCSE and A Level examination syllabuses encourage pupils to use a variety of ICT tools in their compositional work. The computer sequencer comes into its own in this age group as independent work by pupils is encouraged. The notion of the music 'workstation' has been a conception since the late 1980s, when all possible functions were built into a single operating environment: a music keyboard with an on-board sequencer, possessing editing functions linked to a storage methodology such as a disk drive. In other words, an integrated music keyboard environment that does away with a separate computer. However, such an instrument has greater usefulness and reliability as a performance tool, rather than a composition environment, as it is not usually possible to connect a printer to achieve a score transcription without using a computer. Dedicated performance equipment is usually more portable, more reliable in operation, and very often, significantly cheaper than computer-based music systems, although sometimes lacking in functionality.

The diversification of post-16 music education provision in recent years is linked to significant developments in the further and higher education sectors. The commercial relevance of vocational training has gained importance with an increasing availability of NVQ and degree qualifications in both popular music and music technology. The growing interest in popular and commercial music in the further education sector will continue to impact on the school music curriculum. The

Music Technology A Level qualification, which began in the mid-1990s, supports technological composition and production. This examination course would be unthinkable without engagement with ICT. The importance of the music industry is evidenced by the £3.7 billion attributed to total domestic spending in the UK on music in 1997 (NMC, 1999). The danger for music education is that the growth of courses in music that link closely with the technological aspects of the subject will encourage ICT to be seen as an end in itself, and not as a means to achieve a musical outcome engaging aesthetic responsiveness.

The challenge of new developments

The global telecommunications network that enables computers around the world to share information is known as the Internet. Communications technologies include telephones, fax, and electronic mail or email. The term Intranet is also used to define a network of computers, but that term is applied to the computer network within an organisation, e.g. that of a local authority, or a school. The Internet will assume an increasingly important role in supporting the professional development of teachers as well as transforming the educational opportunities of children.

The British Educational Communications and Technology agency (BECTa) is playing a leading role in establishing ICT support materials for music teachers. BECTa is the lead agency for the National Grid for Learning (NGfL). The NGfL seeks to enable all pupils and teachers to interact, providing content to support teaching and learning in all relevant localities, including schools, colleges, universities, libraries, the workplace and the home. The government has dedicated over £1 billion to support the use of ICT in schools in the United Kingdom through the National Grid for Learning and the New Opportunities Fund training initiative. The Prime Minister hopes to harness the powers of technology to 'bring the world into the classroom' (TTA, 1999a). Much of the funding will support training and support for teacher education and ICT.

Recent years have seen rapid advances in computer technology linked with much more intuitive interfacing for users. The computer environment has promoted the multimedia learning experience and access to information has been transformed. The financial constraints that affect resourcing remain a concern (Rogers, 1997), but tumbling prices and increasing functionality will promote greater access to ICT. There is some indication that schools may develop teaching environments with multiple computer workstations to cater for the individual needs of pupils. For example, Wilce (2000) has reported on a secondary school where all thirty PCs in a computer room are equipped with a sequencing package. Importantly, the computer room is used in conjunction with activities undertaken in usual music classrooms, and allows pupils to work on their arrangements with immediate aural feedback. The computer laboratory cannot replace a traditional music-making environment, but can extend the teaching and learning possibilities available to pupils.

Patterns of music distribution are set to change in the next few years with the dramatic fall in price of recordable CDs, which are becoming as inexpensive as audiocassettes. It is now possible for pupils effectively to 'publish' their compositions on the World Wide Web (WWW). The MP3 technology also allows audio files to be easily distributed over the Internet. As MP3 files are much smaller than conventional audio files, download times are shorter and the files themselves occupy considerably less hard disk space. Independent MP3 players are now available and downloaded music is obtainable away from the computer. Schools can share musical material, and pupils can freely exchange musical ideas, irrespective of geographical considerations.

The challenge for the future is to provide appropriate training for all staff to extend and enhance the musical experiences of their pupils, using a range of Information and Communication Technologies as appropriate. The Internet will allow the dissemination of teaching and learning materials, and the NGfL will serve as a co-ordinating agency in encouraging teachers to share good practice. The integration of ICT in the music curriculum should be a primary concern, so that the pursuit of technologically based activities is not compromised by electronic equipment dictating inappropriate approaches to teaching and learning. Engagement of musical understanding is a prerequisite for suitable musical activities and the importance of aesthetic engagement and understanding is vital in an artistic context. Technology should remain as a tool that serves musical activities. With the advances in technology and the strengthening opportunities for training and development, the challenge has never been greater, but the potential reward of making musical activity readily accessible to all pupils, irrespective of age or previous experience or ability, has never been closer.

Questions for discussion

1   In what ways can ICT provide opportunities for children to develop their musical skills and concepts?
2   Which classroom music activities are best supported by ICT?
3   To what extent do you consider that ICT places limitations on the creative music process?
4   What are the resource implications for effective ICT in the music classroom? Examine this with relevance to your particular circumstances.

References

British Educational Communications and Technology agency (1998) *Music Technology in Action*, Coventry: BECTa.
Busen-Smith, M. (1999) 'Developing strategies for delivering music technology in secondary PGCE courses', *British Journal of Music Education* 16, 2: 197–213.
Colley, A., Comber, C. and Hargreaves, D. (1997) 'IT and music education: what happens to boys and girls in coeducational and single sex schools?', *British Journal of Music Education* 14, 2, 119–27.
Department for Education and Employment and Qualifications and Curriculum Authority (1999a) *Information and Communication Technology: The National Curriculum for England*, London: HMSO.

Department for Education and Employment and Qualifications and Curriculum Authority (1999b) *Music: The National Curriculum for England*, London: HMSO.

Department of Education and Science (1985) *Information Technology from 5 to 16. Curriculum Matters 15*, London: HMSO.

Ellis, P. (1997) 'The music of sound: a new approach for children with severe and profound and multiple learning difficulties', *British Journal of Music Education* 14, 2, 173–86.

Folkestad, G., Hargreaves, D.J., and Lindström, B. (1998) 'Compositional strategies in computer-based music-making', *British Journal of Music Education* 15, 1, 83–97.

Glover, J. and Young, S. (1999) *Primary Music: Later Years*, London: Falmer Press.

Hennessey, S. (1995) *Music 7–11*, London and New York: Routledge.

Hennessey, S. (1998) *Coordinating Music across the Primary School*, London: Falmer Press.

Hodges, R. (1989) 'Creative keyboards: the ubiquitous electronic keyboard in the primary classroom', *Music Teacher* 68, 5, 28–9.

National Council for Educational Technology (1996) *Primary Music: A Pupil's Entitlement to IT*, Coventry: NCET.

National Council for Educational Technology (1997) *The Music IT Pack*, Coventry: NCET.

National Music Council (1999) *A Sound Performance: The Economic Value of Music to the United Kingdom*, London: NMC/KPMG.

Odam, G., Paterson, A. and Walters, D. (1999) 'Creative dream – three', *Yamaha Education Supplement* 31, 15–17.

Odam, G. and Walters, D. (1998) 'Dreaming or awake?', *Yamaha Education Supplement* 28, 13–15.

Rogers, K. (1997) 'Resourcing music technology in secondary schools', *British Journal of Music Education* 14, 2, 129–36.

Salaman, W. (1997) 'Keyboards in schools', *British Journal of Music Education* 14, 2, 143–9.

Teacher Training Agency (1999a) *ICT: Identification of your Training Needs*, CD-ROM, London: TTA.

Teacher Training Agency (1999b) *The Use of ICT in Subject Teaching*, London: TTA.

Wilce, H. (2000) 'Technology tempo', *Times Educational Supplement*, Music and the Arts Curriculum Special, Spring: 10–11.

Further reading

The following Internet sites provide the latest information on ICT. The Virtual Teacher Centre (VTC) includes teaching resources for integrating ICT and music, and hosts web-based conferencing in music that enables teachers to share ideas and experiences.

British Educational Communications and Technology agency (BECTa)
     http://www.becta.org.uk
National Grid for Learning (NGfL)   http://www.ngfl.gov.uk
OFSTED http://www.ofsted.gov.uk
Qualifications and Curriculum Authority (QCA)   http://www.qca.org.uk
Teacher Training Agency (TTA)   http://www.teach-tta.gov.uk
Virtual Teacher Centre (VTC)   http://vtc.ngfl.gov.uk

14 Resources and activities beyond the school

Pauline Adams

Redefining the curriculum: historical implications and new areas of development

The National Advisory Committee on Creative and Cultural Education was set up to formulate recommendations to the Secretary of State on 'the creative and cultural development of young people through formal and informal education' and to make proposals for 'principles, policies and practice' (NACCCE, 1999: 4). The resulting report, *All Our Futures* is set in the context of global economic and social change and has offered a real opportunity for re-examining the past and looking towards the future in arts education. To be a functioning and useful member of this rapidly evolving society requires the nurturing of individual expression, often through self-directed learning and creative activity, as well as a developed awareness and understanding of the wider society, in a global context. Indeed, themes concerned with the development of the individual in the context of wider society can be found in many educational ideas and philosophies which have historically underpinned the school curriculum.

For example, one of the biggest influences on the construction of education systems, curriculum and pedagogy, has been the workplace. Mass education, introduced during the latter part of the nineteenth century, was mainly concerned with providing a better educated workforce to play its part in the developing industrial society. David Hargreaves (1982) suggests that the main aims of education at this time were social control and maintenance of the class system. However, he also acknowledges the more humanistic and philanthropic motives which have since contributed to other educational reforms. Such reforms have often significantly shifted educational thinking to individualism, with the pupil at the centre of learning. The philosophical treatise of Rousseau in the eighteenth century stressed the importance of individual self-development and influenced the thinking of future reformers. Important 'child-centred' work such as biographical studies (Pestalozzi), the theories of educational idealists (Dewey) and the exploration of developmental psychology (Piaget) have all shaped the thinking of teachers during the latter half of the twentieth century. The culture of individualism was also at the heart of the Plowden Report (1969) which had an enormous impact on primary schools, on teachers and on training programmes.

The recent statutory introduction of Citizenship into the National Curriculum from September 2002 is an attempt to weld the development of the individual into the wider needs of society and community. The citizenship orders are intended to 'provide coherence in a way in which all pupils are helped to develop a full understanding of their roles and responsibilities as citizens in a modern democracy' and to 'play an important role, alongside other aspects of curriculum and school life, in helping pupils deal with difficult moral and social questions which arise in their lives and in society' (DfEE/QCA, 1999: 4).

Furthermore, while academic qualifications are still much valued as employment currency, a number of 'buzz' words have entered the vocabulary of governments and employers. These include 'flexibility', 'adaptability', 'creative thinking skills', 'communication', 'social skills' and 'cultural awareness and understanding'. Since new and different patterns of work are rapidly evolving in employment, alongside the information and communications technology revolution, the purpose of education requires new consideration if it is to prepare young people for the part they are to play in contemporary society, and maximise their chances of employment, economic survival and individual fulfilment.

Through these national initiatives there is an opportunity to re-examine the possibilities for, and benefits of, engaging schools in the wider society, through professional partnerships and the promotion of interaction between pupils and members of the community. As Hargreaves suggests, while the child-centred curriculum has undoubted benefits, teachers also need to ask themselves key questions such as 'what kind of society do we want, and how is education to help us realise that society?' (1982: 92). The arts play an important role here in 'celebrating what we all have in common with our fellow human beings, in our rich diversity of cultures and traditions' (DEA, 1998).

Music teachers have always played a central role in developing the communication and social skills of their pupils. For example, the extended curriculum has provided opportunities for participation in choirs, bands, orchestras and preparation for public performance within and beyond the school. Collegiality, loyalty to the group and social interaction are all developed within such corporate activity. Satisfaction in performance arises both from how well the individual contributes to the whole, and from their knowledge of the pleasure gained by the audience. It follows that musicians, as individual performers, also become aware of their role within the wider community.

In the classroom too, educational practice in music over the past thirty years has gradually moved away from the narrow 'transmission of culture' to one of active participation, performance, creativity and self-expression. Music teachers have been instrumental in this change, finding ways in which to engage large classes of pupils in whole group and small group practical work, often in unsuitable accommodation and with limited resources. Good teaching has encouraged pupils to develop keenly focused critical appraisal of their own work and that of others, and has provided the knowledge and skills for pupils to make significant progress. The broadening of curriculum content has also reflected the cultural diversity within Britain and within the wider global context, challenging teachers in new and different ways. For some, contact with musical styles and genres outside their own training has opened up pathways to developing additional musical resources and skills for the classroom.

With such an important emphasis on bringing children into contact with the musician's fundamental activities of performing, composing and listening, the opportunity to work in partnership with arts organisations, individual musicians and those involved in other areas of the performing arts has been welcomed and has allowed both teachers and pupils access to a richer palette from which to draw inspiration. However, for those who acknowledge the benefits of engaging with agencies and providers beyond the school, questions begin to emerge about the current formal curriculum, its structure and approach. For example, the legislative framework of the National Curriculum constrains 'flexible' possibilities, and the introduction of National Testing has tended to channel curriculum design towards achievement in particular areas of learning and knowledge. Furthermore, those music teachers who have experienced the challenge of negotiating with heads and colleagues when trying to arrange times for rehearsals for large musical events, or to set up partnership projects which require longer sessions, have often experienced at first hand the inflexibility of the school day. The formal curriculum with its allocated slots of time and prescribed content does not sit easily alongside the buzz words of 'flexibility' and 'adaptability'.

The music teacher has traditionally been responsible for balancing compulsory timetabled music as a subject for all against the extended curriculum, which is usually optional and voluntary. Partnerships with community organisations and professional arts bodies have added yet another new organisational challenge by introducing a new strand into the music curriculum. For example, the recently published QCA and Arts Council document *From Policy to Partnership: Developing the Arts in Schools* suggests that 'as with any school/community partnership, the length of time artists, pupils and teachers spend together can vary enormously, from a single session to a residency lasting a week or a year, depending on what is required' (2000: 11–12).

In the National Curriculum, which is currently hierarchical and divided into core and foundation subjects, more guidance is needed. One of the key questions raised in the QCA document relates to organisational and logistical issues, but offers no insight into how teachers are to manage and balance such projects against the wider curriculum. Primary schools might have the flexibility to organise such work. However, the structure of the secondary curriculum presents a more difficult challenge when co-ordinating the timetable for different year groups, finding longer periods of time for developing ideas, the availability of artists, and so on. Without greater commitment to redefining the curriculum models within the present school system and to supporting a change of ethos within schools, governments can be rightly accused of proposing fine precepts for the twenty-first century while showing themselves to be unable to take the bold and imaginative leap required to effect real and significant change.

Within the context of current initiatives such as citizenship, creative and cultural education, there is real potential for developing the individual in society and community through collaborative projects beyond the school.

Re-examining the role of community: definitions and possibilities

The notion of a stable local community is a thing of the past in much of the United Kingdom. In some areas, such as the East End of London, there has always been rapid demographic change. In such an ethnically diverse, multi-dimensional and complex society it is perhaps more difficult to define the meaning of the word 'community'. Anthony Everitt draws on a report from a seminar on community music to illustrate the difficulties participants had in defining the word 'community':

> despite much discussion there was no consensus on the definition of 'the community' or indeed, who should define it . . . Boundaries are contestable and difficult to set: communities can be small, large, isolated, concentric or overlapping . . . Generally people thought it better to resist such definitions as they could become straitjackets.
>
> (1997: 85)

Instead a wider view of community is encouraged, inside or outside any geographical locality, set in the context of an inter-cultural and global society communicating with communities and their religious, social and political values through new technologies.

The idea of artists working in the community sprang from the creation of arts centres in the late 1960s, where participatory workshops allowed for a sharing of ideas and encouraged a much more equal partnership between artists and clients. For music this might have taken the form of a production, where the workshop leader encouraged experimentation and improvisation, and facilitated new skills to create a performance piece. There is a connection in this approach to that of some school music teachers of the time, who were defining the music curriculum by taking into account the interests and skills of pupils, including 'popular music' styles, and building experimental and improvised music making into their planning and teaching. This connection is further exemplified by Anthony Everitt:

> The object of this work was not that the community artists should feel that their job was to take art to the people, for that is in essence the relationship between the professional and the amateur: rather, believing that many people's power of expression was stunted or suppressed, their task was to place their talent at the disposal of others and to collaborate with them on a basis of equality.
>
> (ibid.: 83)

For teachers, who are professional educators, the role of facilitator seems to be somewhere between that of being responsible for the content of the curriculum and the learning outcomes of pupils in their particular subject, while balancing this against opportunities for 'negotiated' learning, where pupils can be active participants, and where their individual, creative and imaginative contributions can be acknowledged and valued.

Music teachers can learn much from the outreach work offered by local community organisations, and the innovations and developments for and by young people within the wider community. For a musician and teacher of music, the discoveries can be endless and fascinating. There is much music to be found which firmly retains its traditional roots, preserving and handing on musical forms and techniques as learned in the past. There is, however, music which retains something of its traditions by re-inventing them in a different form, appealing to individual ideas about style and social identity. Musical genres other than Western ones have filtered through into community and school ensembles, and steel bands, gamelan orchestras and samba bands can be heard across Britain alongside the more traditional ensembles. Schools too can benefit from music which is truly community-driven and where keen and enthusiastic locally based musicians can bring their particular brand of music to a school audience.

In the past much community work, including music, was funded by local authorities though often on a patchy and *ad hoc* basis. There is now funding from a wider number of sources, including national funding bodies, arts education agencies and organisations, and business and industry. Regional discrepancies in funding and a lack of recognition of and support for the growing diversity within music making have resulted in some criticism of the Arts Councils of Great Britain as unfair in their funding allocations and choosing to support 'elitist' groups. Following recent government commitment to securing money for the arts, it has to be seen whether or not it will implement a more coherent system and improve sustainability and development across professional organisations, community groups and schools.

Lottery funding has provided new arts centres for some schools. There are opportunities here for schools to reach out into the community with multi-purpose use of buildings, and sharing of resources for arts experiences for all age groups.

Redefining the artist: changing patterns of work for the professional, with reference to orchestras and opera companies

Professional and community based artists are adapting their practice to promote partnership through education programmes. The term Fordism was first used by Antonio Gramsci in 1971 to describe factory production techniques, such as those employed by Henry Ford. What has this to do with organisations such as orchestras and their players? The following informal statement made by a professional orchestral musician during a conversation may give a clue: 'I have sat in this orchestra for twenty years being told what to do and how to do it! I have never improvised or composed or been musically engaged stylistically in other cultural styles and genres outside the orchestral repertoire, until fairly recently.'

In contrast, post-Fordist principles are marked by the development of a qualified and highly skilled labour force used in flexible employment patterns. The words 'highly skilled and flexible' seem here to be the key to surviving change. This may seem a strange and tenuous way in which to view the changing patterns of work for orchestral players, but there are parallels. A number of orchestras are self-managing, having responsibility for marketing and finance, and their players are often involved in projects outside their concert commitments. Contracted work, including first call contracts, are the norm for most orchestral players, many of whom are often not full-time, which means that professional musicians have to explore other avenues in order to earn a living. Orchestras have, through the necessity for survival, adopted a more eclectic style of working. Live concerts on the web are now becoming a real possibility and the word 'flexibility' for some orchestral musicians has become synonymous with 'education work'! The consultation document *Orchestral Education Programmes: Intents and Purposes* highlights changing expectations 'that publicly-funded arts organisations should develop programmes in order to further develop the Arts Council's chartered objectives of developing and improving knowledge and practice in the arts and to increasing the accessibility of the arts to the public' (Lowson, 1999: 1).

Publicly funded arts organisations, including orchestras, have also been expected to incorporate education work into their programmes. It could be strongly argued that the burgeoning of orchestral education programmes has been in response to market forces. In a survey undertaken by the Arts Council of England in 1997, 78 per cent of publicly funded arts organisations were involved in education work, and 68 per cent of whom had a dedicated education officer.

Julia Winterson looks at the aims of the pioneering creative music workshops of the 1970s which involved professional players giving direct support to teachers and enhancing music in the classroom. She perceives the large-scale education projects of the 1990s as 'developing into a full scale industry of their own' and as 'a systematic economic activity' (1996: 61). Such developments, for whatever reasons, have also provided opportunities for a number of musicians to become more involved in, and open to music outside their usual experiences, and to relate directly to schools and the wider community.

Recently published research and consultation reports are examining the interface between the world of the professional and that of the school or community. The Education, Research and Development Initiative (ERDI), supported by the Education and Training Department of the Arts Council in England, was set up in 1995 with a view to exploring ways in which education could be more effectively integrated into and across arts organisations. However, while Education programmes are now reasonably well established, relatively little research has been undertaken into their effectiveness in terms of meeting the needs of the host organisations and their impact on the artistic activity of both clients and providers.

Important and revealing research undertaken by Saville Kushner for the Calouste Gulbenkian Foundation explored the thoughts and responses of children to music, and to professional musicians during a collaborative project undertaken with the City of Birmingham Symphony Orchestra. Kushner believes that important challenges arise out of the differing cultures, traditions and values within orchestral practice, compared to those developed within the school system. He poses the important question, 'How do performing musicians judge the quality of their education work – because here the measure of what is good and worthwhile grows out of different problems and values?' (1991: 14). The reality of school and classroom, where the personal assumptions of adults may be severely challenged and where the culture and values of pupils are vastly different from those of their prospective teachers, presents a range of complex issues. All those who engage with young people need to consider their own teaching agenda alongside the knowledge and interests of their clients. Sue Cottrell's summary of a report and survey commissioned by the London Arts Board in 1994 concludes that 'while musicians do not need formal teaching qualifications to achieve successful outcomes in schools, they do need some teaching skills' (1998: 284). Kushner also suggests that 'artists need to develop educational theories of their arts in schools activities' (1991: 81). The implications are that the professionals organising projects need to develop a careful rationale for partnership which allows all individuals to develop within the context of the wider community of artist, teachers and pupils.

A small number of programmes are in place (or at the discussion stage) which will allow access to some form of training, in order to bring theoretical underpinning to education and community work and to explore the role of the animateur. Peter Renshaw, who has led pioneering work in this field at the Guildhall School of Music and Drama, believes that the process should begin in the conservatoires. His view of such institutions as being 'embedded in a legacy of tradition, characterised by hierarchical structures that reflect the paternalistic style of management and artistic leadership still prevalent in many symphony orchestras and opera companies' (1999: 285) supports the notion that although orchestras and opera companies are making inroads into education and community work, existing structures and procedures continue to prevent any real focus on personal and artistic development.

Some arts organisations and training institutions have begun to work alongside musicians whose musical skills are rooted in different genres and traditions. Julia Winterson (1996) is concerned that orchestras use music from other cultures because they feel it more accessible for their clients, or to give 'official sanction', and that there is a danger of 'cultural imperialism'. However, musicians of all nationalities have a vested interest in other musical styles, structures and procedures and there have been many productive artistic collaborations between composers, performers, teachers and music students. It is heartening that the complexities within different musical traditions are being explored and appreciated and that discourse and exchange are taking place. There is opportunity here for high quality musicianship to be shared, and for personal and artistic development. If professional musicians are to be engaged within community settings, they need to be aware of and appreciate the music of others.

The interweaving of newfound skills into a musician's repertoire does not necessarily detract from the overall artistic vision of an orchestra or opera company. Professional players consulted as part of research undertaken by the Arts Council of England (Lowson, 1999) viewed their education and artistic work in different ways. Some felt that education and community work should be closely related to the work of the orchestra, not an attempt to 'mould' the orchestra to community needs. However, many felt that their community work could embrace the 'distinctiveness' of the orchestra while at the same time reflecting the needs of the community.

The consultation also considered how performers viewed the place of education in the management structure. It was generally agreed that there should be a commitment from the top of the organisation and that education work needed greater investment if project work were to be developed through better consultation and appropriate planning. It therefore seems to be imperative for education officers to be involved in meetings at management level if school and community work are to be seen as important to the artistic life of any professional body. It is at this level that existing structures and programming policies can be examined alongside development strategies for education and community links.

The thoughts of those professional musicians who are committed to working with people in the community and pupils in schools are well documented in project evaluation reports. The following informal comments of an orchestral player sum up the commitment of a growing number of professionals to a role within community arts: 'In my opinion the work done in this area is crucial to the development of future arts organisations, performers and audiences, and the general artistic and social welfare of the nation.' These are noble words which raise important questions about what defines community and about what role professionals might take within community. Given the growing trend of using professional or community groups in education the training and preparation of teachers and professionals for such collaboration is increasingly important.

Reviewing music training: performers and teachers

The type of training which is most useful to teacher and professional for collaborative community projects is patchy and often contradictory. A number of musicians who have received a university or conservatoire training are now entering the teaching, orchestral or opera professions, having experienced a broader musical education than their predecessors. The introduction of composition and performance into the school curriculum, and its inclusion at examination level, are beginning to impact upon higher education training. Some conservatoires and universities have introduced a wider range of modular options into their training programmes, including education, world musics, ethnomusicology, jazz, composition techniques, music technology and stylistic awareness of music written for different purposes, such as film. This type of training would seem to be ideally suited to allow both performers and teachers to take advantage of the flexible and wide-ranging nature of education projects involving professionals or community artists.

However, in order to attract premium funding, music conservatoires are required to ensure one-to-one instrumental teaching with a view to training students for the professional route. The pressure to ensure that funding is secured and that demands are met may affect the design of courses which have broadened their curriculum content. The current HEFCE requirements (1999) seem at odds with the new and more flexible patterns within orchestral and operatic life, and with the emphasis of the Arts Councils on the development education programmes by professional bodies.

Postgraduate teacher training, which ideally wishes to attract well-trained and competent musicians into the education profession, is keen to increase its numbers of applicants from conservatoires. Secondary pupils deserve teachers who are highly skilled within their subject and who have the space and time to continue their own personal musical development. For those well-trained musicians who choose the teaching route it is often difficult to find the time required to maintain a high standard of playing, although many perform or make music in a semi-professional or amateur capacity.

However, while it is expected that conservatoire-trained musicians are good players and performers, it is also crucial to ensure that personal musical development not only continues with high quality instrumental and vocal tuition, but also in a broad range of musical and artistic practices. Indeed, the balance between breadth and depth of musicianship is a delicate one if teacher and performer training is to be best managed to service collaborative projects.

For primary teachers, who are expected to meet the requirements of the National Curriculum for Music, teacher training courses provide little support. The RSA report *The Disappearing Arts?* brought together evidence to show what is currently happening in the arts at the initial teacher training stage, and the extent of arts provision for continuing professional development. Statistical information showed that the average number of taught hours of music (OFSTED sample of eight providers in 1996–97) on a BEd/BA course was thirty, and on a PGCE course sixteen. There was widespread evidence that teacher training institutions were abandoning specialisms in arts subjects and that many newly qualified primary teachers had little confidence in teaching music.

If partnership with outside organisations is to be encouraged, teachers need to feel confident about the purpose of such collaborations and to be able to bring their own music education perspective to any project. There is an argument here for ensuring that trainees who are secondary or primary music specialists, or primary generalists, are introduced to the challenges and possibilities of working with professional and community artists.

Renewal and discovery in partnership

The implications for collaborative partnerships between schools and professionals are as follows.

1   There are important benefits in terms of individual development within the wider community of teachers, pupils and professionals.
2   There is a need for mutual understanding between schools and professionals (as each other's 'clients').
3   This mutual understanding needs to be underpinned by a sound philosophy and supported by suitable training for both teachers and performers.

4   There is a need for imaginative curriculum models and timetabling to take full advantage of such projects.
5   There is a need for rigorous research into the effectiveness of collaborative projects from the perspective of all 'clients'.

The coming together of artists, dancers, musicians and teachers to devise exciting and creative projects for pupils seems desirable at a time when there are national initiatives promoting the development of the individual within the community. It is also desirable at a time when there is a reduction in arts teaching time within primary schools and when, according to research undertaken by Ross and Kamba, music continues to remain unpopular with pupils, particularly at Key Stage 4 (1997).

The primary school, where confidence in music teaching is often not high, can benefit from the support of professional and community musicians, who may bring skills and knowledge to teachers and pupils. Some professional organisations see their role as one of supporting the National Curriculum for Music, but it should also be remembered that while primary teachers may not be musicians they may be sound educationists with their own specialisms and sophisticated pedagogy. Professional orchestral players are not usually trained teachers, nor are they often trained to work creatively with music. However, the combination and acceptance of the different talents and skills of professional and teacher can form the basis of powerful collaborative projects, which may provide a significant experience for all participants.

In secondary schools the one hour a week music lesson with thirty-plus pupils in one room, with the occasional possibility of working in smaller groups may not always be the best way of structuring the subject. A partnership project where three or four musicians, including the teacher, can spend time with smaller groups over a number of half-days, days or even over a week, may be a more focused and productive approach to engage young people in the creative process.

For some teachers it would be difficult to relinquish regular weekly contact with pupils, but operating in a more open system, based on flexible timetabling of the school day, could be of greater value in terms of both subject satisfaction and musical progress for pupils. Contact with professional and community musicians who have developed a clear rationale and philosophy to underpin their work, alongside the individual skills of the teacher, can be inspirational and motivating for pupils.

Many schools are still housed in old buildings which seem unattractive and unsuitable for the kinds of collaborative projects discussed in this chapter, yet an old power station in London was recently renovated to exhibit an eclectic range of art and sculpture in new and exciting ways. We are told that Tate Modern – an example of the renaissance of an outdated site as a creative centre – is a flagship for the nation. It is now surely time to create School Modern, where the old ways of doing things can be transformed, into relevant and meaningful experiences for young people in the twenty-first century.

Questions for discussion

1   Is current curriculum organisation conducive to effective arts education? How could the curriculum be organised to maximise the benefits of partnerships with professional/community musicians?

2   What are the implications for professional/community musicians, teachers and pupils if effective partnerships are to flourish? What are the implications for teacher and conservatoire education?

References

Cottrell, S. (1998) 'Partnerships in the classroom', *British Journal of Music Education* 15, 3, 271–85.

DfEE/QCA (1999) *The National Curriculum for England*, London: DfEE/QCA.

Development Education Association (1998) *A Framework for the International Dimension for Schools in England*, London: DEA.

Everitt, A. (1997) *Joining In: An Investigation into Participatory Music*, London: Calouste Gulbenkian Foundation.

Hargreaves, D.H. (1982) *The Challenge for the Comprehensive School*, London: Routledge and Kegan Paul.

HEFCE (1999) *Funding of Specialist Arts Institutions*, London: Higher Education Council for England.

Hogarth, S., Kinder, K. and Harland, J. (1997) *Arts Organisations and their Education Programmes*, London: the Arts Council of England.

Kushner, S. (1991) *The Children's Music Book: Performing Musicians in School*, London: Calouste Gulbenkian Foundation.

Ministry of Education (1969) *The Plowden Report of Primary Education*, London: HMSO.

Lowson, S. (1999) *Orchestral Education Programmes: Intents and Purposes, Report of the Consultation Process*, London: the Arts Council of England.

NACCCE (1999) *All Our Futures: Creativity, Culture and Education*, Suffolk: DfEE Publications.

Peggie, A. (1997) *Musicians Go to School: Partnership in the Classroom*, London: Arts Board.

QCA/The Arts Council for England (2000) *From Policy to Partnership: Developing the Arts in Schools*, London: Qualification Curriculum Authority and the Arts Council of England.

Renshaw, P. (1999) 'Teaching – or learning? Sustaining a learning culture in arts training institutions', *ISM Journal*, 280–90.

Rogers, R. (1997) *The Heart of the Matter: Education Research and Development Initiative*, London: the Arts Council of England.

Ross, M. and Kamba, M. (1997) *The State of the Arts*, Exeter: University of Exeter, School of Education.

RSA (1998) *The Disappearing Arts? The Current State of the Arts in Initial Teacher Training and Professional Development*, London: RSA.

RSA (1999) *Opening Minds: Education for the 21st Century*, London: RSA.

Shaw, P. (1996) *Mapping the Field: A Research Project on the Education Work of British Orchestras*, London: Association of British Orchestras.

Tambling, P. and Harland, J. (1998) *Orchestral Education Programmes: Intents and Purposes*, London: the Arts Council of England.

Winterson, J. (1996) 'So what's new? A survey of the education policies of orchestras and opera companies', *British Journal of Music Education* 13, 3, 259–70.

Further reading

Kushner, S. (1991) *The Children's Music Book: Performing Musicians in School*, London: Calouste Gulbenkian Foundation.
Peggie, A. (1997) *Musicians Go to School: Partnership in the Classroom*, London: Arts Board.

15 Music education and individual needs

John Witchell

Introduction

When training to be a teacher I remember being challenged by my education tutor for using the word 'wants' instead of 'needs'. To be frank, I hadn't really thought much about the difference; however, thirty years on I am a little clearer. What pupils may need and what they want are not always the same, but both have to be addressed if teachers are to engage with learners. For instance, a teacher may believe that pupils 'need' to learn how to read music and design activities that reinforce concepts about notation. However, there are not many pupils who would necessarily want to learn to read music for its own sake. More likely they would prefer something that they regard as relevant to them personally. Nearly thirty years ago Robert Witkin produced evidence that indicated that 78 per cent of pupils ignored music altogether when suggesting ideas for their own curriculum. They simply did not 'want' the music that they had experienced in lessons (Witkin, 1974: 145).

Although curriculum design has improved enormously since then, it is not difficult to provide stereotype examples of music teaching that pupils could consider irrelevant. For example, some teachers may cling on to high ideals of Western classical music at the expense of other styles. Others may gear their teaching to the most able pupils and pay insufficient attention to the less able. Perhaps some teachers emphasise extrinsic musical features rather than intrinsic ones by concentrating on the development of technical skills rather than exploration of musical ideas. Some may over-emphasise popular music that pupils might regard as an encroachment on their own cultural territory. Others may try and provide something for everyone, but in so doing perhaps compromise the quality of experience. The teachers may have good intentions, but they do not always match the individual needs and aspirations of their pupils.

Planning for individual needs

Good music teachers have always motivated their pupils by firing their enthusiasm in ways that are the envy of teachers of many other subjects. *The Arts Inspected* (Office for Standards in Education, 1998: 1–3) celebrates this by providing clear examples of good teaching. Likewise, revisions to the National Curriculum in the year 2000 reinforce the entitlement of pupils to a relevant, challenging and balanced curriculum that raises their achievement because it is based on an understanding of their needs. Statutory guidance is explicit in identifying what this means for all subjects:

> When planning, teachers should set high expectations and provide opportunities for all pupils to achieve, including boys and girls, pupils with special educational needs, pupils with disabilities, pupils from all social and cultural backgrounds, pupils of different ethnic groups including travellers, refugees and asylum seekers, and those from diverse linguistic backgrounds. Teachers should take specific action to respond to pupils' diverse needs by:
>
> a) creating effective learning environments
> b) securing their motivation and concentration
> c) providing equality of opportunity through teaching approaches
> d) using appropriate assessment approaches
> e) setting targets for learning.
>
> (Department for Education and Employment, 2000)

These issues are also unpacked in the report *All Our Futures: Creativity, Culture and Education* (National Advisory Committee on Creative and Cultural Education, 1999: 6–15). Young people have unique capacities that must be developed so that they can build lives that are purposeful and fulfilling. One of the roles of education is 'to help them find their future and understand their pasts'. It serves to help them discover their own strengths, passions and sensibilities, and develop social, spiritual and emotional qualities of their characters. The report suggests that developing young people's creativity by helping them to explore and understand their own cultural assumptions and values is essential in helping to meet the challenges in an increasingly complex and technological society. This, however, has to be based on a commitment to the unique value and central importance of the individual.

Principles into practice

In his book *Teaching Music Musically* Keith Swanwick has identified three guiding principles of teaching that engage the learners because they focus on intrinsic qualities of music (1999: 44–57). 'Care for music as a discourse' protects the intrinsic qualities of music. 'Care for the musical discourse of pupils' respects the music and culture that pupils bring with them into the classroom. Finally, 'care for musical fluency' ensures that the pedagogy of music teaching is approached systematically and with regard to the individual needs of the learners. These principles are based on pupils' responsiveness to music and the unique interaction between individual and art form as the process of making music unfolds. Pupils' musical development and their accumulation of understanding, skills and knowledge are also critical. Knowing how pupils acquire their musical understanding provides insight into what they can and cannot do. Being aware of what pupils have already learnt is a logical basis for identifying learning objectives, planning activities and working out assessment procedures.

Swanwick's principles can be illustrated in an approach to developing a unit of work for Key Stage 2, taking, for instance, the song 'Old Joe Clark' as a starting point. First, the pupils could learn the song by copying the teacher in short phrases. If a few have problems in pitching, a strategy could be devised to attend to this. Perhaps the class could sing phrases in a more comfortable range or lower achievers could be placed next to higher achievers. Next, the class could develop the music by tapping the beat, or creating a simple rhythm and adding percussion instruments. The development of an accompaniment could be approached as a whole class activity with short periods allowed for group or paired work. The extent of this would depend on the previous experience, needs and abilities of the pupils. Some aspects would be revisited to reinforce the learning for lower achievers, but extension opportunities would be devised for higher achievers.

Teachers need to have sufficient confidence and flexibility to develop activities in the light of children's response. In planning they need to consider issues such as how to improve the quality of the singing by repetition, modelling, attention to breathing, posture, articulation and tone quality, but always in relation to the expressive possibilities of the music. It may be useful to explore musical devices such as drones that enhance the sense of performance and illuminate other musical strands, including texture, mood and structure. In talking with the children about the music, questions could be devised to tease out everyone's understanding. For example, 'what happens to the music when the instruments are added? Is the song serious or funny and why?' The children could then provide their views on the most and least effective aspects of the performance. Perhaps they may like the words, or the use of the instruments, or they may identify areas for development, such as improving the sense of a steady pulse on the drum.

Further extension work could be provided, not only to stretch the pupils, but also to enrich the musical experience, place it in context and encourage them to take ownership. The class could work in small groups or pairs, composing their own pieces using selected notes over a drone. They could listen to music that included drones such as 'Marta's Dance' from 'Riverdance', or the middle section of Tchaikovsky's 'Dance of the Reed Flutes' from the 'Nutcracker' Suite. Stepped questions about the music could include some for everyone, for example 'how many instruments are playing at the opening?' More open-ended questions could extend the pupils' awareness by asking 'In what ways does the music suggest a dance and how does the composer create this intended effect?'

Therefore connections are made as the pupils respond to the music. As the unit of work unfolds, the intrinsic qualities of the music are seen to be relevant to their individual needs and interests. The emphasis is on making music for its own sake, but based on the needs of individual pupils. Useful guidance on expectations in music, assisting teachers in identifying levels of attainment in relation to national benchmarks has been developed in recent years (School Curriculum and

Assessment Authority, 1997a, 1997b). There are also many useful publications available that are based on this holistic approach to teaching music.

Special Educational Needs: learning difficulties

Recognised characteristics of good teaching include having high expectations, challenging pupils and adopting a fast pace to lessons. However, in the case of pupils with learning difficulties, the teacher also has to ensure that expectations are realistic. Bearing in mind that musical talent sometimes stands out from a child's general abilities, it is also accepted that children with special educational needs require a carefully structured approach to learning. One reason for this, as David Ward has suggested, is that many children have too many unstructured experiences in their lives (1989: 99).

The balance between structure and freedom is critical. Too much emphasis on the mastery of technique for its own sake stifles pupils' imagination. In contrast, freedom without control results in incoherent musical outcomes at best and musical anarchy at worst! The knack is to plan carefully by identifying objectives, intended outcomes and appropriate activities that address the needs of all pupils in a group, but that also promote pupils' curiosity and motivation. Adopting an holistic approach that integrates performing, composing and listening promotes the natural evolution of musical development. By having also a clear understanding of all the pupils' needs, capabilities and potential, the teacher ensures that good progress is made. A positive approach for teachers is to look for *abilities* rather than *disabilities*.

The view of the original National Curriculum Music Working Group (Pratt and Stephens, 1995: 43) was that teachers should identify those activities across the Programmes of Study and through the Key Stages which best allow their pupils to do the following:

- experience a sense of achievement and worth;
- develop confidence;
- make an identifiable individual contribution;
- be sensitive to the musical activities and creation of others.

The guidance goes on to suggest that specific strategies can be used to meet the special educational needs of pupils. They include:

- adapting material, for example, pupils with non-verbal communication may well be able to hum or use body sounds;
- adapting or selecting instruments for pupils with severe physical disabilities, for example, hand chimes may be easier to use than instruments with bars;
- selecting other resources, such as large print or raised notations for the partially sighted;
- selecting software programmes and technology that do not require additional manipulative and cognitive skills, for example, systems such as 'Soundbeam'

enable children to manipulate musical sounds through their gestures within a beam of sound, rather than through the control of a musical instrument;

- changing the order of the curriculum for pupils with progressive illnesses of the nervous system.

The musically gifted and talented

Help is also available for teaching the musically gifted or talented. Musically gifted pupils are likely to get things right the first time, memorise music quickly and be fluent readers. They may have good co-ordination, a sense of perfect or relative pitch, a spontaneous creative impulse, an unusual affinity to a particular instrument, sensitivity to music itself, initiative, determination and involvement in extra-curricular music making (UK Council for Music Education and Training, 1982: 8). Knowing this, do we always provide sufficient challenge for the gifted in ordinary class lessons? While additional help may be sought, perhaps by enabling the study of a musical instrument, involvement in extension activities or attendance at a specialist school, practical strategies for teaching in the mainstream school are less clear. Is it reasonable to expect primary classroom teachers to be able to identify and stretch musically gifted children when they have insufficient musical training themselves, or when other priorities, such as developing numeracy and literacy skills, reduce the time available for music and other foundation subjects? How successful are secondary music teachers in incorporating strategies for the musically talented when they perhaps teach in the order of six hundred pupils a week?

Planning for differentiation

Accepting these constraints, we have nevertheless made significant advances in our approach to differentiated teaching and learning. Deborah Eyre distinguishes between two elements of differentiation: planning and opportunism (1997: 39). Planning for differentiation includes strategies based on resource, task, support or response (Dickinson and Wright, 1993: 1–25). Differentiation by outcome is less dependent on planning, but more on effective methods of assessing pupils' achievements. Opportunism goes a stage further because it depends on the teacher building on an unplanned opportunity to move children forward. It involves greater risks as teachers stray from their plan of work, but it lies at the heart of creativity, especially in an expressive subject like music.

In order for teachers to be able to adopt this flexible approach one might argue that they need a thorough understanding of the subject. While a prerequisite for specialist teachers, it is perhaps an unrealistic expectation for primary generalist teachers. In research undertaken by Eyre and Fuller (1993), teachers said they were less willing to deviate when teaching a subject with which they were either unfamiliar or under-confident. Since the introduction of the National Curriculum teachers have become reluctant to digress from their plans. In music teaching this can be seen in a reluctance to explore the unpredictable elements of surprise.

Yet there is evidence that achievement in music and standards of teaching are improving in primary schools where many of the teachers also teach all the other subjects. This supports the notion that higher achievement can be brought about through imaginative, creative teaching based on knowledge of children's learning as well as subject expertise. Without undermining the value of knowing the subject, it is equally important to be able to have the generic teaching skills that provide a 'scaffold' which supports pupils' progression (Vygotsky, 1978). There are many examples of children relishing the delight of musical creativity, supported by imaginative teachers who are not necessarily specialists, but who know how to provide scaffolds for them to learn.

Guidance from the Qualifications and Curriculum Authority illustrates ways in planning differentiated schemes of work (Qualifications and Curriculum Authority, 2000). The approach requires thought about what is to be taught to most pupils, the additional support that some pupils will need and the extension work that will challenge the more able. Each unit of work is planned on this basis: consideration is given to the nature of the activities in relation to the learning objectives and intended outcomes, and how they can be designed to reinforce the learning of lower achievers and increase the challenge for higher achievers.

Differentiated performing

Teaching an activity to a whole class without building in different levels of demand is likely to generate some bored pupils at the margins. Performing activities are particularly vulnerable to being approached in a uniform way. Performing that has been planned on the basis of what pupils already know and how they can be nurtured to the next stage of understanding stands a better chance of success. For the least able, the teacher needs to have a clear idea of their musical skills, knowledge and understanding, so that they can participate at their own level. The *Code of Practice* for pupils with special educational needs should ensure that teachers have specific strategies at hand. It should also identify additional support in the classroom for those pupils on higher stages of assessment (Department for Education, 1994). However, even with this support, the music teacher should consider how the performing activity is relevant for the less able. For instance, parts for ensembles can be specially adapted or written. Teacher–pupil interaction may also include more emphasis on copying, repeating and developing musical memory in short questions and answer phrases. Rhythmic ostinati and the use of pentatonic patterns often enable less able pupils to achieve satisfying musical results. Nevertheless these approaches cannot be undertaken spontaneously: reinforcement needs to be planned into the work. Bolt-on or one-off ideas are of limited value and are not the same as developing flexibility in order to explore musical ideas.

In contrast, more able pupils can often be challenged through extension activities. 'More able' may mean those who have instrumental/vocal tuition, those who work quickly and are good at most things, or simply those who choose to do harder work. Extension work does not simply mean more practice of the same ideas:

nor is it unplanned rehearsal in a practice room without any goals. It cannot be assumed that able pupils are more hard-working than others. Left unsupervised, they are likely to drift off task as much as any others. Deborah Eyre (1997) has identified twenty ways to create challenge for able children. Many of them involve placing more responsibility in the hands of the learner as well as increasing the demand of the work. Within the programmes of study for music there are opportunities for pupils to take a lead in rehearsal and to direct performances. In the same way, they can help others in composing by applying their higher technical skills and sharing their musical ideas. Teachers can increase the demand of performing and composing tasks by encouraging able pupils to invent their own additional parts – descants, harmonies or bass parts. Transposition for appropriate instrumental players involves them in higher level problem-solving skills. Applying musical techniques to open-ended composing tasks can be taken as far as the pupils can comfortably handle. For example, if the majority of pupils are exploring riffs, the more able can be hooking them together to form a more coherent musical composition. The sky is the limit, since when given the opportunity to choose, able pupils often select difficult and challenging routes, and enjoy taking risks.

Differentiated listening

Listening activities can also be differentiated. By its very nature, listening underpins all other musical processes. But activities can be focused to encourage pupils to apply their aural acuity in response to what they hear. Approaches to listening can be varied according to the objectives of the activity. For instance, music being listened to at assembly is unlikely to promote differentiated and measurable outcomes. In contrast, focused listening in lessons provides opportunities for pupils to demonstrate their own understanding. Open and closed questions can be devised so that all pupils can respond without losing confidence. Teachers and pupils can then make judgements about what has been heard and how it has been understood.

In offering help in assessing musical attainment, Keith Swanwick has identified a framework of four cumulative layers of musical understanding. His model is applicable to all areas of musical development, but can be illustrated as a basis for the planning of listening activities around the individual needs of pupils (Swanwick, 1997). The four layers can assist teachers to devise questions at an appropriate level and tease out the pupils' understanding. At the first level pupils are able to distinguish between sound qualities and/or instruments. An appropriate question would be to ask the pupils to describe the differences between instruments or voices playing. At the second level pupils can also identify expressive features. A question might be 'what is the effect of the reduced texture in the middle section of the piece?' In addition, at the third level pupils are aware of structural relationships. For instance, 'what happens to the main melody when the chorus returns for the final time?' At the most advanced level pupils can also make independent critical appraisals. An open-ended question here could be 'In what ways does the piece succeed in describing the storm? Give your musical reasons.'

In a mainstream class perhaps only a minority of pupils would be able to respond and answer questions at higher levels. But many teachers have found ways of devising differentiated listening tasks. One teacher proudly boasted a strategy for listening as applicable to pupils in Year 7 as well as those at A Level! A local entry level music course for less able pupils at Key Stage 4 has devised listening tasks that do not require literacy skills for those with severe learning difficulties (Hertfordshire Local Education Authority, 1999). However, further work is needed in the primary music curriculum. Although listening is used extensively, it is not always approached in such a systematic way.

Differentiated composing

Composing in the classroom is an area of music that has transformed our perspectives of teaching and learning. With roots in a child-centred approach that espoused creativity it has provided the basis for naturally differentiated learning where the outcomes are largely determined by the input of the learner. The teacher adopts a facilitator rather than director role and pupils are encouraged to find and use independent learning and social skills as well as musical skills. In many ways this approach has enriched the music curriculum. Composing reaches the internal processes within the art form and often enables pupils to take control of their learning: it can empower them.

But although composing in the curriculum involves all pupils, it does not necessarily address their individual needs. The problem is essentially an organisational one, especially in secondary schools. A false assumption was that, given a composing task, groups of children could work independently in practice rooms, or in groups around the main teaching room and make progress at their own pace by organising their musical ideas together. For many years we pursued this format. Notwithstanding the fact that the approach can be successful, an unacceptable amount of composing in the classroom deteriorated into noisy and lengthy sessions, during which pupils' attention wandered, either because they were out of sight, or because there were simply too many sounds in the environment. A teacher cannot be in all places at once: while the judicious use of practice rooms is a sensible resource, extensive time without teacher input naturally strains pupils' ability to stay on task. Pupils with learning difficulties are most likely to suffer under these circumstances, but those who are easily distracted, or who are content to sit on the sidelines will also be affected. Likewise, there are inevitable limitations to the amount of noise that thirty children can cope with in group work restricted to one classroom. We delude ourselves if we think that pupils, even the most gifted, can select and organise musical sounds with attention to expressive shaping while there is an almighty din around them! A further problem has also arisen from this format. By concentrating on their facilitator role, some teachers are losing their director skills and are less comfortable in teaching whole classes.

The problem was not so pronounced in primary schools because approaches to composing were often generated from whole-class circle activities, or work in the music corner. Group work was also less of a problem in other arts subjects in secondary schools such as drama, mainly because teachers often planned shorter, time-related activities within individual lessons. By learning from good practice in other creative subject areas it may be possible to improve our approach to composing, thus ensuring that we attend to the individual needs of all pupils. The following examples illustrate how, by observing some basic organisational principles, more rigour can be injected into composing.

First, the composing task can be broken down into manageable portions to ensure that pupils have a range of appropriate skills to utilise. For instance, when setting the task it is best to focus on specific devices within a given genre, perhaps by exploring a scale (pentatonic, whole-tone, mode), a riff, or a sequence. In setting words to music, pupils will be able to manage the task more easily if they are taught some basic principles of song forms, word underlay and melodic patterns. Given complete freedom with few limitations, many pupils will struggle to produce coherent musical ideas.

Second, it is necessary to demonstrate the technique or concept being explored. Modelling a task with a whole class, perhaps involving a small group for demonstration purposes, is likely to promote a successful outcome and provides useful input to commence a topic.

Third, consideration should be given to the balance between whole-class, group, paired and individual learning. Should groups be selected on the basis of friendship, gender, ability, or should they be designed to ensure that all pupils have maximum chance to contribute? This may mean that some of the more able pupils are placed with less able and that they will be expected to develop their own personal skills in helping others.

Fourth, the activity needs to be carefully timed: the pupils must be aware that they will be expected to demonstrate their understanding by reporting back to others immediately after the time runs out. Formative assessment, appraisal and pupils' self-assessment are at this point critical techniques in revealing their understanding and ensuring that they are accountable for what they do. Ten or fifteen minutes are often long enough for the pupils to work on a composing task. Without wishing to rush them, a faster pace with realistically high expectations from teacher and pupils will promote speedier progress. It will also enable the learning to be treated more holistically, the composing element being part of a framework that integrates listening and performing.

The setting up, planning and delivery of composing activities are key levers in addressing the individual needs of learners. It may well be that a lack of a systematic approach to composing is a significant factor in the concern about achievement in music at Key Stage 3. George Odam has provided a detailed approach to the teaching of composing, as well as listening and performing in *The Sounding Symbol* (1995). As well as identifying organisational approaches he has emphasised the connections between the processes involved in composing and the way we use our brains. His fascinating research provides sufficient evidence to tell us that the open-ended nature of composing is a wonderful way of helping all individual children find their musical voice and fulfil their expressive potential.

Entitlement and access

These considerations are likely to be irrelevant if they are not based on social inclusion and equality of opportunity. A statement of access in the National Curriculum preserves the entitlement of all children, regardless of cultural background or ability, to a broad and balanced education built on their needs. In many ways music lends itself to providing opportunities for everyone by celebrating cultural diversity. A large number of schools enjoy the diversity of musical styles from around the world, African drumming groups, gamelan and samba bands are being established in many areas, and examination syllabuses now include a greater range of genres. However, we have not yet reached the stage where music education truly recognises and facilitates the cultural traditions that pupils bring with them to school. This is evident when art forms from minority ethnic groups are not promoted in the curriculum. Naturally, in preparing schemes of work it is necessary to ensure a balance of styles. However, pupils should not feel alienated from what they are taught. If we do not make the connections between what and who we teach, how are we respecting pupils as individuals?

The wider curriculum

In a similar way, are we ensuring that all pupils are able to access instrumental/vocal tuition? Although more funds have been injected into music service provision, there is still great disparity of provision in the country. In all this one has to work within what is possible rather than what is ideal. But the point is that we should not assume that we are able to deliver everything, even though we make worthy policy statements about access and entitlement. We still have a long way to go in ensuring that principles of inclusion and equal opportunities are implicit in the way we regard the individual needs of learners in instrumental tuition, ensembles and choirs in the wider curriculum.

Conclusion

In 1914 John Dewey laid down some principles of democracy in education (Dewey, 1916). In his view, young people should be educated, not for the existing state of affairs, but rather to make possible a better future for humanity. At the dawn of a new century we are still being challenged to rethink the purposes, methods and scale of education required for future generations. In the report *All our Futures: Creativity, Culture and Education*, Ken Robinson reaffirmed the importance of creativity as a central point in the curriculum (National Advisory Committee on Creative and Cultural Education, 1999). Music's unique role in developing imagination and creativity is well understood, but we have not yet reached a position whereby all pupils have equal access. The purpose of this chapter has been to argue that entitlement to music education must be preserved at all costs. The music curriculum should be designed to include all children whatever their abilities and background. Opportunities in music should be equally available to all.

Teaching strategies should be built on principles of inclusion, both in the recognition of cultural diversity and in the way that making music is designed around the individual learning needs of the pupils. Teaching music is a difficult and complex skill that requires a balance between subject knowledge and the ability to motivate children. An understanding of how children learn, their individual needs, previous experience and potential is essential in all this. But above all, music teaching must contribute to the humanity of all children so that its impact is sustained throughout their lives. That is a good aim for all schools and music teachers. It should also be our bottom line in ensuring that music in schools meets the individual needs of all pupils.

Questions for discussion

1   Identify different ways of organising and planning music lessons and discuss the advantages and disadvantages in relation to the individual needs of children.
2   How can the individual needs of pupils be addressed in instrumental/vocal group teaching?
3   In what ways can teachers develop a music curriculum that balances the constraints of time with the priority of addressing the individual needs of children?
4   What strategies are particularly effective for teaching children with special educational needs, or the gifted and talented? What problems need to be solved in order to ensure successful outcomes?

References

Department for Education (1994) *Code of Practice on the Identification and Assessment of Special Educational Needs*, London: HMSO.
Department for Education and Employment (2000) *The National Curriculum: Handbook for Teachers in England*, London: HMSO.
Dewey, J. (1916) *Democracy and Education*, New York: Macmillan.
Dickinson, C. and Wright, J. (1993) *Differentiation: A Practical Handbook of Classroom Strategies*, Coventry: National Council for Educational Technology.
Eyre, D. (1997) *Able Children in Ordinary Schools*, London: David Fulton.
Eyre, D. and Fuller, M. (1993) *Year 6 Teachers and More Able Pupils*, Oxford: National Primary Centre.
Hertfordshire Education Authority (1999) *Achievement in Music Project*, Wheathampstead: Hertfordshire County Council.
National Advisory Committee on Creative and Cultural Education (1999) *All Our Futures: Creativity, Culture and Education*, London: NACCCE.
Odam, G. (1995) *The Sounding Symbol: Music Education in Action*, Cheltenham: Stanley Thornes.
Office for Standards in Education (1998) *The Arts Inspected*, Oxford: Heinemann.
Pratt, G. and Stephens, J. (1995) *Teaching Music in the National Curriculum*, Oxford: Heinemann.

Qualifications and Curriculum Authority (2000) *Music: A Scheme of Work for Key Stage 3: Teacher's Guide*, London: QCA/DfEE.

School Curriculum and Assessment Authority (1997a) *Expectations in Music at Key Stages 1 and 2*, London: SCAA.

School Curriculum and Assessment Authority (1997b) *Exemplification of Standards at Key Stage 3*, London: SCAA.

Swanwick, K. (1997) 'Assessing musical quality in the National Curriculum', *British Journal of Music Education* 14, 3, 205–15.

Swanwick, K. (1999) *Teaching Music Musically*, London, Routledge.

UK Council for Music Education and Training (1982) *Musical Giftedness in the Primary School*, London: Pullen Publications.

Vygotsky, L.S. (1978) *Mind in Society*, Cambridge, MA: Harvard University Press.

Ward, D. (1989) 'The arts and special needs', in M. Ross (ed.) *The Claims of Feeling: Readings in Aesthetic Education*, London: The Falmer Press.

Witkin, R. (1974) *The Intelligence of Feeling*, London: Heinemann.

Further reading

Eyre, D. (1997) *Able Children in Ordinary Schools*, London: David Fulton.

National Advisory Committee on Creative and Cultural Education (1999) *All Our Futures: Creativity, Culture and Education*, London: NACCCE.

Odam, G. (1995) *The Sounding Symbol: Music Education in Action*, Cheltenham: Stanley Thornes.

Swanwick, K. (1999) *Teaching Music Musically*, London, Routledge.

Part III

Professional development in music education

16 Teacher development in music

Vanessa Young

> We have come to realize in recent years that the teacher is the ultimate key to educational change and school improvement. The restructuring of schools, the composition of national and provincial curricula, and the development of benchmark assessments – all these are of little value if they do not take the teacher into account. Teachers don't merely deliver the curriculum. They develop it, refine it and interpret it too.
>
> (Hargreaves and Fullan, 1992: ix)

The centrality of the teacher's role in shaping the education of pupils can hardly be in question, and yet the dubious quality and effectiveness of teacher development in the arts generally and in music in particular have long been acknowledged. Gifford (1993) cites a number of national and international reports from the 1980s which express this concern including the important Gulbenkian Foundation Report: Arts in Schools (Calouste Gulbenkian Foundation, 1982). More recently, two new reports: *The Disappearing Arts?* (RSA, 1998) and *All Our Futures: Creativity and Culture in Education* (NACCCE, 1999) have once again drawn our attention to the real crisis both in Initial Teacher Education (ITE) and Continuing Professional Development (CPD).

For primary school teachers, the problems (which seem to be perennial) are well documented, particularly in relation to the non-specialist. Here, it is the combined and compounding issues of teacher competence and confidence that are central. These feelings of inadequacy seem to spring from a conviction on the part of trainees (and later, teachers in service) that they themselves are not musical. This perception is no doubt formed as a consequence of inadequate school experiences of music as pupils (Calouste Gulbenkian Foundation, 1982; Mills, 1993). They then receive inadequate training – both initial and in-service. In school they encounter teachers who also feel inadequate and all parties proceed in turn to provide inadequate experiences for their pupils. Thus the cycle of inadequacy is effectively perpetuated (Gifford, 1993).

The problem for secondary teachers appears to be different, although there are in fact a number of overlapping issues. Most secondary ITE is postgraduate and trainees therefore enter their course with a music degree. Swanwick and Paynter (1993) point out that these degree experiences may well be very varied.

Traditionally, secondary school music teachers were recruited from universities which often adopted a conservatoire model (with an emphasis on individual performing skills), or ignored the role of direct musical experience altogether (placing all their emphasis on musical theory or the history of music). These courses still exist. At the other end of the spectrum, however, trainees may now arrive with expertise in music technology or world musics. Although there have been many changes to music degree programmes over the past thirty years and a 'gradual alignment of institutional objectives' in terms of music degree programmes (Swanwick and Paynter, 1993), the sheer variety of formative experiences could have a significant effect on trainee attitudes and therefore their responses to teacher education. For example, a traditional 'conservatoire' approach where players are prepared for entering the music profession would give a very particular teaching and learning experience with an emphasis on technical mastery and excellence of performance. This would run counter to the nature of music education in mainstream state secondary schools where experience needs to be more rounded musically to include all aspects of musical production and perception as well as reproduction.

In the school context, the secondary trainee or teacher experiences further difficulties in terms of how the subject is perceived; the relative status of class music to extra-curricular/'shop-window' music and the sheer isolation of one-person departments.

One cannot consider the whole topic of teacher development without looking at the educational (and therefore political) climate in which it exists. In the past ten or fifteen years education has undergone unprecedented change. That change has encompassed a number of significant trends which together have created (or perhaps arisen from) a much tougher, harder-edged culture. It is worth examining some of these trends in further detail and considering the implications for teacher development in music.

Prescription: 'the what'

The top-down, prescriptive approach of (interestingly) both previous and current governments has meant that the relative autonomy enjoyed by teachers through the 1970s and early 1980s has become a thing of the past (Hargreaves and Evans, 1997). The National Curriculum now not only dictates content in terms of subjects, areas of study and assessment criteria, but in some cases (i.e. numeracy and literacy hours in primary schools), the recommended methodology to be used by the teacher to 'deliver' the curriculum is perceived as prescribed. With no clearly articulated rationale, certain subjects have been accorded high status, while by definition, others have been marginalised. Even within the 'high status' subjects themselves, certain aspects (i.e. numbers, reading and writing) have been elevated at the further expense of the so-called 'minority' subjects. Music, it could be argued, may be the biggest casualty of this prescription of content, particularly in the primary sector.

This prescription of curriculum has in turn impacted on both ITE and CPD. In ITE, there is a stringent and demanding National Curriculum for primary students in the core subjects, which now includes ICT (Information and Communication Technology), with rigorous assessment standards (DfEE, 1998). In parallel with the impact in schools, this has had devastating effects on other curriculum areas. Most blatantly, hours for foundation subjects have been cut, indeed in some institutions the subjects themselves have been cut (RSA, 1998) and assessments removed or reduced to mere tokens, in order to devote more time to helping students meet the required standards in the core subjects. This is likely to be exacerbated even further with the recent introduction by the TTA (Teacher Training Agency) of highly demanding tests in numeracy, literacy and ICT which both primary and secondary students have to pass in order to obtain qualified teacher status (QTS). Ubiquitous and relentless OFSTED inspections of ITE courses that target English and Maths finally ram the point home just in case HE (Higher Education) institutions entertain alternative priorities. This prescription of content, while affecting all foundation subjects, seems to have had a particular impact on music and the arts. Due to the falling status of these subjects in school, this discipline area is perhaps perceived as the most dispensable in a crowded timetable.

More insidiously but no less seriously, students during school experience can find themselves infected and demoralised by the practice and attitudes of teachers in schools where the foundation subjects have lost their status and position in the curriculum. Again, this has significant implications for music. When questioned, our primary ITE students often report that they have been told not to plan for music as it is 'covered by a specialist', or done '*en masse*', or 'not on the curriculum this term', or even 'not done at all'. Furthermore, they are given little or no opportunity to either observe the teaching of music (good or otherwise) or teach it themselves. This phenomenon in turn affects the content of the trainees' courses. Formal reflection on school practice and experience becomes a hollow affair when so few students have anything to share. Links, therefore, between theory and practice are difficult to make.

In CPD, the situation is also worrying. The setting up of National Priority Areas and the abandonment of local priorities under GEST in 1991 ensured that the agenda for CPD was firmly in government hands; and that the agenda today largely excludes foundation subjects. From LEAS all over the country there are anecdotal reports of cancelled courses. At the last annual conference of the National Association of Music Educators (NAME), LEA members reported the state of in-service training and professional development in their regions:

> Members painted a fairly bleak picture. Many people who are delivering INSET are on short-term contracts. Many have to split their role up to 50% whole school and therefore only 50% on music. It's very hard for teacher colleagues to get out of school and twilight sessions are common. Others are compromising on a 3.00pm start. All INSET has to be related to school development plan priorities. It was felt by some to be sensible to jump on bandwagons like literacy and numeracy.
>
> (NAME, 1999: 35)

And now, what might be considered the last bastion of in-service provision is in danger of falling. Funding for CPD in Higher Education, which previously came from the Higher Education Funding Council for England (HEFCE) is now in the control of the TTA – an agency which in its turn is under government control. The afore-mentioned report: *All Our Futures* (NACCCE, 1999) highlights an analysis of the TTA funding for award-bearing in-service training from 1989 to 2001. It reveals that of the estimated numbers for all the TTA funded courses, only about 1 per cent is to be allocated to courses or modules on art, music, dance or drama. The percentage of that 1 per cent likely to be devoted to music alone presents a startling picture of the dearth of opportunity for professional development currently available to teachers of classroom music.

Pragmatism: 'the how'

As well as the 'what?', the 'how?' of teacher development has also undergone a significant shift. The 'approved' approach is pragmatic rather than ideological; practical rather than theoretical; providing technical training rather than education (Young, 1996; Goodson, 1997). There are plenty of indicators of this trend, most notably the introduction of school-based training for trainee teachers with its emphasis on skills and competencies and the eschewing of critical thinking that it implies. Swanwick and Paynter remarked that: 'we face a continual onslaught by those who seem to regard higher education with suspicion and teacher education as largely unnecessary, beyond having a first degree and picking up a few tips from a mentor "on the job"' (1993: 6). This is particularly problematic for primary generalist trainees in music. Lack of knowledge on the part of mentors (and class teachers) leads to inadequate guidance and a paucity of role models.

The erosion of long-term masters level courses in favour of short-term part-time courses and modularised degrees (Golby, 1994) is another indicator, and seems to reflect the denigration of theory and sidelining of scholarship over the years by those in political power (Goodson, 1997).

This means–end approach to teacher development with its attack on abstract thinking could be construed as a means of distracting teachers from asking 'why?' by concentrating their minds on simply 'how' to deliver the new curriculum (Young, 1999). This is one way of creating a compliant profession. As Helsby observed a number of years ago:

> The current structures for teacher education would not seem tailored to support the necessary development of critical capacities, reflective practice or a meaningful interchange with colleagues to agree a shared set of values and professional knowledge; rather they seem organized to facilitate uncritical implementation of government policies, casting the teacher in the role of 'agent of the NC'.
>
> (1995: 329)

Performance : 'the so-what'

This emphasis on skills training which has now become such big business (Hargreaves and Fullan, 1992) complements the third major trend which is about carrying out (performing) those skills and measurement of performance success. The notion of 'performance' in education is not a new one of course. For a number of years we have been talking about pupils' 'performance' in SATs or comparing schools' 'performances' in the league tables. Students' 'performances' in classrooms have been assessed against tightly defined criteria and teachers' 'performances' both in and out of the classroom have been a key focus for appraisals.

It is only recently, however, that the performances of schools, teachers and pupils have been so inextricably bound up together. With the Performance Management Framework (DfEE, 1999), a teacher's career development is now heavily dependent on measurable performance against measured pupil outcomes which relate to predetermined criteria and targets. All of this is designed to link to the school's development plans, including the OFSTED action plan.

It does not, however, stop there. As Day points out: 'Professional development in the 1990s is no longer a privately pursued optional extra, but a publicly implied accountable part of every teacher's working life' (1993: 87). The key words here are 'publicly' and 'accountable'. In 1996, the TTA Corporate Plan (TTA, 1996) revealed concern that the benefits of CPD were not immediately visible (i.e. measurable). This arose from a MORI survey commissioned by the Agency which suggested that although 89 per cent of teachers thought their experiences were useful or very useful, only 26 per cent of them could claim that they had had any direct impact on their classroom practice. As a result, the TTA proposed that evaluation of CPD should, in future, focus much more specifically on outcomes in the classroom. Recent bids for funding by CPD providers therefore had to justify their proposals in terms of potential outcomes in the classroom. Furthermore, they had to demonstrate how these outcomes would be measured. This presents considerable difficulties for masters level courses which are designed to do more than provide 'tips for teachers'.

One could argue of course that this call for tangible results is a very reasonable expectation. There has to be some accountability for public funds and if CPD is not about improvement in the classroom, what is it for? The TTA are, after all, merely echoing a statement made by the DES over twelve years earlier:

> At the heart of evaluation is the effect on pupils. Given that the ultimate purpose of most INSET is directly or indirectly to improve the quality of learning, the evaluation process must seek ways of showing this to be happening.
>
> (Morrison 1992: 158)

The key phrase here however is 'directly or indirectly'. English (1995) highlights the enormous difficulty of attributing outcomes in the classroom to in-service training activities when he poses questions such as:

- How long might it take any changes to manifest themselves?
- Can it be guaranteed that any observed changes are a direct result of the in-service training?
- Is it likely that a single factor has brought about the change or might there be several contributory factors?

'Deep' (as opposed to 'surface') knowledge needs a 'gestation period' in order for learning to be 'transformed', never mind the time that it could take for that knowledge to manifest itself in terms of pupil outcome. In addition, questions could well be asked about the nature and desirability of the changes and who defines the criteria. It might be more relevant and certainly more realistic to ask where the 'change' is located – in the teachers themselves or in the pupils they teach? – and therefore at what point it should be demonstrated. In 1987 Eraut (quoted in Harland *et al.*, 1993) advised that we should distinguish between 'INSET evaluation' which should focus on the link between INSET and teachers' attitudes and behaviour, and 'school evaluation' which should focus on the link between school policy and practice and pupils' attitudes and achievements. This is a crucial distinction.

Parochialism: 'the where'

The 1980s also saw significant changes in the actual location of the design and provision of CPD activities. Traditional, menu-driven courses, centrally designed and provided, which teachers could opt into (or not), became a thing of the past. Devolution of funds for in-service training dictated that teacher development should be at the very least, school-focused (i.e. on the needs of the school and only on the needs of the individual in so far as they pertained to school needs). In reality, this often meant 'school-based'. The devolution of funds away from LEAs to schools coupled with the five 'Baker Days' as they were then known, led inexorably to training that not only took place on the school premises, but was often led by a member of the school staff. While this approach can be valuable, adopted universally and indiscriminately it can result in cosy, uncritical parochialism. Drawing on their experiences in North America, Bollough and Gitlin argue that: 'Confining continuing professional activities to individual school contexts in this way can inhibit critical thinking by discouraging the scrutiny of institutionally accepted roles and relationships' (quoted in Helsby and McCulloch, 1997: 150).

Three more recent government initiatives have served to underline this trend towards introspection. The first was the introduction of the school development plan not long after the first publication of the National Curriculum. While a useful management tool, with its function of lending coherence to a whole range of internal and external factors, this very 'tidiness' carried the danger of making schools even more 'inward-looking'. The second initiative has already been mentioned – the move towards school-based training of teachers. Swanwick and Paynter (1993) maintain that: 'the assertion that standards of teaching can be improved or even maintained by simply adopting a simple "apprenticeship" model has no empirical or logical support'. The report *All Our Futures* also expresses concern about this model, concluding that: 'Central training sessions are almost always better than subject training which takes place in schools' (NACCCE, 1999). The particular problems encountered by primary trainees within this model in relation to music have already been highlighted.

The third initiative is the TTA's commitment to promoting the idea of teaching as a research-based profession, giving funding directly to teachers to carry out their own classroom-based research. On the face of it, this seems a good idea and goes some way to answering the accusation by Hargreaves and others that educational research (as traditionally carried out in HE institutions) is an 'esoteric activity of little relevance to practitioners' (Hargreaves, 1996). The notion of teacher as researcher implies a process that is:

- reflective;
- teacher-initiated;
- intrinsically motivated;
- sharply relevant to the classroom;
- action-orientated.

It is possible, however, that Stenhouse (1975) who advocated this idea over twenty years ago would have some qualms about this. First, the TTA are only likely to support research that relates to their own (i.e. the government's) agenda. Remembering the problem of prescription, we can see that this does not bode well for music as a subject for classroom research. A more serious problem might, however, be the lack of external perspective that this notion of the lone teacher researcher implies. With an external course, teachers are encouraged to 'step outside' their day-to-day situation. They are required to listen to other approaches, different viewpoints, and alternative strategies. Their existing understanding is deepened, stretched or even challenged by learning about the work of others, including experts and authorities in the field. This new knowledge generates new hypotheses which are then 'tested' in the school setting and further insights into the field of enquiry are gained, allowing a more informed, critical analysis of the work of others. In other words, there is a dialectic between theory and practice which promotes objectivity and which at its best leads to profound change within the teacher (and therefore also within the classroom) that is intrinsically generated and based on knowledge.

Professionalism v proletarianism: 'the who'

So what about the teachers themselves – both pre-service and in-service? What is the effect of all these other trends on them as individuals and on the profession as a whole? Goodson (1997) reminds us that teaching is seen as a profession precisely because of its basis on thorough research and theoretical bodies of knowledge. It implies the freedom to take an unfashionable stance, examine long-held assumptions and challenge the status quo. This notion of professionalism, however, seems to be under threat:

> The meaning of 'professional' has slid away from the rich suggestiveness of say 'professional judgement' or 'professional integrity' towards the narrower end of its continuum, where it is synonymous with 'proficient' as in 'they made a proficient job of it' . . . Professional development covers management training from those teachers already heads or senior teachers and refers primarily to the acquisition and extension of skills needed to implement and assess the national curriculum for all others.
>
> (Golby, 1994: 71)

Helsby and McCulloch go further:

> In these circumstances of apparently increased control of teachers' working lives and potentially low morale for schools, it might be expected that the imposition of an exclusive and tightly prescribed National Curriculum, with a rigorous system of inspection and national testing, would mark the final disintegration of the tradition of professional autonomy in the school curriculum. In this scenario, the teacher's role would be reduced to that of a mere technician, carrying out the plans of others and held accountable for certain quantifiable and pre-specified outcomes.
>
> (Helsby and McCulloch, 1997: 4)

Hargreaves puts it even more strongly when he refers to the deterioration and deprofessionalisation of teachers' work, which he describes as having become routinized and de-skilled:

> In England and Wales, policy makers tend to treat teachers rather like naughty children; in need of firm guidelines, strict requirements and a few short, sharp evaluative shocks to keep them up to the mark. In the United States, the tendency is to treat and train teachers more like recovering alcoholics: subjecting them to step-by-step programs of effective instruction or conflict management or *professional* [my italics] growth in ways which make them overly dependent on pseudo-scientific expertise developed and imposed by others.
>
> (Hargreaves, 1994: xlv)

He points out that this kind of rhetoric of professionalism simply seduces teachers into consorting with their own exploitation.

Helsby (1995) refers to the movement from professionalism to proletarianism. She highlights the work of Bowe and Ball (1992) who distinguish between 'readerly' and 'writerly' texts and corresponding modes of behaviour. 'Readerly' behaviour results from imposed prescription where teachers are (or perceive themselves to be) merely implementers. 'Writerly' behaviour, on the other hand, results from texts in which there is scope for creativity and interpretation. These are useful terms to which we shall return.

In terms of the teacher as an individual, it seems that lack of autonomy has been accompanied by a denial of individualism. The needs of the institution, or more widely, the needs of the system, subsume the needs of the individual. Hartley (1989) points out that professional development is determined by individual needs only in so far as those needs relate to those of officialdom. The problem does not stop there. The prescriptive nature of the changes in education means that there has been little room for dissent. In fact, individual dissent is simply interpreted as resistance (Hargreaves and Fullan, 1992; Smyth, 1995). This issue was underlined recently by the Prime Minister, Tony Blair, who at the Labour Party Conference (October 1999) referred to teachers as 'forces of conservatism' who were standing in the way of educational reform! (O'Hear, 1999).

Discussion

If we reflect on all of these factors and trends we will be forced to see them not as discrete phenomena, but as indicators of an overall shift in ideology over the last two decades that is hugely significant. Moreover, the infra-structure that is now in place is not providing a framework upon which to hang these various initiatives, but rather a web which will tie one initiative inextricably into another, making them mutually dependent and thereby ensuring their continued existence. If this makes rather a sinister image I make no apology. We need to be aware of the political stranglehold the government (and its various quangos) has on education – not just in terms of a vague unease, but in all its problematic minutiae, if we are to begin to see our way out of the rather depressing current situation for teacher development in music. It is difficult to suggest a piecemeal approach with atomised strategies. This is likely to make little impression on the current edifice which is now in place. What is needed is a complete dismantling of existing structures and a return to first principles with regard to teacher development.

First, if we are not to become a profession of mere technicians delivering a centrally prescribed curriculum, we need to maintain a critical perspective. A critical approach demands open and receptive (rather than defensive) schools and teacher training institutions as well as confident teachers and students who have time to reflect and question, in other words, a culture which welcomes enquiry.

This commitment to enquiry in turn implies provisionality and therefore uncertainty. If we support the notion that 'ownership of the curriculum is a prerequisite to understanding' (Kushner, 1994: 42), then the curriculum needs to be regarded as a hypothesis to be tested, rather than as a syllabus to be followed; pedagogical approaches need to be continually 'trialled' rather than prescribed; learning outcomes need to become valued for their unpredictability as much as for their predictability; and we need to once more acknowledge that what we teach is not necessarily what pupils learn (Stenhouse, 1975).

> There are those who choose the swampy lowlands. They deliberately involve themselves in messy but crucially important problems. When asked to describe their methods of inquiry, they speak of experience, trial and error, intuition and muddling through. Other professionals opt for the high ground. Hungry for technical rigour, devoted to an image of solid technical competence, or fearful of entering a world in which they feel they do not know what they are doing, they choose to confine themselves to a narrowly technical practice.
>
> (Day, 1993: 91)

In short, we need to choose the 'swampy lowlands' as opposed to the 'high ground', what Stake *et al.* describe as 'existentialism' rather than 'instrumentalism' (quoted in Kushner, 1994).

All this of course requires teacher (re)empowerment coupled with a great deal of trust – both challenging notions in the current culture of 'top-down' bureaucratic *mistrust*. Some might argue of course that the profession had its chance before education was so comprehensively politicised, and frankly 'blew it'! They might have a point. Certainly, past practices were far from ideal. The legacy of teachers of music who themselves had a poor educational experience at the pre-service as well as in-service stage (Swanwick and Paynter, 1993) and the resultant cycle of inadequacy that that generated have already been discussed. No – we do not want a return to some mythical 'golden age'. What we need to do instead is to identify and reclaim the best practices in this area and give them the attention they deserve in the context of what must be seen as a more enlightened understanding of what constitutes effective learning in music *per se*. It is worth acknowledging that one of the ironies of the current lack of status of music and the arts is the relative lack of scrutiny that this implies. Arguably, this allows for a measure of freedom denied to other 'high-profile' curriculum areas. Let us take advantage of this admittedly double-edged advantage to rethink a few things. What would good teacher education in music look like?

Let us consider two specific examples. The first refers to pre-service teacher education and the second describes an in-service experience. Both I think go some way towards helping us to answer our question.

The first arises from a paper on pre-service teacher training in music for primary generalists in Queensland, Australia. Gifford (1993) reports on an investigation into the effectiveness of a particular music course. Having confirmed the trainees' low perception of their competence and confidence as music teachers, the findings paradoxically suggest that any limited gains in music and music teaching skills from the course were offset by a corresponding dip in the students' enjoyment of music and the value they placed on music education. The research examined a number of factors including pre-course experience, preferred learning styles, the music classroom environment and the music courses themselves. Not only did they find their courses too theoretical, too teacher-directed and the content too difficult to master, but their school experience was not seen as either helpful or relevant in terms of preparing them to teach music in school.

Gifford concludes that the course experienced by these students was very much more akin to what Swanwick (1988) describes as 'instruction' rather than 'encounter'. A key characteristic of 'instruction' is the pre-specification of performance objectives and by implication then, measurement of the expected outcomes. What happens in between them has to be a rational, linear set of instructional strategies to bring these to fruition (a model which we instantly recognise in the current school curriculum). Music education by 'encounter', on the other hand, is more likely to involve experiencing music and developing a relationship with it. With a musical 'encounter' Swanwick argues:

> Music is not dissected into little bits for the purpose of practice or analysis but presented and taken as a whole . . . Graded exercises, sequential steps, programmed learning, instructional objectives, musical analysis and formal assessment procedures are of no consequence here.
>
> (1988: 128)

Gifford proposes for the primary ITE students, experiences much more akin to 'musical encounters'. Central to this notion of musical encounter is music criticism. The role of 'teacher as critic' is therefore much more highly valued than that of 'teacher as model' (i.e. teacher as skilled performer). Evaluation of the success of students within this approach would be based on the extent to which they are able to respond to their pupils' work in an artistic, musically sensitive way.

In making the distinction between 'instruction' and 'encounter', Swanwick is drawing on the work of Stenhouse who argues that higher levels of learning demand from the teacher 'the task of continual refinement of "a philosophical under-standing of the subject he is teaching and learning, of its deep structures and their rationale"' (quoted in Swanwick, 1988: 130).

It is worth noting here that Stenhouse talks about 'teaching and learning' on the part of the teacher in the same breath, as if they were inextricably linked processes – the refinement of teaching being dependent on a continuous process of reflection which deepens understanding which in turn enhances teaching.

In the second example, Kushner (1994) contrasts the National Curriculum and, all that that implies, with collaborative projects involving professional musicians and schools. Kushner sees these two phenomena as representing two ends of the spectrum: the first:

> a nationally engineered, standardized approach to a curriculum devised in non-school settings and imposed with the force of law; the other a locally diverse basket of activities devised in collaborations between teachers and professional musicians in school and joined on a voluntaristic basis.
>
> (Kushner, 1994: 34)

Kushner claims that the most immediate need is for the professional development of music teachers, not for compliance with a national strategy. In contrast to the prescription and implied certainty of the National Curriculum, the 'artist in school' project allows for the curriculum to be negotiated (i.e. to be treated provisionally); it relies on the capacity of the teacher to act as both critic and as professional (in the original sense of the word), reflecting upon and analysing the experience before adapting teaching strategies and content in a continuous cycle of enhanced understanding and curriculum renewal. This approach is, according to Kushner, 'the stuff of professional development'.

There seem to be some parallels to be drawn from these two examples in terms of their recommendations:

- neither rely on pre-specified objectives or outcomes;
- both have the advantages of a locally devised curriculum which is organic and developed continuously by those directly involved in it;
- in both, the involvement of all, whether pupil, student or teacher is concerned in genuine musical activity whether as performers, composers or critics, with the opportunity to develop relationships with the music;
- both involve students and teachers in the 'writerly' as well as 'readerly' behaviours to which we have already alluded;
- both imply the revival of original values of what it means to be a professional.

Conclusion

What we might conclude from this is the holistic, complex and interdependent nature of educational experience for pupil *and* teacher. For too long, perhaps we have separated out the processes of teaching, pupil learning, curriculum development and teacher development in our scramble to make the world of education a tidier (and therefore better) place. If we want to develop deep learning approaches at all levels in education we need to do something more risky. Hallam and Barnett (1999) in relation to higher education, talk about the need to provide students with 'pedagogical space to develop their own ideas, to inject something of themselves into their learning and to make and to substantiate . . . their own truth claims in and on the world' (quoted in Mortimore, 1999: 148). What holds good for students holds good for pupils holds good for teacher development in all its guises – in fact holds good for all *learners*.

In meta-cognitive terms, we need to recognise when and where learning takes place (and indeed when and where that recognition itself takes place). Learning is not something that happens 'out there' when something is done to us. If we trace back and identify those moments when a real shift in our understanding has taken place, we realise that these are 'eureka' moments which happen often when we least expect them, but which move us qualitatively onwards in terms of our understanding. It is impossible to prescribe these moments, plan for them or even predict them. The best that teachers can do is to provide the optimum conditions for these moments to take place. This applies at all levels whether we are teachers of children, teachers of trainees or teachers of teachers.

This does not mean, however, 'lighting the blue touch paper and standing well back' in a 'non-interventionist' kind of way. It does not mean that there is no place for instruction or feedback. Nor, importantly, does it imply that all teacher development should take place within the school context. If a measure of criticality is high up on the agenda, then this implies an injection of ideas that challenge existing assumptions. We do, however, need to think carefully about where this 'external' input comes from. As Day (1993) points out, schools often lack the culture, teachers often lack the energy or the knowledge, consultants are often ruled by the profit margin and LEAs are often forced to peddle the latest government initiative. Even HE is subject to commercial and accountability pressures.

Ultimately, wherever the provision for teacher development is located, we need to transform our understanding of it from a training model to a learning model. This implies involving teachers once again in 'writerly' behaviours. We do have an official national (and therefore externally prescribed) curriculum for music it is true, but one could argue that the main value of this is the extent to which its formulation has involved all those concerned with music education in discussion and debate. Any future value therefore lies in its interpretation and therefore 're-writing'. Many people in education, understandably, are crying out for stability and an end to constant change and the introduction of new initiatives. On the contrary, I would argue that the curriculum – whether in schools, LEAs or teacher training institutions – should *never* stop changing; it should *never* be finished; we should *never* be satisfied. Change and development are perceived as threatening precisely because they are imposed by others and therefore imply a loss of control. We must all reclaim the initiative and adopt 'writerly' behaviours, re-writing the curriculum every time we engage with it so that development comes not courtesy of the DfEE, OFSTED, TTA or even QCA, but of ourselves.

Questions for discussion

1   How do we provide the optimum conditions for those 'eureka' moments which move us qualitatively onwards in terms of our understanding?
2   If teacher development experiences are not to be outcome-led, how do we ensure that music teachers are 'accountable'?
3   What strategies can we use to make sure that evaluation of teacher development focuses not on that which is easily measurable, but on that which is significant?

References

Bradley, H., Conner, C. and Southworth, G. (1994) *Developing Teachers Developing Schools*, London: David Fulton Publishers in association with the University of Cambridge Institute of Education.

Bullough, R.V. and Gitlin, A.D. (1994) 'Challenging teacher education as training: four propositions', *Journal of Education for Teaching* 20, 1, 67–81.

Calderhead, J. and Gates, P. (1993) *Conceptualising Reflection in Teacher Development*, London: The Falmer Press.

Calouste Gulbenkian Foundation (1982) *The Arts in Schools*, London: Gulbenkian Foundation.

David, T. (ed.) (1999) *Teaching Young Children*, London: Paul Chapman Publishing.

Day, C. (1993) 'Reflection: a necessary but not sufficient condition for professional development', *British Education Research Journal* 19, 1, 83–93.

DfEE (1998) Circular Number 4/98 *Teaching: High Status, High Standards*, London: DfEE.

DfEE (1999) *Performance Management Framework*, London: HMSO.

English, R. (1995) 'INSET: initiating change or merely supporting it?', *British Journal of In-service Education* 21, 3, 295–301.

Erant, M., Pennycuick, D. and Radnor, H. (1987) *The Local Evaluation of INSET: A Meta-evaluation of TRIST*, Sussex, University of Sussex.

Gifford, E. (1993) 'Teachers: old problems, new insights and possible solutions', *British Journal of Music Education* 10, 1, 33–46.

Golby, M. (1994) 'Doing a proper course: the present crisis in advanced courses', *Teacher Development*, May, 69–73.

Goodson, I. (1997) 'Trendy theory and teacher professionalism', *Cambridge Journal of Education* 27 1, 7–22.

Hanley, B. (1993) 'Music teacher's education: new directions', *British Journal of Music Education* 10, 1, 9–21.

Hargreaves, A. (1994) *Changing Teachers, Changing Times: Teacher's Work and Culture in the Postmodern Age*, London: Cassell.

Hargreaves, A. and Evans, R. (eds) (1997) *Beyond Educational Reform: Bringing Teachers Back In*, Buckingham: Open University Press.

Hargreaves, A. and Fullan, M. (1992) *Understanding Teacher Development*, New York: Cassell.

Hargreaves, D.H. (1996) *Teaching as a Research-based Profession: Possibilities and Prospects*, TTA Annual Lecture, London: TTA.

Harland, J., Kinder, K. and Keys, W. (1993) *Restructuring INSET: Privatisation and its Alternatives*, Slough: NFER.

Hartley, D. (1989) 'Beyond collaboration: the management of professional development policy in Scotland 1979–89', *Journal of Education for Teaching* 15, 3, 211–23.

Hayes, D. (ed.) (1996) *Debating Education*, Canterbury: Canterbury Christ Church College.

Helsby, G. and McCulloch, G. (1997) *Teachers and the National Curriculum*, London: Cassell.

Hoyle, E. (1974) 'Professionality, professionalism and control in teaching', *London Educational Review* 3, 2, Summer, 13–19.

Kushner, S. (1994) 'Against better judgement: how a centrally prescribed music curriculum works against teacher development', *International Journal of Music Education* 23, 34–45.

Mills, J. (1993) *Music in the Primary School*, Cambridge: Cambridge University Press.

Morrison, M. (1992) 'Time for INSET, time to teach: evaluating school-based development in an infants school during a period of change', *Teacher Development*, October, 157–69.

Mortimore, P. (ed.) (1999) *Understanding Pedagogy*, London: PCP.

NACCCE (1999) *All Our Futures: Creativity and Culture in Education*, London: DfEE.

NAME (1999) *Conference Report '99*, National Association of Music Educators 3, 35–7.

O'Hear, A. (1999) *Times Educational Supplement*, 29 October, letter.

RSA (1998) *The Disappearing Arts?* London: Calouste Gulbenkian Foundation.

Smyth, J. (ed.) (1995) *Critical Discourses on Teacher Development*, London: Cassell.

Stenhouse, L. (1975) *An Introduction to Curriculum Research and Development*, London: Heinemann.

Swanwick, S. (1988) *Music, Mind and Education*, London: Routledge.

Swanwick, S. and Paynter, J. (1993) 'Teacher education and music education: an editorial view', *British Journal of Music Education* 10, 1, 3–8.

TTA (1996) *Corporate Plan*, London: TTA.

Young, V. (1996) 'Issues in staff development: the school experience', in D. Hayes (ed.) *Debating Education: Issues for the New Millennium?*, Canterbury: Canterbury Christ Church College.

Young, V. (1999) 'Continuing professional development', in T. David (ed.) *Teaching Young Children*, London: Paul Chapman Publishing Ltd.

Further reading

Day, C., Calderhead, J. and Denicolo, P. (1993) *Research on Teacher Thinking: Understanding Professional Development*, London and Washington, DC: The Falmer Press.

Goodson, I.F. and Hargreaves, A. (eds) (1996) *Teachers' Professional Lives*, London and Washington, DC: The Falmer Press.

McBride, R. (ed.) (1996) *Teacher Education Policy*, London and Washington, DC: The Falmer Press.

17 Comparative perspectives

Philip Tate

Introduction

One of the major benefits of studying aspects of music education in a country different from our own is that it helps us to reflect on, and better understand, our own music education provision. It may be that one wishes to address a particular problem in one's own system of music education by looking at other approaches. Such study could lead eventually to possible recommendations for the teaching and learning of music or changes in policy. Comparative music education as a field of study is also valuable in its own right, contributing, through discussion of common issues, to greater international understanding in music education.

It is important to recognise that many studies which have been classified under a comparative education heading are not actually comparative: 'Such studies do not compare, but rather describe, analyse or make proposals for a particular aspect of education in *one* country other than the author's own country' (Postlethwaite, 1988: xvii). In order to accommodate such single nation studies the British Comparative Education Society changed its name in 1983 to the British Comparative and International Education Society. A reading of the *International Journal of Music Education* from its inception reveals few genuinely comparative studies. Indeed, the 'comparative segment' established by Laurence Lepherd in the May 1985 issue continued for only two further issues. Of course, systematic comparative research is more difficult than single country study because the researcher has in effect to conduct, analyse, and evaluate at least two sets of data before drawing conclusions.

Kemp and Lepherd (1992), however, have been critical of some international and comparative music education research and suggest a major problem in the field is that some researchers have not given enough attention to the development of appropriate theory and methodology for their work. It is arguable that single nation studies, which are not overtly comparative, will, whether consciously or not, involve the writer (and subsequent readers) in making comparisons. At a professional level care needs to be taken with informal comparing especially if one decides to implement changes in practice on the basis of such reports. For Kemp and Lepherd such a situation is unsatisfactory because this kind of approach lacks the rigour necessary for meaningful and objective comparison. Because of the difficulties associated with comparative work, attention has been given to the possibility of developing a comparative education methodology.

If one is to evaluate another country's provision for music education and compare it with our own, it is important to be aware of some of the 'perils' as well as the 'promise' (Maclean, 1992) of comparative work. The first part of this chapter introduces the field of comparative education. Following this, some international and comparative music education studies are reviewed and, finally, issues relevant to those who may engage in such research in the future are discussed.

Comparative education as a field of study

Historical views of comparative education reveal an interesting line of development beginning in ancient times (Noah and Eckstein, 1969; Brickman, 1988). It is, however, within the last 200 years that formal comparisons between education systems have been made. Three major contributions to the field of comparative methodology since World War II can be found in the works of Bereday (1964), Noah and Eckstein (1969) and Holmes (1965, 1981). Although differing in approach, each represents an attempt to develop the field in terms of method rather than content (Kelly *et al.*, 1982).

Bereday, in his *Comparative Method in Education* (1964) gave importance to the systematic collection and cataloguing of data, interpretation and juxtaposition leading to comparison. For him comparative study was, although inevitably involving description, more than simply listing factual information; the researcher should attempt to explain similarities and differences through careful analysis. Hypotheses can be generated by themes emerging from data or alternatively by what he terms a 'problem approach' which involves the selection of a theme or topic whose variance is examined within each of the educational systems under scrutiny. He considered residence in countries being studied as important in order to give the researcher as much understanding of the context (e.g. 'foreign' language and culture) in which he or she is working. This would, he believed, help a researcher avoid potential bias which an inquiry conducted from afar might attract.

In their *Towards a Science of Comparative Education* Noah and Eckstein (1969), while acknowledging Bereday's work, offered an alternative approach to method. Unlike Bereday they emphasised the importance of early consideration of hypothesis without which they felt studies would lack clear focus. With clear hypotheses specific data can be collected, minimising problems of managing large amounts of redundant data which may result from a more general approach. Their scientific method, critical of qualitative approaches, favoured quantitative methods which they believed would lead to greater objectivity in analysis and comparison and minimise cultural bias. They did not share Bereday's concern for the need of the researcher to acquire linguistic proficiency or experience in the 'foreign' culture under investigation. Other writers on comparative education were critical of approaches which emphasised quantitative methods. Stenhouse (1979) argued that although statistical accounts of educational systems might claim greater objectivity, they lose the critical perspective of the researcher which is inevitably linked to his or her cultural background.

The work of Brian Holmes draws on the ideas of Popper and Dewey and his approach to method is explained in his *Problems in Education: A Comparative Approach* (1965) and *Comparative Education: Some Considerations of Method* (1981). Holmes bases the latter on articles he wrote during the previous twenty-five years and the volume offers a comprehensive insight into his work in comparative education. Holmes believed that Dewey's problem-solving approach could be applied in comparative education contexts. The stages of his method may be summarised as (a) the identification and analysis of 'a problem' allowing the researcher to focus on particular kinds of relevant data; (b) classification of data under various categories including aims, finance, structure and organisation, curricula and teacher education; (c) identification of 'ideal-normative' models to assist comparison of overt aims and possibly different internal actions and attitudes; and (d) analysis and comparison leading to prediction of the impact on practice which adopted or proposed policy might have (Holmes, 1981). Holmes also rejected the positivist approach implicit in the work of Noah and Eckstein because their 'techniques are based on the assumption that general propositions are valid regardless of the context in which they are to be applied as policy' (ibid.: 68). Prediction of outcomes is a key element in Holmes' belief that the comparatavist is able to contribute to piecemeal social engineering, as suggested by Popper, rather than large-scale social planning.

The inter-disciplinary nature of comparative education has led to some difficulty in the field establishing itself in its own right. Broadfoot suggests that comparative education is 'not a discipline: it is a context' allowing for 'the interaction of perspectives arising out of a number of social science disciplines' (1977: 133). The debate about method has, since the early 1980s, shifted towards an acceptance that it is unlikely that there is or should be an 'ideal' way to conduct comparative education research. This shift, together with other factors, has contributed to a widening of approaches to comparative study. For example the questioning of structural-functionalism and the acceptance of conflict theory have moved theorists away from earlier attempts to define a single methodology focusing instead on the content of the field (Kelly *et al.*, 1982). Furthermore, the growing interest of comparative researchers in other research traditions such as anthropology and ethnology has led to the development of alternative approaches which were more suitable for studies looking at actual teaching and learning processes.

International and comparative music education

Within the field of music education one finds that an interest in international and comparative music education is not restricted to the twentieth century. In the eighteenth and nineteenth centuries there were a number of musicians and music educators interested in music education practice in foreign lands. In 1770 Burney began the first of his tours to gather information for a general history of music. He visited schools in Venice for the training of musicians and sought to replicate such an institution in England. He was also impressed with a school in Bohemia where 'little children of both sexes from five to eleven years old . . . were reading, writing, playing on violins, hautbois, bassoons and other instruments' (Burney, quoted in Rainbow, 1990: 123). Lowell Mason, the pioneer of American music education, visited Europe in 1837 to observe methods of teaching music and search for materials to assist him in the development of his singing curriculum for the Boston school system.

John Spencer Curwen and John Hullah at the end of the nineteenth century both travelled abroad widely to investigate singing in schools and their findings were published in two reports. These reports have more recently been published under the title *School Music Abroad* in the *Classic Texts in Music Education* series introduced by Bernarr Rainbow. Curwen was keen to compare standards in singing between children in England and those in other countries and also to see if teachers abroad faced similar difficulties encountered by their counterparts in England. Curwen was also interested in evaluating the 'extravagant' claims made with reference to the excellence of school music in Germany – claims which were, he concluded, unfounded. Both these music educators saw a clear purpose for their investigation hoping that the reports they made 'will serve their purpose if some who are in charge of the singing in our schools gather hints as to the direction which their work should take' (Curwen, 1901: 26).

In 1887 Curwen visited the US cities of Albany, Chicago and Philadelphia. In Philadelphia he found, due to the continuing influence of the Quakers, that apart from in kindergarten classes, singing was not present in the public schools he visited. In Chicago he observed, in a number of high schools, the kind of behaviour problems which may ring true with music educators today. Problems included a lack of interest in singing and a certain 'listlessness'. Interestingly Curwen perceived a mismatch between the content of lessons and the age of the students as the cause of the problems. He suggested a solution – exercises in diction, time, tune, harmony analysis, form analysis, advanced modulator work and weekly sight reading tests, and then 'the pupils emulation would be aroused' (ibid.: 156). The observations he made were quite detailed and addressed issues of what might be termed nowadays as those of 'quality', commenting on teacher expertise, singing tone, intonation, style, feeling and taste.

What these music educators had in common was a desire to observe practice in other countries with a view to enhancing or improving that in their own. The possibility, given the different cultural circumstances, of borrowing ideas from one country and transplanting them into another is called 'cultural borrowing'. The term is not necessarily a negative one; indeed, it is reasonable to agree that the aim of comparative education and comparative music education is, as mentioned earlier, to gain insight into one's own practices through looking at another's. This issue is discussed below and relates to another issue, namely, that of cultural bias.

A framework for studies in comparative and international music education

Kemp and Lepherd (1992) provide a useful model or framework for the classification of international music education studies both single nation and comparative. This framework included global statements, distinctions between systemic and non-systemic cultural transmission.

Global statements

'Global Statement' type studies address those issues in music education which are of relevance to an international audience. For example, a group of papers by various well-known music educators introduced by Dobbs and Kemp (1997) published in the *International Journal of Music Education*, attempted to clarify issues regarding music as a 'universal language'.

Systemic and non-systemic cultural transmission

Here a distinction is made between systemic studies, that is formal systems of music education which exist within a country's overall education system, and non-systemic studies, i.e. music education which does not involve formal tuition in schools. This model does not of course preclude some overlap and studies could explore the relationship between the two. For example, a possible area for study could be to look at the relationship between 'in school' and 'out of school' instrumental tuition. Campbell (1989), in her article 'Music learning and song acquisition among Native American Indians', although focusing on non-systemic approaches does discuss possible implications of her findings for music educators in schools.

Systemic education: overview and thematic

Kemp and Lepherd divide systemic education studies into overview or thematic in a national context. These studies may be either single-system studies or comparative. As compared to single-system national or thematic studies, comparative studies, of either kind, have been fewer, although in single-system studies informal comparisons may be found. Some of the well-known major single-system studies are Choksy (1974) of Hungary, Taylor (1979) of England, Gates (1988) of the USA and Lepherd (1988, 1994) of China and Australia. Lepherd has played an active role in seeking to develop a suitable methodology for such studies based for the most part on that of Holmes (1981) and Bereday (1964) mentioned earlier. Lepherd has also edited a publication *Music Education in International Perspective* (1995) in which music educators from seven countries (one from each of the main geographical regions), including the USA and England, using the same approach, give accounts of their respective country's music education system. Although using the same framework, the contributors display obvious differences in writing style and approach. Lepherd acknowledges this and sees it as a positive situation leading to more lively and interesting reading. Although no attempt is made at comparison, the uniformity of presentation enables that possibility. It should be noted that although Lepherd has done much towards trying to develop the field of comparative and international music education his own work has focused almost exclusively on single-system studies.

Thematic studies

In contrast to comprehensive overviews, other smaller studies may focus on particular themes. Within this classification Kemp and Lepherd include smaller papers which may include brief overviews, e.g. Abdoo (1984). More recent examples may be found in Kiester (1993) of Japan, Karjala (1995) of England, and Brahmstedt and Brahmstedt (1997) of China. Again, these single nation studies contain a great deal of description with some informal comparisons or suggestions for the researchers' home country. For example, in her 'A look at Japanese music education' Kiester (1993) suggests that the USA should adopt aspects of the Japanese system with the aim of achieving greater rigour in sequencing. Her study provides some interesting detail and description although there is little on the quality of the teacher–pupil interaction. Photographs of students in uniforms prompt questions regarding the range of schools visited and how the apparent lack of cultural diversity found in Japanese schools might affect issues regarding music education.

One of the more interesting reports is Reimer's (1989) overview of music education in China. In the article he sketches a broad outline of the country's music education system, making appropriate disclaimers regarding sampling due to the vastness of the country and the schools he was 'allowed' to visit. As an advocate of 'aesthetic music education' or 'comprehensive musicianship' Reimer evaluates the music teaching he observed in Chinese schools in these terms. He is critical of the approach found in many Chinese schools where the music curriculum is dominated by an emphasis on skills rather than what he terms 'aesthetic education'. He devotes a significant portion of his article to comparing music education standards and programmes in China with those in the USA. The report is lively and, despite possible criticism for being rather subjective, shows that there is tension between just recounting of facts, which some studies tend to do, and more interesting analysis and comparison.

As mentioned earlier, genuine comparative music education studies, whether overview or thematic, are rarer than single nation studies. Kemp and Lepherd cite a number of comparative studies which research a variety of areas, for example, teacher education (Cykler, 1960), and the professional training of musicians (Bartle, 1988, 1990). Stowasser (1993) describes her observations of music education in Australia, North America and Great Britain. She makes it clear that her report is qualitative in nature and not systematic and hopes that it raises issues for future discussion. She identified an emphasis on creative work in British secondary schools and noticed that while there was evidence of exemplary work in this area there was a wide disparity in the quality of such work between different schools. In America she identified an emphasis on performance at the expense of more comprehensive music programmes at secondary level.

Richmond (1997) compared and contrasted the US experience of universal access to music education with public music education practices in England, Germany and Japan. In this research, Richmond drew on research data from two published reports for his comparison (National Endowment for the Arts, 1993 and National Center for Educational Statistics, 1995). The comparison showed that provision for arts education could be implemented in both highly and less centralised systems of educational delivery. As a result of his comparison Richmond was able to put forward the view that the decentralised nature of American schooling need not be a barrier to equality of provision in music education.

There are also highly specific experimental comparative studies, which may be included in this category, e.g. Costa-Giomi's study of the recognition of chord changes in 4- and 5-year-old American and Argentine children (1994) and Moore's (1987) study on the effects of age and nationality on auditory/visual sequential memory of English and American children. More recently Hentschke (1993) investigated and compared responses to music of English and Brazilian children, finding the former were able to describe music which they heard in richer detail and with more evidence of musical understanding than the latter.

Campbell's wide-ranging study *Lessons from the World* (1991) focuses on the concepts of ear training and improvisation. She presents a history of the development of the (systemic) American public (state) school music and accompanying teaching and learning practices and compares them with traditional (non-systemic) practice from a range of cultural samples representing parts of Asia, Africa and the West. She demonstrates a rationale for and the importance of ear training and improvisation in all musics and most importantly, in the final section of her book, offers pragmatic suggestions regarding how these skills may be developed in the contemporary music classroom and studio.

Issues to consider

Perhaps one of the greatest barriers to meaningful international and comparative music education studies is the tendency to oversimplify and make inappropriate generalisations. An awareness of the issues presented below, by researchers wishing to research in this field, will help to minimise these tendencies.

The notion of comparison itself does involve some consideration of the question 'what is comparable?'. Satori refers to the discussion about apples and pears; traditionally they are not comparable. However, in some respects they are (fruits), and in others they are not (shape). He suggests that meaningful comparison can only take place between entities which share similarities as well as differences. There comes a point when the differences between entities may be so great that sensible and meaningful comparison becomes difficult, if not impossible. Satori sees careful classification as the most effective means of differentiating between what is similar and what is different. It follows from this that would-be comparative music education researchers should give careful consideration to their choice of what to compare.

Educational comparisons

In England the concept of educational comparisons has generated much discussion, some of it acrimonious, about the possibility of comparing various forms of educational achievement (for example, school examination results). Politicians in the late 1980s began to realise the political use to which 'comparisons' could be put. Maclean, for example (1992) points out that Kenneth Baker, the then Education Secretary, used international league tables in a press release in 1988 to question standards of mathematics teaching in England and Wales. Arguing from the perspective of Holmes, Maclean draws attention to the assumption in the comparison that mathematics was 'a universal and culturally neutral subject', an assumption which, he claims, was false, thus making the comparison flawed.

More recently in a periodical report we find that 'England beats France' (Pyke, 1998: 1) – not at football, but at reading, writing and arithmetic at the primary level; such comparisons could be used to confirm existing policy affecting possible future curriculum development initiatives, i.e. England is 'better' than France in these areas, thus there is less pressure on the 'winning' side to improve. This illustrates the more controversial side of comparison: the 'peril' rather than 'promise' of comparative education (Maclean, 1992). It seems unlikely that such international comparisons in classroom musical achievement would ever attract such a newspaper headline. However, looking for similarities and differences between music education systems and teaching can be of value, providing that any such comparisons are mindful of methodological issues.

Cultural bias and cultural borrowing

Every researcher belongs to a culture. This may limit his or her ability to see other cultures objectively, leading to the possibility of cultural bias which Bereday called 'the plague of comparative methodology'. For example, Maclean (1992) is critical of a study of teaching and learning in New York City schools by HMI because, he suggests, they approached their evaluation as if they were undertaking an inspec-tion in an English school. Comparative music education researchers may question whether it is appropriate to use, say, Western models of music education as a 'universal' conceptual framework with which to evaluate school music in all parts of the world. Westerlund (1999), for example, asks whether Western music educators are able to develop the necessary understandings to appreciate the 'modes of meaning which constitute traditional African Music'. Campbell (1989) draws our attention to Sloboda's view that there might be some universal cognitive basis for music which transcends individual cultures, but cautions that one still needs to consider that the function of music may differ in varying cultural contexts. One should, where possible, share interpretations of observations with those one has observed. It is crucial that one's values and beliefs are made explicit when conducting research in other cultures to avoid ethnocentric bias in the interpretation of findings. One possible way of avoiding problems of cultural bias or misunderstanding may be to undertake joint research which includes members from countries being investigated as part of the research team.

Another related issue is the extent to which educational practices in one country may be 'transplanted' into another – so-called 'cultural borrowing'. As mentioned earlier, one of the main advantages of comparison with foreign approaches is that it enables us to critique our own practice in the light of another. It may well be that we identify particular practices, methods, curricula or indeed whole schemes of music education in which we see the potential for transplantation. The model for the adoption of class instrumental teaching in American schools is a good example of 'cultural borrowing', the idea coming, as it did, from England. In 1910 Mitchell observed a highly successful string-teaching programme called the Maidstone Movement. The movement, sponsored by an instrumental manufacturing and music publishing company, began in Maidstone, England, and over a period of time spread to some three thousand schools. Mitchell successfully transplanted the idea in Boston public schools in 1914. The practice resulting from these ideas can still be found in American public schools today (Deverich, 1987). The ideas of Kodaly and Orff are perhaps some of the best examples of methods which have been transplanted into many different countries. It is important to recognise though that *adaptation* has been necessary for successful transplantation. The 'Hungarian' nature of the content of Kodaly's method did not readily transfer to other cultural locations – indeed, regarding American use of his method, Kodaly himself addressed the issue of adaptation suggesting that content could be based on the large collection of American folk songs to be found in the Library of Congress (Keene, 1982). When making recommendations which involve cultural borrowing, researchers need to also make clear suggestions as to how such 'borrowing' might successfully take place by giving ideas regarding adaptation.

Recently the 'transplantation' of Western approaches to music education as a result of colonialism has been questioned. For example, Oehrle (1993) suggested that overseas approaches to South African music education still had an inappropriately large influence on practice to the detriment of traditional approaches. Akapelwa (1989) investigated the processes of Western ideas on human musicality and compared them with those of indigenous music in postcolonial Zambia, finding some incompatibility. Wiggins (1996) investigating music instruction and practice in Ghana found that certain verbal concepts used in Western music to assist in musical study were inapplicable when studying traditional Ghanaian music.

It is possible working in a global environment that some words do not exist or meanings are clouded through translation into different cultural contexts. An example is found in the work of Muckle (1987) who noted that Russian music teachers in general schools held a different concept of 'creativity' to that of their English counterparts. For the Russian teachers, creativity related to 'a quality of response' rather than creating new pieces of music. Even in a study between England and America, use and meaning of language need to be considered. My own research comparing school music in New Jersey and South East England showed that the New Jersey music teachers, unlike their English counterparts, tended to equate 'composing' strongly with the possession and/or development of traditional notation skills. Such considerations would be important in, say, survey research where questions relating to composing would need to take into account concepts such as improvisation, working by ear, with or without notation, and whether standard and/or non-standard student devised notation is employed.

Comparison may be problematic when concepts, variables, etc. are placed in classifications which differ with respect to the 'same' categories of data leading to 'false comparison'. For example, a comparative study between schools in, say, America and England where age was an important variable, would need to take into account that grades do not correspond with English 'years'; this problem is easy to resolve. However, we encounter further difficulty when we find that, unlike in the English system, American students may be 'held back' from proceeding to the next grade if their work is unsatisfactory. In other words grade does not necessarily correspond to age in the American system. Matching samples may also cause difficulties due to differences in the structure and organisation of schools, making it difficult to give unambiguous cross-cultural meaning to such terms as 'comprehensive school', 'high school', and 'college'. Again, using an America/England example, the American 'middle school' age range differs with the English middle school and there is no equivalent in the English system of the 'junior high school'. The use of the term 'secondary school' could be misleading, indicating as it does a variety of year/grade structures in different country settings.

Some of the more practical problems may involve, as in my own recent study, management of large amounts of data, and also the issue of travel costs. While experience of the 'foreign' culture is an important preliminary part of the research process, finding the time to actually do it may be problematic. One possible avenue which offers considerable opportunity for comparative research is through international exchange programmes for academics.

Conclusion

Studies in comparative and international music education have tended to focus on single nation studies at the macro level. However, it is the quality of the musical experience in the classroom which ultimately determines the success or failure of any music curriculum 'in action'. There is, therefore, a gap between the large-scale 'national system' approach, as exemplified in the work of, for example, Lepherd (1988) and an often less systematic exploration of the musical transaction in classrooms, e.g. Reimer (1989) or Kiester (1993). The value of 'national system' or 'nation–state' approaches is not in question as they do offer insights into important defining parameters of music education at national level. Future studies, however, could move towards bridging the gap between macro and micro studies. Those interested in researching the actuality of classrooms will benefit from an understanding of approaches used by those undertaking large-scale nation–state studies. Schools do not operate in a vacuum and classroom-based research which gives due attention to setting studies in appropriate national/cultural contexts will be stronger than those which do not. Although it has been shown that there is some controversy regarding the relative merits of quantitative as against qualitative methods, researchers should feel free to use whatever methods best suit their purpose; polarisation of methods is counterproductive and a variety of methods might be used in one study.

Considerable resources are devoted to music education in many countries of the world and some have developed national curriculum initiatives. As has been shown, comparative music education is a field of study which offers excellent opportunities for understanding music education practice as it exists in its many forms and cultural contexts throughout the world. Music educators have at times been accused of being rather insular, however, an interest in aspects of music education as implemented in other countries does at the very least guard against myopia and self-absorption. The International Society for Music Education has recently designed new strategies to increase membership of the organisation and build 'a world-wide community of music educators' (ISME, 1999). The Society's publication, *The International Journal of Music Education* (*IJME*), continues to be a major forum for the presentation of studies of interest to an international audience. Lepherd noted in 1992 that although international studies in music education have increased since the 1950s, systematic comparative study in the field was relatively underdeveloped – the same holds true today. It would be a positive step forward to see an increase in the number of quality *comparative* studies in the field published in the *IJME* and other journals with an international readership. Such studies will have the potential to play an important part in improving international music education practice in the twenty-first century.

Questions for discussion

1   Choose an aspect of music education which would be open to international comparative investigation. Design a conceptual framework for such a study, including possible variables and suggestions for appropriate methodologies.
2   Discuss whether it is really possible to avoid 'cultural bias' in international comparative music studies. To what extent might an awareness of the concept help, or perhaps hinder, contemporary comparative work in this area?
3   Consider the advantages and disadvantages of adopting a comparative (at least two countries), rather than single country approach to international music studies. Are there particular types of research questions which would be served better by one or other of these approaches? Give examples.

References

Abdoo F.B. (1984) 'Music education in Japan', *Music Educators Journal* 70, 6, 52–6.
Akapelwa, E.Z.M. (1989) 'Problems of music education: a comparative study', PhD diss., Queen's University, Belfast.
Bartle, G. (1988) 'The grass on the other side of the fence . . . two contrasting models for the organisation of music education for the beginner performer', in J. Dobbs (ed.) *International Music Education: ISME Yearbook Vol. XV*, 196–202.

Bartle, G. (1990) 'How 1,250,000,000 people train their performing musicians: a microscopic view of the training of pianists, opera singers, orchestral musicians, conductors, organists and sound recording technicians in six countries', *International Journal of Music Education* 15, 31–6.

Bereday, G.Z.F. (1964) *Comparative Method in Education*, New York: Holt.

Brahmstedt, H. and Brahmstedt, P. (1997) 'Music education in China', *Music Educators Journal* 83, 6, 28–30.

Brickman, W.W. (1988) 'History of comparative education', in T.N. Postlethwaite (ed.) *The Encyclopaedia of Comparative Education and National Systems of Education*, Oxford: Pergamon Press, pp. 3–7.

Broadfoot, P. (1977) 'The comparative contribution – a research perspective', *Comparative Education* 13, 2, 133–7.

Campbell, P.S. (1989) 'Music learning and song acquisition among Native American Indians', *International Journal of Music Education* 14, 24–31.

Campbell, P.S. (1991) *Lessons from the World: A Cross-cultural Guide to Music Teaching and Learning*, New York: Schirmer Books.

Choksy, L. (1974) *The Kodaly Method*, Englewood Cliffs, NJ: Prentice-Hall.

Costa-Giomi, E. (1994) 'Recognition of chord changes by 4 and 5 year old American and Argentine children', *Journal of Research in Music Education* 42, 1, 68–85.

Curwen, J.S. (1901) *School Music Abroad*, London: J. Curwen and Sons.

Cykler, E. (1960) 'Some salient areas of comparison in the training of music teachers in Austria, Germany, and in the United States of America', *International Music Education* 2, 31–5.

Deverich, R. (1987) 'The Maidstone Movement – influential British precursor of American public school instrumental classes', *Journal of Research in Music Education* 35, 1, 39–55.

Dobbs, J. and Kemp, A.E. (1997) 'Editorial', *International Journal of Music Education* 29, 1.

Gates, J.T. (ed.) (1988) *Music Education in the United States: Contemporary Issues*, Tuscaloosa: University of Alabama Press.

Hentschke, L. (1993) 'Musical development: testing a model in the audience-listening setting', PhD diss., University of London, Institute of Education, London.

Holmes, B. (1965) *Problems in Education: A Comparative Approach*, London: Routledge and Kegan Paul.

Holmes, B. (1981) *Comparative Education: Some Considerations of Method*, London and Boston: Allen and Unwin.

ISME (1999) *The International Society for Music Education Newsletter* No. 6.

Karjala, H. (1995) 'Thinking globally, teaching in England', *Music Educators Journal* 81, 6, 32–4.

Keene, J. (1982) *A History of Music Education in the United States*, Hanover: University Press of New England.

Kelly, G., Altbach, P. and Arnove, R. (1982) 'Trends in comparative education: a critical analysis', in G. Kelly, P. Altbach and R. Arnove (eds) *Comparative Education*, New York: Macmillan, pp. 503–33.

Kemp, A.E. and Lephard, L. (1992) 'Research methods in international and comparative music education', in R. Colwell (ed.) *Handbook of Research on Music Teaching and Learning*, New York: Schirmer, pp. 773–88.

Kiester, G. (1993) 'A look at Japanese music education', *Music Educators Journal* 79, 6, 42–8.

Lepherd, L. (1985) 'Comparative music education: viewing the forest as well as the trees', *International Journal of Music Education* 5, 47–9.

Lepherd, L. (1988) *Music Education in International Perspective: The People's Republic of China*, Darling Heights: Music International Queensland.

Lepherd, L. (1992) 'Comparative research', in A.E. Kemp, *Some Approaches to Research in Music Education*, Reading: International Society for Music Education, pp. 33–56.

Lepherd, L. (1994) *Music Education in International Perspective: Australia*, Toowoomba: University of Southern Queensland Press.

Lepherd, L. (ed.) (1995) *Music Education in International Perspective: National Systems*, Toowoomba: University of Southern Queensland Press.

Maclean, M. (1992) *The Promise and Perils of Educational Comparison*, London: Tufnell Press.

Moore, R.S. (1987) 'Effects of age and nationality on auditory/visual sequential memory of English and American children', *Bulletin of the Council for Research in Music Education* 91, 126–31.

Muckle, J. (1987) 'Dmitriy Kabalevsky and the three Wales: recent developments in music education in the Soviet general education school', *British Journal of Music Education* 4, 1, 53–70.

National Center for Educational Statistics (1995) *Arts Education in Public Elementary and Secondary Schools*, Washington, DC: US Department of Education, Office of Educational Research and Improvement.

National Endowment for the Arts (1993) *Arts in Schools: Perspectives from Four Nations*, Washington, DC: National Endowment for the Arts.

Noah, H.J. and Eckstein, M.A. (1969) *Towards a Science of Comparative Education*, Toronto: Macmillan.

Oehrle, E. (1993) 'Education through music: towards a South African approach', *British Journal of Music Education*, 10, 255–61.

Postlethwaite, T.N. (ed.) (1988) *The Encyclopaedia of Comparative Education and National Systems of Education*, Oxford: Pergamon Press.

Pyke, N. (1998) 'England beats France', *Times Educational Supplement*, 6 December, p. 1.

Rainbow, B. (1990) *Music in Educational Thought and Practice: A Survey from 800 BC*, Aberystwyth: Boethius.

Reimer, B. (1989) 'Music education in China: an overview and some issues', *Journal of Aesthetic Education* 23, 1, 65–83.

Richmond, J.R. (1997) 'Universal access for the universal language', *Arts Education Policy Review* 99, 2, 22–9.

Satori, G. (1994) 'Compare why and how: comparing, miscomparing and the comparative method', in M. Dogan and A. Kazancigil (eds) *Comparing Nations, Concepts, Strategies, Substance*, Oxford: Blackwell, pp. 14–34.

Stenhouse, L. (1979) 'Case study in comparative education: particularity and generalisation', *Comparative Education* 15, 1, 5–10.

Stowasser, H. (1993) 'Some personal observations of music education in Australia, North America and Great Britain', *International Journal of Music Education*, 22, 14–28.

Taylor, D. (1979) *Music Now*, Bristol: The Open University Press.

Thomas, R. Murray (1995) *International Comparative Education: Practices, Issues and Problems*, 2nd edn, Oxford: Butterworth-Heinemann.

Westerlund, H. (1999) 'Universalism against contextual thinking in multicultural music education – Western colonialism or pluralism', *International Journal of Music Education*, 33, 94–103.

Wiggins, T. (1996) 'The world of music in education', *British Journal of Music Education* 13, 21–9.

Further reading

Arnove, R.F., Altbach, P.G. and Kelley, G.P. (eds) (1992) *Emergent Issues in Education: Comparative Perspectives*, Albany, NY: State University of New York.

Kemp, A.E. (1992) *Some Approaches to Research in Music Education*, Reading: International Society for Music Education ISME International Office.

Kemp, A.E. and Lepherd, L. (1992) 'Research methods in international and comparative music education', in R. Colwell (ed.) *Handbook of Research on Music Teaching and Learning*, New York: Schirmer, pp. 773–88.

Lepherd, L. (ed.) (1995) *Music Education in International Perspective: National Systems*, Toowoomba: University of Southern Queensland Press.

Maclean, M. (1992) *The Promise and Perils of Educational Comparison*, London: Tufnell Press.

Postlethwaite, T.N. (ed.) (1988) *The Encyclopaedia of Comparative Education and National Systems of Education*, Oxford: Pergamon Press.

Thomas, R. Murray (1995) *International Comparative Education: Practices, Issues and Problems*, 2nd edn, Oxford: Butterworth-Heinemann.

18 Research and development in music education

Sarah Hennessy

The importance of research

- How can creativity in music be developed in all children?
- What are the most effective ways in which teachers can facilitate (teach) composing?
- What is the relationship between improvising and composing?
- How do composing skills develop?
- Can participation and learning in music raise self-esteem?
- To what extent does language, or movement or visual art contribute to the development of musical understanding?
- What motivates and sustains learners?
- What strategies can teachers use to encourage children to reject gender stereotypic attitudes in music?
- How might music education contribute to a curriculum for global citizenship?
- Does learning about the music of other cultures contribute to greater understanding of those cultures?
- How effective is music technology in developing musical thinking and/or skills?

These are some of the kinds of questions that my student teachers attempt to address in their research assignments: they are questions that arise from their experience of learning to teach in primary schools. They are not easily answered and certainly not easily researched, but they do focus on pressing issues for teachers in schools.

'The ultimate test of a set of educational ideas is the degree to which it illuminates and positively influences the educational experiences of those who live and work in our schools' (Eisner, 1991). In this chapter I intend to focus on issues of research in relation to teaching and learning in music, principally in the school context. However, it should be noted that the educational ideas that Eisner refers to and their field of influence should also encompass people involved in education as teachers and learners in other, less formal settings of home or community. The glib term 'lifelong learning' over-simplifies a complex map of contexts and conditions in which we learn. Not all learning takes place in situations where the intention to learn is declared or obvious. We may learn a great deal by accident, and learn very little by design. We learn as much indirectly as directly: what we know and what we understand, what we like and don't like, what moves us, what music tells us about the world of feeling, how it expresses or defines our values and identifies us in relation to others. Music is learned and understood in the act of making music (*musicking* in Christopher Small's sense (1998)) rather than in only what we can notate, describe or explain.

The popular view of the researcher as an objective, dispassionate even clinical collector and measurer of data sits rather awkwardly alongside the reality of classrooms, learning processes and music making itself. 'Real-world' music education (Maidlow and Bruce, 1999) needs to look at the social, environmental, and cultural contexts in which teachers teach and students learn. Parents, peers and the media are at least, if not much more, influential in determining attitudes and motives towards learning. Issues of race, class, disability and gender need as much attention as cognitive processes in developing our understanding of what is going on when we engage with music.

For school-based teachers there can be a tension between the idea of the lone, perhaps gifted artist developing his or her own means of expression, and music as a social activity in which all children can participate and develop their musical thinking. This is gradually changing as music education becomes more diverse both in and beyond school. However, many teachers' own music education is likely to have favoured the former whereas the conditions in which we teach in school are more often the latter. The tension arises when we attempt to integrate the two. Most specialist teachers have been taught their skills, if not their musical attitudes and values within a historically established system which exercises a powerful influence on teaching styles and assessment criteria. The master–apprentice model of teaching and learning is deeply embedded in music teachers' thinking: the music teacher as instructor or musical director is a much more familiar image than that of facilitator, mediator and critical friend. So pervasive is this first model that headteachers and teachers of other subjects find great difficulty in accommodating any other. However, with an increased focus on composing in the curriculum of English schools this model has been challenged and teachers have had to develop new, perhaps more flexible and responsive approaches and attitudes.

Researchers in music education must also deal with this tension and not only look at and assess finished 'work' (the performance, the text, the final composition) but concern themselves with how the learner arrives there and what happens along the way. Attitudes, informal modes of learning, peer learning, motivation and the less tangible ideas surrounding musical creativity, imagination, and thinking skills, learning contexts and previous experience will all help to 'muddy the water'.

Teachers and creative music-makers engage in research activity continually. Eisner proposes that music is a way of 'describing, interpreting and appraising the world' (Eisner, 1996: 1). Burns, an eminent sociologist, entitles a collection of his published papers *Description, Explanation and Understanding* (1995). This title describes the development of his own work over forty years *and* the research process itself. These three activities are inextricably linked – we cannot explain without a clear picture of the subject and through explanation we arrive at interpretation and understanding. Clearly, the intentions and the modes of communication are quite different for a composer and for an educational researcher but I would not negate the usefulness of considering that the processes are similar. Thinking of composing as problem solving or research doesn't help us to become better composers but it might help, as learners and teachers, to recognise that there are stages of the creative process which parallel those of other contexts and disciplines, and which need to be given time and attention. On the other hand, Swanwick (1994: 71) reminds us that an essential difference between the artist and the researcher is that the latter cannot change the 'data' 'to fit an intuitive hunch of how it [a piece of music] might become . . . Research is one way of subjecting intuitive insights to analytical scrutiny'.

One of the millstones that music education has round its neck is the perception that real research is scientific, hard-nosed, quantitative and irrefutable. Scientific analysis (in caricature) involves dissecting a fixed subject, variables can be controlled or eliminated and results can be clearly and irrefutably measured. Of course, good quality research is much more complex, dynamic and even serendipitous than this. Music education research is relatively young and there is a sense in which researchers have adopted the notion that, in order to be taken seriously and to acquire status, the more 'scientific' the methods, the more credible the research will be. This has led to a methodological hierarchy which places 'scientific' quantitative research at the top and oversimplifies the differences between and among different methodologies.

I believe that this perception has contributed to a tension which has arisen between the apparent demands of the academic research community (represented in recent years by the Research Assessment Exercise); a strongly expressed view held by certain people close to government that most educational research (and particularly the empirical and qualitative kind) is of questionable quality and not useful (Tooley and Darby, 1998); and the needs and interests of the teaching profession who may be inclined to be sceptical and mistrustful of research findings, seeing them as alienating, unrelated to and unrepresentative of the real world of the classroom, or in some sense telling teachers what they feel they already know.

Despite the current government's attempts (through increasing prescription, testing and inspection frameworks) to make it otherwise, teaching is still very much a qualitative process and researchers need to be able to call on a range of methods if their descriptions are to reflect and illuminate what goes on, and if their explanations are to offer insight into how teachers might develop or change their practice in knowledgeable ways.

> Educational inquiry will be more complete and informative as we increase the ways in which we describe, interpret and evaluate the educational world. Which forms of representation become acceptable is as much a political matter as an epistemological one.
>
> (Eisner, 1996)

In researching music education there is the additional problem of gathering data which is temporal, transitory, provisional and multi-sensory. Understanding young children composing or responding to music involves more than listening. It demands 'thick description' (Geertz, 1973): gestures, facial expressions, body language and group behaviour are invariably as important in understanding children's understanding as what they utter (verbally and musically). Researchers in classrooms need to adopt a range of approaches and practices in order to illuminate what is essentially dynamic, active and practical.

The focus of research

As a teacher educator I spend a great deal of my time helping student teachers, and experienced teachers who are research students, to develop their knowledge and understanding of the nature of teaching and learning in music. In this process they are motivated by their own experience and observations, and encouraged to use published research to illuminate and clarify the focus of their research questions. I have noticed more recently that student teachers of music are often drawn to investigate how music contributes to the development of the whole child, how learning activity in music promotes positive attributes (e.g. 'good' behaviour, language development, positive social interaction) in the learner. This appears to have coincided with a quite sudden decrease in opportunities for musical activity in English primary schools due to an intense focus on literacy and numeracy teaching. Specialist music students return from their primary school placements with dismal stories of their difficulties in securing regular teaching time in which to develop their own practice. The studies they then undertake are often aimed at strengthening their arguments for the importance of music for all in the school curriculum. They believe that if it can be proved that music has a direct, positive effect on children's thinking skills (especially language acquisition and numeracy), physical, social and emotional development, then we can demand better resources, more time and increased status.

Part of my role in supporting students is to guide their reading and recommend appropriate academic sources to explore, support, clarify and challenge their own thinking. It continues to be the case that there is no shortage of literature which advocates music for all, which argues for the distinct and unique qualities which music offers to developing the mind, the body, social, emotional, aesthetic and spiritual well-being (Hennessy, 1998a, 1998b; Glover and Ward, 1993; Mills, 1992; Odam, 1995; Swanwick, 1988). Claims are made for music's power to promote co-operation, collaboration, co-ordination, self-discipline, confidence, increased self-esteem, and so on. Most writers, and I include myself, would also make a strong case for the teaching of music for its own sake: the intense pleasure and enjoyment it can generate for both listeners and makers, the centrality of music to all cultures in defining, redefining, challenging and celebrating who we are and what we aspire to for ourselves and our community.

However, in all this rhetoric, advocacy, proselytising and articulate rationales there is very little evidence of any kind of empirical research which seeks to establish the validity of such claims, or even to find out to what extent they might be found to be evident. Perhaps this is unnecessary when there is reasonable consensus within the profession of music's value, even if it doesn't always change policy or attitudes in the educational community as a whole. It is also the case that without research we cannot develop our understanding nor influence policy or practice through new insights or new questions.

My contention is that it is not difficult to make the case for music, or to argue for a curriculum which places practical, creative music making at its centre. What is lacking is research which looks at the teaching and learning processes involved. What is needed is more knowledge and understanding of good music teaching. Maria Spychiger (1998) comments, 'Good music teaching has been the strongest specification as regards the conclusivity of positive extra-musical outcomes from [extended] music education.' From the well-publicised research she was involved with in Switzerland in the early 1990s (Spychiger *et al.*, 1993), she concludes that what is needed are well-educated music teachers, a high status for music in the curriculum and the evaluation of the quality and outcomes of music teaching. 'Accompanying research, process-oriented rather than outcome-oriented, will contribute to the ongoing development of the discipline, in practice as well as in theory' (1998: 201). In this same debate Janet Mills adds, 'if we are to exploit the potential of music to improve the mind, we need researchers . . . to help isolate the conditions under which this happens' (OFSTED, 1998: 205).

One of my concerns with much of the research that has been carried out by psychologists into brain function, and music learning processes, is that it tends to focus on the Western classical tradition both in terms of the music learned and performed, and the style of teaching. In these contexts the pedagogy is often teacher-centred (e.g. the Kodaly method) and involves a high degree of skill-training, as opposed to being learner-centred and focused on the acquisition of skills and understanding for individual creativity. This of course makes the control of variables more manageable and the evaluation of the effects of teaching on outcomes, 'tidier'. It is less difficult to observe improvement in singing intonation over time, or fluency of coordination, than it is to gather evidence on musical thinking processes in improvisation, or listening. There is a danger that researchers will be attracted to what is evidently researchable rather than struggling with the 'messier questions'.

Research in teaching and learning

In the UK there are several distinct but overlapping contexts for research and researchers: schools, university departments, local and central government evaluation and inspection, government departments, and charitable and arts organisations who sponsor or commission studies. These contexts not only define what is researched but how it is carried out. They may also be in conflict with each other so that political, economic and educational agendas may unduly influence the kind of research which is supported and published.

The introduction of the National Curriculum for England and Wales (1992 for Music) and the attendant funding for in-service courses gave rise to a great deal of activity focused on professional development for primary generalists, consultancy training for primary specialists, resources and training in the use of technologies for secondary music teachers and, to a lesser extent, courses for composition and new (unfamiliar) repertoires. Significant independent research to validate, evaluate, or challenge their effectiveness seems largely absent. There is a great deal of writing to advocate the emphasis on creativity and music for all: rationales, justifications, and suggested frameworks for teaching, but limited examples of research, beyond descriptions of individual practices, which might offer some real insight into what impact all this activity has on children's learning. Longitudinal, qualitative studies are needed to discover what impact recent and current practice has on children's learning in music. This practice includes not only what is taught and its impact on learning, but also how it is taught and what teachers understand about their pupils' responses.

In primary education the context for music education has certain distinctive features which affect the kind of questions which researchers need to address. The music curriculum has been strongly influenced by the 'music for all' movement which argued that all class teachers should teach music at least to their own class. This idea was supported by the Plowden Report in 1967 and gained momentum through the influence of John Paynter and others who, although not working specifically in the primary sector, promoted and developed ways of working freely and creatively in music which avoided an emphasis on traditional 'craft' skills. This was taken up enthusiastically by educators keen to find a solution to the loss of 'floating' specialists in primary schools, and to the perceived, and actual, elitism of traditional music education, a tradition which focused on performing (largely singing), knowledge about music, and music theory. In the eagerness to demystify music subject matter for primary generalists, games, graphic notation and group composition have all become widespread in primary classrooms. But without the underpinning of some musical understanding through which music is made, they remain enjoyable activities but may only accidentally give rise to coherent, progressive learning. There has been no research which looks systematically at the effects of these teaching approaches on children over time.

A principal way to implement 'music for all' was, and still is, through using music specialists as consultants, usually in their own schools. Sandy Allen (1988, 1989) investigated 'to what extent the claims made for music consultancy [could] be substantiated by empirical evidence'. She highlighted the sophisticated and relatively expensive (in staff time) nature of implementing a consultancy model. As it is designed to change attitudes and practice among staff, certain favourable conditions had to be in place. Despite the very convincing arguments in support of the consultancy approach (equity of provision, better continuity, better match of teaching to learners and greater curriculum integration), Allen's research was not able to provide any conclusive evidence of its efficacy in the schools she sampled. Her conclusion was that consultancy does have the potential to improve the quality of music education, but the conditions in which it can succeed are still greatly dependent on the skills of the 'consultant', a climate conducive to professional development among the staff, and support by the management.

Despite the limited research evidence, this approach to primary music teaching received strong support from the professional community (Glover and Ward, 1993; Hennessy, 1995, 1998b) and quickly became the orthodoxy in the years immediately prior to and during the implementation of the National Curriculum for Music in England (DfEE, 1992). Reviews of inspection findings, and Her Majesty's Inspectors' (HMI) recommendations, endorse this approach. Over a seven-year period (285 Primary schools, 1982–89) it was found that 'music-making of quality was better developed where there was at least one teacher with sufficient expertise . . . to give leadership in the school' (DES, 1991). In 1993/94 (OFSTED, 1995) it was reported that the majority of classes observed were taught by the class teacher and 'the standards achieved . . . are satisfactory or better in 96% of KS1 and 75% of KS2 lessons'. It is difficult not to be persuaded of the value of all teachers being involved in music teaching, but more research is needed to develop the practice and evaluation of different patterns of initial training as well as professional development. Independent research is needed to evaluate the efficacy of professional development for serving teachers in music. The most important question is 'do children receive a better education in music?' as a result, 'better' meaning more engaging, exciting, relevant, imaginative, demanding . . . *more* musical.

We still have little evidence to tell us how the increased focus on composing in the curriculum has affected all children's musical development across the ability range. If it is having an impact on the creative work of students who go on to study music at conservatoires or universities, is it also making a difference to the vast majority who, in the past, enjoyed the music of others as consumers? What evidence is there that more children, as a result of their more practical music education, are practically engaged in music?

Peter Mortimore (Director, London University Institute of Education), in his address to the 1999 BERA (British Educational Research Association) conference, presented his analysis of the current state of research in education. He high-lighted areas that have been neglected or under-researched in the education field generally: learning theory, different pedagogies, the impact of ICT on learning, and the relationship between assessment and learning. All of these are similarly under-researched in the field of music education. In the absence of substantial independent research in these areas, the work of centralised, politically driven, inspection findings are in danger of going unchallenged and their criteria for evaluation uncontested.

The implementation of the statutory curriculum for music (in 1992) and the attendant official monitoring and inspection have led to a particular kind of evidence being available: that of inspection evidence and reviews undertaken by subject HMIs. The nature of inspections gives rise to large amounts of 'snapshot' evidence which may well distort our knowledge of what is going on both in terms of quality, quantity and effectiveness.

An early independent study of the impact of the National Curriculum (NC) for Music in England (Lawson *et al.*, 1994) focused on primary schools and the issue of resources. Through looking at management and policy issues with head teachers and subject issues with music coordinators they found that, at that time, there were only a small number of schools (out of thirty-nine in all) that had a comprehensive scheme of music education in place for all children. Teachers felt overwhelmed by the requirements and were least likely to be addressing listening and appraising in lessons.

A more recent five-year survey looked at post-primary provision in Northern Ireland (Drummond, 1999). Teachers expressed a deep ambivalence in their attitude and commitment to non-examination teaching and often considered extra-curricular activity to be more important than classroom work. Drummond concluded that consideration should be given to making music an optional subject at an earlier age than is current practice. These kinds of findings are received with ambivalence by the music education community. Is research in danger of undermining our fragile status in statutory education? There seems always the lurking fear that if research finds intractable problems with the provision of music education in school then perhaps the policy makers will act; music is an expensive subject to support, so perhaps leave it to the private or at least the extra-curricular sectors.

Gordon Cox's study (1999) of secondary music teachers found a more positive picture in which, although there were the expected problems of overwork and lack of career structure, teachers were positive about the effects of the NC. Low status was compensated for by the personal reward gained from music making with young people and from influencing the ethos of the school community.

Janet Mills, one of Her Majesty's Inspectors of Schools (HMI) has contributed several articles based on inspection findings (e.g. 1997). She reports that in the first year of the NC's introduction, lessons in primary schools were better than teachers expected, and that music lessons were significantly better taught than those inspected in other subjects, while at Year 7 they were significantly worse, making 'uncomfortable reading for music specialists'. The issue of the dip in quality and engagement at KS3 (11–14 age range) has continued to be raised by inspections. Mills (1996) focused on five extreme examples of unsuccessful approaches adopted by secondary teachers with new Year 7 classes: 'sheep and goats'; 'they do nothing at primary school'; 'back to basics'; 'praise them regardless'; and 'no keyboards before Christmas'. She concludes that links between primary and secondary schools need improvement to foster continuity and higher expectations, and that planning needs to be diagnostic, differentiated and demanding. Again, it is longitudinal studies which will properly address and investigate such issues with the aim of improving practice.

Mills also used national data and case studies to look at GCSE take-up (6.5 per cent of Y11s). She found that there was a positive correlation between the quality of KS3 teaching and GCSE numbers and that with increased attention to the quality and relevance of the KS3 curriculum this percentage could be raised. Quality and relevance are of course value judgements and are therefore subject to individual, cultural and local interpretation. Arriving at a consensus of what constitutes quality is closely linked to cultural values relevant to a particular social group, i.e. that which is served by a particular school or group of schools. I am not aware of any research which has attempted to explore this.

In *The Arts Inspected* (1998b) Mills presents several case studies as examples of good practice (as defined by OFSTED) in teaching, and identifies features which characterise it: high expectations, direct instruction, verbal analysis, eliciting demonstrations and overt encouragement. Models of 'good practice' are seen as a useful way to encourage teachers to reflect on and develop their own teaching, although criteria for what constitutes good practice are often assumed rather than discussed or made explicit. However, even here it is not clear how successful such published examples and models are in achieving the desired aim of dissemination and development.

There has been little independent research looking at the range and quality of music learning in school to enrich our understanding and help to develop the relationships between theory, policy and practice. In searching for evidence of recent research on pedagogy, it was surprising to find little of real substance. Many papers describe practice but rarely attempt to analyse the role of the teacher or the impact that a particular teaching strategy or design of a musical task has on learners. A research project currently underway is investigating how teachers teach composing (and in particular the value of keyboards), and their students' views of what constitutes progress (Odam and Paterson, unpublished conference paper, 1999). Robert Bunting (1987, 1988) used two case studies (pupils following a GCSE music course) from his own teaching to investigate the musical thinking which took place during the composing process and the role of the teacher. He identifies the need for a balance between 'instructor' and 'mediator' and wrestles with the problem of control, i.e. whose composition is it?

The teacher's role is rarely the focus of attention in music education research. The influence of constructivist views of learning appears to have had less impact on the teaching of music than other curriculum subjects. This may be because specialist teaching has been so dominated by the teacher-as-musical-director image. The teaching of composing at all levels has demanded a radical rethinking not only of what is going on when children compose, but also how teachers should interact with, instruct and guide the process. Although the role of mediator and facilitator is a well-established one in primary teaching it, seems not to have permeated the practice of music teachers so successfully. In a paper on the common ground between music learning and language learning, Harrison and Pound (1996) looked at the value of improvising with primary teachers and their pupils. They found that teachers needed help with 'intervention strategies which would promote . . . musical development while preserving [the] freedom to improvise'. Again, there is some literature aimed at developing thinking in this area (Hennessy, 1998a), but no published empirical research. Such research could contribute usefully to our understanding of the relationships between learners, and between learners and teachers.

Reaching our audience

If educational research is ultimately aimed at improving practice then our principal audience must be teachers and policy-makers. Rena Upitis (1999) proposes that we should make our research more accessible and be prepared to produce not only 'multiple texts, but multi-representational forms – aural (and oral), visual, written, acted, and so on'. She goes on to state the need for 'lively and coherent language that avoids the kind of jargon that distances the reader from the writer (sometimes on purpose)'. Dissemination of research through academic journals and conferences is important for peer review and generating discourse, dialogue and critical debate; however, it is dangerous to assume that the press and other reporting media will represent findings and recommendations in a careful and thorough way to a wider audience, which includes teachers. One only has to look at the fall-out from the 'Mozart Effect' to recognise this.

Researchers themselves need to communicate their investigations and findings to the community which is most likely to apply and develop new ideas and initiatives, i.e. teachers and policy-makers. This community is not particularly homogeneous – and less so in music, perhaps, than those of other subjects. This is because, certainly in the UK, school-based curriculum teaching has been seen as quite distinct from instrumental teaching even where it takes place in the same school with some of the same students. Teachers are often trained in separate institutions (although this is beginning to change) and in different traditions. Many instrumental teachers are not qualified teachers and are not expected to work in classrooms or follow the school curriculum framework. They often work with small self-selecting groups or individuals. Classroom teachers must have a professional qualification and teach a wide range of subject matter through composing, performing and listening activities to the whole range of abilities in a school. A third grouping has emerged more recently: community musicians who work 'in residence' or on short-term projects in schools. This group is made up of performers and composers who work independently and for outside institutions although their funding may derive from joint bids with schools, education authorities or arts organisations. For all these groups there can be a problem of isolation: many music teachers (both school-based and instrumental) work in very small departments or teams: they may work entirely alone in their specialism. Consequently, it is less likely that such teachers will have opportunities to discuss, or hear about new developments in research, let alone be involved in research activity themselves. Lack of knowledge of current issues and new thinking, and lack of challenge to one's practice lead to fossilisation.

The dissemination of research findings and recommendations is one important issue. The other is the need to involve music teachers and learners in the research itself: identifying problems and questions, learning to analyse and reflect on one's own professional practice, sharing experience and expertise. In a study of student teachers' developing confidence to teach music in primary schools (Hennessy, 2000) it emerged that the very act of being involved in a research project contributed to their development. They were more aware of their own learning and more assertive in their demands for practice opportunities in school. Research in which teachers are equal partners in the process, and whose classrooms provide the context and subjects of a study, has the ability to empower teachers. The work on musical appraising carried out at Huddersfield University (Flynn and Pratt, 1995) exemplifies this approach. A group of primary teachers worked with the researchers to develop criteria for identifying and assessing this aspect of the curriculum. Through analysis of their own practice and evidence from their pupils, they arrived at a series of statements which described a broad range of activities which involved appraising skills. The disempowerment caused by increasing prescription and centralised policy-making discourages innovation, experimentation and creativity in teaching.

My purpose in this chapter has been to raise some of the issues which arise from the context in which I and my students work and learn. My research interests emerge from teaching, observations of, and conversations with learners, as well as the larger professional community teachers and researchers both in school and higher education. The dynamics of teaching and learning demand a constant preoccupation with asking questions and the imperative to find better questions. Research, as much as teaching, only has value and relevance if it contributes to making a positive difference and contributes to better understanding, better practice, more inclusive and responsive education, and to a healthier and richer cultural life for everyone. If we want teachers to be more creative and take more risks in their teaching, then we must also do this in our research, with the confidence to use methods which properly suit that purpose.

Questions for discussion

1   Often, in the context of your own teaching, there are things going on that you'd like to understand better, things that affect (positively or negatively) the quality of your students' learning. How might you go about identifying these and how might you then evaluate an intervention to change, improve, or capitalise on one or more aspects?

2   What methods might you adopt to evaluate a particular teaching approach, resource, or scheme of work used by yourself or other teachers?

3   In reading this book what issues or questions have resonated with your own experience and thinking?

References

Allen, S. (1988) 'Music consultancy in primary education', *British Journal of Music Education* 5, 3, 217–40.

Allen, S. (1989) 'Case studies in music consultancy', *British Journal of Music Education* 6, 2, 139–54.

Bunting, R. (1987) 'Composing music: case studies in the teaching and learning process', *British Journal of Music Education* 4, 1, 25–52.

Bunting, R. (1988) 'Composing music: case studies in the teaching and learning process', *British Journal of Music Education* 5, 3, 269–310.

Burns, T. (1995) *Description, Explanation and Understanding: Selected Writings*, Edinburgh: Edinburgh University Press.

Cox, G. (1999) 'Secondary school music teachers talking', *Music Education Research* 1, 1, 37–47.

Department of Education and Science (1991) *The Teaching and Learning of Music*, London: HMSO.

DfEE (1992) *National Curriculum Orders for Music (England)*, London: HMSO.

Drummond, B. (1999) 'Classroom music teachers and the post-primary curriculum: the implications of recent research in Northern Ireland', *British Journal of Music Education* 16, 1, 21–39.

Eisner, E.W. (1991) *The Enlightened Eye: Qualitative Inquiry and the Enhancement of Educational Practice*, New York: Macmillan.

Eisner, E.W. (1996) 'Qualitative research in music education: past, present, perils, and promise', *Bulletin of the Council for Research in Music Education* 130, 8–16.

Flynn, P. and Pratt, G. (1995) 'Developing an understanding of appraising music with practising primary teachers', *British Journal of Music Education* 12, 2, 127–58.

Geertz, C. (1973) *The Interpretation of Cultures*, New York: Basic Books Inc.

Glover, J. and Ward, S. (1993) *Music in the Primary School*, London: Cassell.

Harrison, C. and Pound, L. (1996) 'Talking music', *British Journal of Music Education* 13, 3, 233–42.

Hennessy, S. (1995) *Music 7–11: Developing Primary Teaching Skills*, London: Routledge.

Hennessy, S. (1998a) 'Teaching composing in the music curriculum', in M. Littledyke and L. Huxford, *Teaching the Primary Curriculum for Constructive Learning*, London: David Fulton.

Hennessy, S. (1998b) *Coordinating Music Across the Primary School*, London: Falmer Press.

Hennessy, S. (2000) 'Overcoming the red-feeling: the development of confidence to teach music in primary school among student teachers', *British Journal of Music Education*, 17, 2, 183–96.

Hennessy, S., Rolfe, L. and Chedzoy, S. (1999) 'The factors which influence student teachers' confidence to teach the arts in the primary classroom', paper presented at BERA conference, September 1999.

Lawson, D., Plummeridge, C. and Swanwick, K. (1994) 'Music and the National Curriculum in primary schools', *British Journal of Music Education* 11, 1, 3–14.

Maidlow, S. and Bruce, R. (1999) 'The role of psychological research in understanding the sex/gender paradox in music. Plus ça change', *Psychology of Music* 27, 147–58.

Mellor, E. (1999) 'Language and music teaching; the use of Personal Construct Theory to investigate teachers' responses to young people's music compositions', *Music Education Research* 1, 2, 147–58.

Mills, J. (1992) *Music in the Primary School*, Cambridge: Cambridge University Press.

Mills, J. (1996) 'Starting at Secondary School', *British Journal of Music Education* 13, 1, 5–14.

Mills, J. (1997) 'Ofsted music inspection findings', *Primary Music Today* 8, 20–1.

Mills, J. (1998) 'Respondent to Overy, K. (1998) "Music, does it improve the mind?"', *Psychology of Music* 26, 2, 204–5.

Odam, G. (1995) *The Sounding Symbol*, Cheltenham: Stanley Thornes.

Odam, G. and Paterson, A. (1999) 'The creative dream', unpublished conference paper given at the International Conference for Research in Music Education, April 1999, University of Exeter, UK.

OFSTED (1995) *Music: A Review of Inspection Findings 1993/94*, London: HMSO.

OFSTED (1998) *The Arts Inspected*, London: Heinemann.

Priest, P. (1996) 'General practitioners in music', *British Journal of Music Education* 13, 3, 225–32.

Rauscher, F.H., Shaw, G.L. and Ky, K.N. (1993) 'Music and spatial task performance', *Nature* 365, 611.

Small, C. (1998) *Musicking: The Meanings of Performing and Listening*, New England: Wesleyan University Press.

Spychiger, M. (1998) 'Respondent to Overy, K. (1998) "Music, does it improve the mind?"', *Psychology of Music* 26, 2, 199–201.

Spychiger, M., Weber, E. and Patry, J.-L. (1993) *Musik Macht Schule: Biografie und Ergebnisse eines Schulversuchs mit erweiterten Musikunterricht*, Essen: Blaue Eule.

Swanwick, K. (1988) *Music, Mind and Education*, London: Routledge.

Swanwick, K. (1994) *Musical Knowledge. Intuition, Analysis and Music Education*, London: Routledge.

Tooley, J. and Darby, D. (1998) *Educational Research. A Critique*, London: OFSTED.

Upitis, R. (1999) 'Artistic approaches to research', *Music Education Research* 1, 2, 219–26.

Further reading

There are two categories of reading which will help to develop your understanding of approaches to doing research. First, there is an enormous literature on research methods in the social sciences in general and education in particular. A few books have been chosen which deal with more qualitative approaches although in most research both quantitative and qualitative methods are necessary. Second, some recent published texts are listed which report on research projects which represent a variety of methods.

The process of doing research

Alderson, P. (1995) *Listening to Children: Children, Ethics and Social Research*, Ilford: Barnardo's.

Breakwell, G. and Millward, L. (1995) *Basic Evaluation Methods: Analysing Performance, Practice and Procedure*, Leicester: BPS.

Cohen, L. and Manion, L. (2000) *Research Methods in Education*, London: Croom Helm.

Maykut, P. and Morehouse, R. (1994) *Beginning Qualitative Research*, London: Falmer Press.

Strauss, A. and Corbin, J. (1990) *Basics of Qualitative Research: Grounded Theory Procedures and Techniques*, Newbury Park, CA: SAGE Publications.

Swanwick, K. (1994) 'Research and the magic of music', in *Musical Knowledge: Intuition, Analysis and Music Education*, London: Routledge.

Woolf, F. (1999) *Partnerships for Learning: A Guide to Evaluating Arts Education Projects*, London: Arts Council of England.

Research in the arts, and music education

Burnard, P. (2000) 'How children ascribe meaning to improvisation and composition; rethinking pedagogy in music education', *Music Education Research* 2, 1, 7–23.

Cox, G. (1999) 'Secondary school music teachers talking', *Music Education Research* 1, 1, 37–47.

Green, L. (1997) *Music, Gender, Education*, Cambridge: Cambridge University Press.

Matarasso, F. (1997) *Use or Ornament: The Social Impact of Participation in the Arts*, Stroud: Comedia.

Ross, M. and Kamba, M. (1997) *The State of the Arts*, Exeter: University of Exeter.

Journals which publish research include: *British Journal of Music Education*; *Music Education Research*; *Journal of Research in Music Education*; *Psychology of Music*; *Journal of Aesthetic Education*.

Index